Reading Zadie Smith

ALSO AVAILABLE FROM BLOOMSBURY

Reading Zadie Smith

The First Decade and Beyond

Edited by Philip Tew

BLOOMSBURY

LONDON • NEW DELHI • NEW YORK • SYDNEY

Bloomsbury Academic

An imprint of Bloomsbury Publishing Plc

50 Bedford Square	1385 Broadway
London	New York
WC1B 3DP	NY 10018
UK	USA

www.bloomsbury.com

Bloomsbury is a registered trade mark of Bloomsbury Publishing Plc

First published 2013

British Library Cataloguing-in-Publication Data
A catalogue record for this book is available from the British Library.

ISBN: HB: 978-1-4411-8245-6
PB: 978-1-4411-8661-4
ePub: 978-1-4725-0816-4
ePDF: 978-1-4725-0797-6

Library of Congress Cataloging-in-Publication Data
Reading Zadie Smith : the first decade and beyond / edited by Philip Tew.
pages cm
Includes bibliographical references.
ISBN 978-1-4411-8245-6 (hardback)– ISBN 978-1-4411-8661-4 (pbk.)–
ISBN 978-1-4725-1715-9 (epub)– ISBN 978-1-4725-1716-6 (epdf) 1. Smith,
Zadie–Criticism and interpretation. I. Tew, Philip editor of compilation.
PR6069.M59Z65 2013
823'.914–dc23
2013026676

Typeset by Fakenham Prepress Solutions, Fakenham, Norfolk NR21 8NN
Printed and bound in India

in memoriam
Leslie Arthur Tew
(1928–2012)
bene decessit

CONTENTS

ACKNOWLEDGEMENTS

I am most grateful to the organizers of the 41st Anniversary Convention of the Northeast Modern Language Association (NeMLA), held in Montreal from 7–11 April 2010, for their request that I prepare a specially invited double panel, entitled 'Zadie Smith: After the First Decade'. Thanks to all the contributors for their generally prompt responses to my many queries as editor of this volume, and hats off especially to those who wrote on Smith's fourth novel, *NW*, so promptly and perceptively so soon after its publication.

On a personal level my gratitude as ever to my partner, Agnes Bartha, in particular for all her help during a most difficult time when I was editing these essays initially during my father's final illness and latterly after his death. This volume is dedicated to his memory.

A NOTE ON TEXTS

Scholars from Canada, Europe, the UK and the USA contributed essays to this collection, and it seemed both unrealistic and inappropriate to attempt to impose the uniform use of the same editions of Zadie Smith's work, especially given that they might prove difficult for some to obtain. Although the pagination in the different editions used varies greatly and in certain cases there are variants in the text themselves and in their layout, overall this should not present the reader of this volume an insurmountable challenge. Hence the decision for each essay to offer its own list of works cited entitled Bibliography, which refers usually to editions of Smith's work available locally to each scholar. It is hoped that with keen eyes our readers can track down any quotations from Smith's work in their own editions of the texts, a similar task to that which I undertook as volume editor when checking for accuracy and so forth. Where there are cited more than one work by one individual these will be listed chronologically according to date of original publication (regardless of edition used, unless this is revised), and any such works in the same year set out alphabetically by title.

Note to the reader: Bracketed numbers after quotations refer to the page number of the text from which the quote was taken. Full references can be found in the relevant Bibliography.

Introduction

Philip Tew

Reading Zadie Smith has been a fascinating collection of essays to have edited, chiefly because of its overarching ambition, in which I think it largely succeeds, which was to offer readers, over a decade after the author's first novel appeared, a series of original analyses of Smith's writing from a range of academics based variously in Europe, North America and the UK. It is hoped that bringing these readings together will be a catalyst for more responses to Smith's oeuvre. Taken together these essays provide a challenging and sophisticated view of a range of key aspects of Smith's fiction, including criticism of her novels, short stories, journalism and other writing. Some of these originated as papers for a specially invited double panel, entitled 'Zadie Smith: After the First Decade', and were presented at the 41st Anniversary Convention of the Northeast Modern Language Association (NeMLA), which was held in Montreal from 7–11 April 2010. Ironically my own paper for that event was published in modified form elsewhere, so I had to write another essay on an entirely different topic for this volume. Further additional essays were commissioned from scholars that I knew and respected, to both broaden the range of topics and particularly to cover work published by Smith well after this event in the Francophone part of Canada. I also mention this because it reminds me of an associated collision of very different cultures, not of the type the reader might expect, but rather when a British delegate (who shall remain entirely unidentified by gender and also nameless) encountered local by-laws and officialdom in the form of the gendarmerie when arrested for jaywalking. That unfortunate academic had crossed a small, innocuous road outside the hotel on emerging for the very first occasion, and despite protestations of jetlag and lack of knowledge of local customs was issued a hefty fine on the spot. That person felt real trauma, whether really they might be regarded as culpable or not. This seemed to me a fine example of the underlying vulnerability, humanity and imperfection that one can find so readily in our world, and certainly so according to Smith's accounts of contemporary lives.

In following and applying my original guidance to potential partici-pants in the Montreal event (which I admit failed in terms of any caution concerning the careless traversing of thoroughfares), part of this volume's innovative approach is that its contributors do not begin by regarding Smith as primarily a 'postcolonial' writer, with all the essentialist presumptions that might entail, but instead pay attention to what her texts actually do and say. Individually and collectively we listened to her voice and what her words might actually mean, rather than interpreting them according to one or another idealistic or prefigured schema of identity and community. This is in part required because like pretty much all things *and* all individuals, Smith's corpus of work may well contain multiple contradictions. As Marcus Aurelius says aphoristically in the third section of Book IV of *Meditations*, 'The Universe is change; life is opinion' (19). Smith's novels are certainly structured around certain kinds of 'accumulation and repetition' (83), which characteristics she identifies in her essay 'Two Directions for the Novel' when accounting for Tom McCarthy's *Remainder*, a book Smith much admires. In the same essay Smith also considers Joseph O'Neill's *Netherland*, which is defined as 'absolutely a post-catastrophe novel, but the catastrophe isn't terror, it's realism' (73), and arguably this central anxiety is one that Smith shares. So moving rapidly to the essays in the volume, below I will summarize what each one offers.

The first essay, Brad Buchanan's 'The Gift that Keeps on Giving: Zadie Smith's *White Teeth* and the Posthuman', is a sophisticated consideration of the author's first and arguably most successful novel from the angle of how in *White Teeth* Smith adopts and yet challenges the emergent 'posthuman' movement influential in science, cybernetics and cultural theory, and literature and which both contributed to and celebrated the breakdown of traditional humanist descriptions of nature in many disciplines, including work by scholars in discourses such as science, archaeology, anthropology and psychology. Significantly such traditional approaches appeared apparently to incorporate the widespread belief that such thinking might offer a comprehensive universal account of matters such as human beings' shared evolutionary history, their inner lives, and might even incorporate religious practices anthropologically into an understanding of a common human nature. Buchanan foregrounds one resultant theory, Sigmund Freud's highly influential Oedipus complex, together with the ironies implicit in Freud's concept, initiated by the original 'Oedipal rupture of the laws of humanity'. Buchanan explores in detail first how Smith invokes Fukuyama's examination of liberal democracy and its humanistic underpinnings in *The End of History and the Last Man* (1992), and second traces in Smith's novel various aspects including the Nietzschean 'last men' of history, and cloning as a genetic attempt at dominating the universe and controlling the genetic make-up of beings. In so reading the novel Buchanan considers how 'posthumanism' may or may not differ from traditional humanism, about which distinction he argues Smith remains ambivalent, managing for instance to both pay tribute to Freud and his mythical hero, particularly with regards to the relations within the Chalfen and Iqbal families, but equally using Oedipal tropes to provide a critique of an overly complacent humanism, her narrative inflected by both humanism's enduring paradoxes and self-critical movements. Buchanan offers a compelling critique of the fruitfulness of Smith's intellectual engagement with the (post)humanist traditions in the novel, analysing her persistent deployment of Oedipal tropes in service of her undertaking. Buchanan reads the novel's climax as representing an extended interrogation of Fukuyama's assertion that science undermines the possibility of making autonomous moral choices. The second analysis of the same text is Ulrike Tancke's 'White Teeth Reconsidered: Narrative Deception and Uncomfortable Truths', which details first that media and critical establishment purpounded a view that the novel was essentially a positive account of multiculturalism in Britain in the latter part of the twentieth century. Second it establishes a shift towards a growing critical response questioning such assumptions, and third seeks to 're-evaluate White Teeth's pivotal yet ambiguous position in literary studies'. Tancke reads three aspects closely, first the episode when Irie, Magid and Millat visit the 'racist' Mr Hamilton to offer Harvest Festival gifts, second the interlinked vignettes that trace Millat's rebellion and inner psychic pain, and third those sections charting Iroie's problems with self-image and identity. In doing so Tancke offers demonstrations of the vicissitudes of migration and being the offspring of migrants, its often conflictual and painful dynamics, the 'original trauma' (161) in Smith's terms of such migration. The experience of migration emerges as essentially traumatic in nature, fundamentally threatening identity and selfhood, both literally and metaphorically. For Tancke Smith's critique often precisely concerns the apparently fashionable realities of a multicultural context and discourse that so many critics initially celebrated and Tancke insists that Smith demands her reader reassess such commonly held beliefs and widely accepted convictions, using the narrative's ubiquitously ironic and comical tone to further complicates her narrative mechanism of subversion. Through an analysis of a range of such contradictions, White Teeth emerges as a more poignant and profound commentary on contemporary multicultural reality, asking not only very uncomfortable truths not just about British multicultural society, but also about the human condition at large. Tancke writes persuasively of the text's innate seriousness, its indirection and irony that allows its 'surface comedy to highlight a profound poignancy' while testing readerly expectations and moving them beyond their comfort zone, an aspect many early critics not only missed, but resisted. Joanna O'Leary offers another highly original reading of Smith's first novel in 'Body Larceny: Somatic Seizure and Control in Zadie Smith's White Teeth'. O'Leary starts with the debate between those such as Katarzyna Jakubiak and Philip Tew who challenge the initial scholarly and review-based responses that focused very largely on the novel's model of multiculturalism, seeing this as a distraction. Rather O'Leary foregrounds thematically genetic manipulation, its exploration of the desirability of general human, rather than racial, perfection and the potential for an ideal body form, together with the moral dilemmas of manipulating other non-ideal bodies. The parental desire for bodily perfection for their offspring runs counter to their own degraded, often malfunctioning bodies. Such generational conflict animates the narrative. O'Leary considers how Samad Iqbal glorifies and yet simultaneously despises his imperfection, drawn to the Muslim religion he resists, his withered arm becoming part of a pathological form of introjection, as a lost object creating an unshakeable obsession, through which Samad rediscover perversely the erotic desire of his youth, focusing initially on masturbation and subsequently the 'ineffectual, guilt-ridden affair with Poppy Burt-Jones'. Both entail self-loathing, religious hypocrisy. O'Leary moves to Samad's subsequent obsession concerning his fears for the potential harm to his sons offered by corrosive Western cultural mores *and* values that he sees degrading others. Samad idealizes the figure and potential of the child, but his practical response of sending one son home is ineffectual, and ironically painful for him as a father. As O'Leary observes this becomes 'an unplanned experiment on the influence of environment on growth and development and throughout the novel one looks forward to comparing the results when both twins finally emerge from their respective geographical "wombs" of Bangladesh and England'. She outlines the resulting comic contradictions, including Alsana's denial to her husband of her own body, resisting his desire for somatic control. The essay contrasts Samad's vicissitudes with Archie's acceptance of his own bodily and emotional presence, and examines how after Magid's return it becomes evident in all three households how much children inevitably deviate from parental expectations. Ending with the biogenetic theme is crucial since, as O'Leary explains, 'the age of scientific technology significantly complicates the practice of appropriating an external (often child's) body to act as a container for one's aspirations and expectations'.

The next two essays reconsider in much detail Smith's second novel, assessing its merits after an initial period of critical hostility to a number of its elements and its perceived failings. The first is my own (non-Montreal) offering, 'Celebrity, Suburban Identity and Transatlantic Epiphanies: Reconsidering Zadie Smith's *The Autograph Man*' which begins by illustrating a range of less than positive reception by reviewers and critics alike, particularly in the case of James Wood who not only dismisses Smith's adoption of an 'irrelevant intensity' that he finds so characterizes many contemporary writers, but objects to the vacuity of the protagonist, Alex-Li Tandem, to which I object, since it is precisely the trappings of celebrity culture together with contemporary society's associated deadening of affect and its rejections of certainty for the power of the symbol that Smith attempts to convey before the novel can attempt an epiphanic transformation which takes place on board an airplane bound for America. I dissect an example Smith uses on the cover of the first UK hardback edition, the lyrics of the musical *Fame* (1980), written by Irene Cara. As I explain, the image abuts its own incomprehensibility in such a culture and yet still one encounters an example of its origin, the human actuality of a symbol made flesh when Alex meets Kitty Alexander, the movie star whom Alex has fetishized. This encounter has various consequences explored in my analysis. Overall my reading traces variously: Alex's avoidance of pain and suffering stemming from in part an avoidance of the trauma of his father's death; his inwardness as a symptom of a generational malaise where both meaning and reality seem fractured and radically elusive; Smith's literary and symbolic avowal of the experiential and equally her concomitant rejection of relativism, essentialism and the excesses of so-called 'high theory'; her capacity to evoke a more complex notion of community than just celebrating the tensions within a range of multicultural identities; references to and the meaning of the gift or *potlatch*; and how the novel foregrounds the effects of a mediatized, affectless, celebrity culture, in order to question the cultural inauthenticity this represents; the ever-present potential for an epiphany concerning one's set of values within such a vacuous system of non-meaning. A different approach animates Tracey K. Parker's '"I could have been somebody": The Articulation of Identity in Zadie Smith's *The Autograph Man*' which considers how when in the second novel popular culture seemingly for Alex and his friends contributes a key aspect to their individual subject position, nevertheless a thematic and authorial interrogation reveals such a culture as becoming more of a personal preoccupation that risks becoming an insurmountable barrier to self-understanding, most especially so when the obsessional and emotional distance created come to dominate interpersonal relationships, evoking for Alex a larger sense of estrangement. Parker traces how in describing a contemporary current consumer and media-driven era in *The Autograph Man* Smith ironically references Jean Baudrillard's theory of the 'hyperreal', which presupposes that the image has increasingly replaced the real, and diverted by such simulacra for many desire has displaced both need and authenticity, creating 'an existence [that] becomes superficial, devoid of substance'. As Parker argues, Smith makes clear that from an early age Alex and his circle of friends are described as representative of a new, sloganizing, televisual generation, absorbing cultural forms and attitudes that shape their lives. Parker demonstrates that Smith, in line with Stuart Hall's materialist critique, applying his theory of encoding/decoding to a hybridized world, allows her readers 'a dialogical process of communication'. According to Parker's reading contemporary subjects are caught in a web of a plethora of readings and discourses of popular culture, leading to a limiting self-consciousness and reflexivity. She details how Alex's obsessions lead him to a fundamental contradiction, defining himself in terms of celebrity, even though he lacks fame. In this analysis, in terms of empathy, emotion or affect he appears to be fundamentally confused as to what is filmic and what is legitimately happening, originating largely in a coping mechanism responding to his father's death. His view of Kitty's films indicates his inability to comprehend, recognize or embrace any sense of authenticity, which lack as Jameson indicated, severs the subject from history. For Parker finally, Honey serves to remind Alex that 'actual life is unavoidable and painful'.

In 'History in Zadie Smith's *On Beauty*' Susan Alice Fischer offers her view that even though the novel 'takes place in a staid, mostly white academic town in the US', the continuing relevance of American history in the nation's contemporary culture, most especially with regard to the fault-lines of ethnicity and the specific legacy of slavery and segregation, are fundamental to an effective reading of Smith's third novel. As Fischer explains, although this is not fundamentally a 'historical novel' in terms of setting, the past informs both the entrenched positions the characters adopt *and* the public policies that lie at the heart of their disagreements. Certainly it contextualizes the disintegration of the mixed-race marriage of Kiki and Howard Belsey, for both of whom the critical question is whether 30 years of love would prove sufficient to hold together their marriage after Howard's repeated infidelity. The public arena is framed by arguments over affirmative action and more locally at Wellington, whether outside 'discretionary' students be allowed, a policy opposed by Sir Montague Kipps, a visiting black conservative scholar. As Fischer explores, Monty's views allow Smith to feature the extremes and posturing of the so-called 'cultural wars' in the academy between left-liberal inclined and more right-wing academics. Underlying this range of issues Fischer traces subtle forms of racism, and 'the legacy of slavery [which] is an underlying, though often silenced or subterranean' reality in all of these lives, most especially Kiki, aspirant black poet and discretionary student, Carl, and a group of migrant Haitian 'rap' style poets. The very house the Belseys inhabit is a reminder and symbol of the past with its 'multicoloured light, which symbolizes the nation's avoidance of recognizing its history and diversity'. Ultimately, Fischer argues that Smith's novel attempts not only to underline the ways that history reverberates in our personal and public lives, but also to suggest a more productive way of debating historically rooted conflicts.

Lynn Wells offers an intriguing and intelligent critique of the author's most recent novel in 'The Right to a Secret: Zadie Smith's *NW*'. Smith's novel represents an authorial change of direction, influenced by Jacques Derrida in terms of secrets constituting a resistance to the panoptic, potentially totalitarian space of collective narratives. Wells emphasizes the withholding of information three central characters – Leah Hanwell, Felix Cooper and Leah's best friend Natalie (Keisha) Blake – all from a council estate in northwest London, notorious for poverty, crime and interracial tension. Wells contrasts variously: Natalie's professional life and apparently successful marriage and children with her clandestine assignations for group sex; Leah's childlessness and supposed attempts at conception with her juvenile lifestyle and surreptitiously birth control, the latter concealed from her partner; and, Felix's positive new stable relationship with a trip across London to buy her a surprise gift for his partner and his sex with an older ex-lover followed by a random incident that leads to his death. All three lives are inflected by the politics of contemporary England, amid the contradictory interplay of the personal and the political. For Derrida any sense of 'belonging' entails a capitulation of the self to the collective. Hence Smith both applauds the novel's capacity to incorporate marginal voices while recognizing it denies the individual the right to silence and privacy. By being doubly secretive, for Wells such characters become 'manifestations of the ethical danger of reducing others to essentialized identities based on race or other factors while denying their uniqueness'. Lacking ambition and under-achieving, Leah exhibits characteristics ascribed to immigrants and non-whites by mainstream culture; Natalie/Keisha is programmatically aspirational, yet lacks any true sense of inner, authentic identity, inhabiting a lifestyle Leah finds hypocritical; and Felix has transcended low-paying jobs, drug-dealing and addiction, to become a mechanic. From the opening scene Leah is associated with the dissident Eve of the novel's epigraph. After multiple abortions she cannot alleviate her guilt, the monuments in a church graveyard of long-dead women who died after multiple childbirths and a Madonna with a swaddled Christ child becoming accusatory. Disorienting scenes are rendered through a Woolfian stream-of-consciousness, Leah's life made comprehensible despite its discontinuous thoughts, memories and observations. Contradictions abound. Ironically Felix's very compassion leads him variously to betray sexually his stable relationship with his current partner, to intervene on behalf of a pregnant woman on the Tube, and refuse to hand over the earrings his partner gifted him, leading to his death that finally allows both Leah and Natalie to respond ethically by identifying his killer.

Wendy Knepper's reading in 'Revisionary Modernism and Post-millennial Experimentation in Zadie Smith's *NW*' argues that the modernist search 'for a new aesthetics responding to war, revolution, terror and global economic crisis seems highly relevant once again' in a post-millennial era characterized by comparable socio-political anxieties concerning the world order. Knepper traces the text's relationship with the experimental novel, including its spatially configured narrative, graphical qualities, stream-of-conscious narration, ludic play with numbers and disrupted chronologies. She positions Smith's book as part of a revisionary avant-garde, reaching beyond traditional realist approaches to mimesis, searching for more effective ways of representing contemporary life, incorporating the visceral, experiential, lived experience. Although Smith appears to eschew both realism and postmodernism, Knepper insists the author attempts a combination of a rigorous 'lyrical realism' with a complex, varied avant-garde prose tradition from Melville through Kafka, Beckett and Joyce to Tom McCarthy. Drawing on Smith's essays on the genre, 'Two Directions for the Novel', 'How To Fail Better' and 'Some Notes on Attunement: A Voyage around Joni Mitchell', Knepper concludes that *NW* embraces an aesthetics that questions prevailing conceptions of individuality and space, demands 'a more rigorous interrogation of subjectivity, which recognizes the mutability and contradictions of self [...]', employing 'strategies of immersion, interaction, intersection and imaginative remapping' and thereby interrogates prevailing racial and cultural othering. Knepper's detailed analysis regards *NW* as immersing the reader spatially in a world that is both serious and playful, thereby challenging literary and cultural expectations and norms, blurring the real and the imagined, the worldly and textual. Smith deploys such 'interactive and immersive' experimental techniques so the reader might 'explore the contested production of localities in a globalizing world' through the imagined, virtual and actual cartographies of 'NW'. Knepper explores a range of elements, most especially Smith's evocation of figure of Black Madonna and experiments with style in the search for 'truer' forms of mimesis.

In 'On Religion: Postsecular Quests, Scriptural Borrowings and Irreducible Beauty in the Fiction of Zadie Smith', Magdalena Mączyńska considers how although interest in religion is expressed as a central concern in all of Smith's fiction, she remains ambivalent about religiosity. Yet in an apparently secular age she understands its shaping influence in contemporary culture. Mączyńska traces Muslim fundamentalism and other similarly fundamentalist belief systems in *White Teeth*, seeing religion as interconnected with issues 'of nationality, race, and class'. In *White Teeth* Mączyńska sees religion as regarded as pathological, and its 'cast of believers, an assembly of social misfits, unassimilated immigrants, and sexually repressed teens, seems to confirm such misgivings'. Violence and retribution underpin religiosity for both the Jehovah's Witnesses and members of the Keepers of the Eternal and Victorious Islamic Nation (KEVIN), while religious impulses and vocabulary permeate others doubtful about or diametrically opposed to faith, such as Samad Iqbal *and* Marcus Chalfen. Smith eschews any absolute division of the sacred and the profane. Although *The Autograph Man* engages with the tensions of Jewish identity, still religion marks social belonging, its tropes found everywhere in everyday life, the possibility of belief incorporated into social practices. Mączyńska illustrates how Smith juxtaposes the Kabbalistic Tree of Life, Taoist concepts and the Kaddish and 'uses religion not only as a theme but also as a metatextual structuring device'. In an interrelated set of themes while Alex sacralizes the mundane, fame and celebrity offer complex and profane elaborations of the sacred.

In *On Beauty* Mączyńska foregrounds the conflict between the secular atheistic modernism of Howard Belsey and the religious views of Monty Kipps, and their respective families. Certain characters who breach these binary positions Smith applauds, including Kiki and Levi Belsey together with Carlene Kipps. Equally aesthetics allows a transcendent sense of the good and the beautiful once accessed primarily through faith. For Mączyńska *NW* interrogates variously attitudes towards fundamentalist Islam, the capitalist commodification of the impulses for faith, and the 'the theme of ritual, whose importance can be seen in Leah's yearning for confession [...]'. Smith also incorporates as longings the aesthetic possibilities of worship and its mystical and spiritual qualities, and as Mączyńska comments: 'Smith freely mixes Christianity, numerology, and animism to meet the particular needs of her modern protagonist'.

In part Christopher Holmes details little-considered aspects of the so-called 'Smith-Wood debate' over the future of the novel and studies their implications in 'The Novel's Third Way: Zadie Smith's "Hysterical Realism"' but he also offers a reading of the importance of understanding that realism and experimentalism are not the only coordinates for situating the contemporary novel. Responding to both her critical writing and her fiction, he argues that in advocating both in criticism and practice for a literary form responsive to contemporaneity, Smith describes the process by which the novel might structure knowing and thinking. He uses her essay on the evolution of George Eliot's *Middlemarch*, to demonstrate Smith's view of how 'novels think or, rather, how they are preparing space for thinking'. The debate with James Wood contextualizes Smith as both distrustful of the ideologies of realism and embracing a formal fluidity that eludes easy categorization, alongside a recognition of the novel as an 'analogue of thought', capable of encountering contradictory ideas. Holmes argues that if the novel transcends

> the tired oppositions between realism and some version of the avant-garde, politics and aesthetics, history and form – then literary criticism appears ripe for a paradigm shift, something akin to the move from programmatic literature to the pursuit of limits as a dynamic of form.

This allows a displacement both of Wood's bête noire, the contemporary novel's 'hysterical realism', and the 'lyrical realism' Smith herself opposes, resituating the central terminology of their literary feud. Holmes dissects this debate, particularly the architectural terminology of Wood's objections, addressing his underlying preference for vitality and 'the rich interiority of the novel'. Holmes suggests Woods perhaps misreads Smith's incorporation of 'the hoax' or experimental mode, and misses both her challenges to the reader's expectations and her preference for a shifting, adaptive aesthetic capable of both knowing and feeling. Her manifesto for the contemporary novel attend to the concepts upon which realism is built so as to suggests its two possible future directions.

In a detailed comparison, Lewis MacLeod explores certain lines of influence on Smith in 'Eliminating the Random, Ruling the World: Monologic and Hybridity in Zadie Smith's *White Teeth* and Salman Rushdie's *Midnight's Children*', arguing that after her precursor's innovative groundwork, Smith's novel cannot be regarded as simply extending or echoing the same characteristics. He explains his 'uneasiness' concerning this reconstitution of *Midnight's Children* hybridity and details that novel's abundant similarities to *White Teeth*, suggestive of a problematically homogenized (rather than hybridized) range of preferences 'in the contemporary literary-academic climate'. MacLeod argues what was innovative in Rushdie is no longer so in Smith. Hence Edward Said's post-imperial multiplicity of cultures and Rushdie's 'chutnification of history' should be reinterpreted. Using conceptually Mary Douglas' *Purity and Danger* and Zygmunt Bauman *Postmodernity and its Discontents*, the essay explores the role of dirt and the desire for purity inherent in classificatory impulses and processes of history and narrative. This is explored in terms of *Midnight's Children*, explaining the various local prejudices, and demonstrating that 'it is clear that both Saleem's chutney and his narrative method are meant as hybridity's answer to this kind of compartmentalized sterility'. For MacLeod neither Rushdie nor his character, Saleem, avoids the quest for purity and order, neither transcends the anxieties about contagion, fears of dirt, which they apparently critique. In a narrative about narrativizing, the formal narrative compulsion resists any disorderliness.

Consequently while detailing severally the similarities of Rushdie's and Smith's novels, particularly in terms of purity and its relationship to history and its various metaphors, MacLeod suggests that the ease of incorporation with which 'Rushdie's fiction and non-fiction can be used to describe Smith's novel ought to suggest something less than hybrid and less than heterogeneous in *White Teeth*'. Rather than being helplessly heterogeneous, Smith's procedures are modelled on Rushdie's encoding of a new kind of orthodoxy focused on a specific mode of hybridity. Additionally Smith's use of diametrically opposed twins and her depiction of fundamentalism run counter to the messiness of history, and she patterns her text precisely, evoking a narrative order or purity achieved by formally reconciling many oppositional elements, such as incorporating Midnight's Children's interest in perfectibility and cloning, and Rushdie's twins motif in the antithetical Magid and Millat. In a general sense Rushdie's excessive influence has an over-determining effect upon *White Teeth*, both mapping and revealing the latter's structures and interior discourse, undermining its larger discursive position. The novel's success indicates predictable and ordered modes of production and reception, a commodified hybridity.

Last, but certainly being far from the least significant among this set of essays, Lucienne Loh explores the writer's shorter fiction in 'Zadie Smith's Short Stories: Being English in a Globalised World', considering in particular the shifting and persistent signifiers of Englishness in a contemporary world where post-war Britain reshaped by unprecedented mass migration from the ex-colonies, elements of an emergent Anglo-American popular culture, and the economic and political unification of Europe. Loh's first section analyses closely two of Smith's Stories, 'Mrs. Begum's Son and the Private Tutor' (1997), and 'Martha, Martha' (2003), reading them in terms of key themes for Smith, including British multiculturalism and working class life in a globalized world. The second section analyses work focused on white English bourgeois liberalism in Britain, in stories with white middle-class women central characters: 'Mirrored Box (1995),

'Picnic, Lightning' (1997), 'The Girl With Bangs' (2001) and 'The Trials of Finch' (2002). The third section considers post-war English masculinity in 'The Newspaper Man', 'Hanwell Senior' and 'Hanwell in Hell'. For Loh Smith's key concerns in depicting various collective and individual perspectives include: a sensitivity to the nuances of the English class system faced with a globalized economy of selfhood, and an awareness that a multicultural society might always become a potentially uneasy experience.

Loh suggests that Smith's year as a fellow at Harvard University in 2002–3 allowed the writer to incorporate into her stories both her increasingly direct knowledge of American life and a profound sense of separation from home which engendered a reassessment of contemporary English life. Immersed in America where the modern short story had evolved greatly, Smith both committed herself to this form, and distinguished its various dynamics and traditions to incorporate into her own writing: an English preference for character driven plots, a sense of irony, and self-deprecation; the formal polish and control American stories; and the influence of a 'Chekhovian' narrative, reflecting endless contingencies and absurdities, refusing judgement, abjuring climax or narrative resolution, thereby creating stories often appearing inconclusive.

Loh also indicates the importance of two essays by Smith concerning her father, a white Englishman and D-Day veteran, Harvey Smith. 'Accidental Hero', testifies to his military experiences and an insistence on not being regarded as having exhibited bravery. 'Dead Man Laughing' concerns Smith's comedic inheritance from Harvey, their shared passion for a particular strand of mordant, popular English comedy found in the comic Tony Hancock and the sitcom 'Steptoe and Son', both grotesquely dark, both detailing a macabre existentialism and an ironic despondency. The lives depicted are at heart almost irredeemably bleak. According to Loh, Smith's work exhibits three key aspects of post-war and contemporary expressions of Englishness: first, multiculturalism and Englishness viewed through a working-class lens in a contemporary, globalized world; second, the perspective of the white English bourgeoisie, particularly white English women who uphold the values and ideologies of this class in lives portrayed as both stifling and selfish, driven by a dogmatic adherence to material preoccupations and prejudices; and finally, preoccupation with the inarticulacy of working-class and lower middle-class English men, with their residual forms of post-war English masculinity.

Bibliography

Aurelius, Marcus. *Meditations*. Trans. A. S. L. Farquharson. London: Everyman's Library, 1992.

Bauman, Zygmunt. *Postmodernity and its Discontents*. New York: New York University Press, 1997.

Cara, Irene. 'Fame' [song lyrics]. 1980. http://www.lyricstime.com/irene-cara-fame-lyrics.html. N. Pag. Web. Accessed 17 February 2013.

Douglas, Mary. *Purity and Danger: An Analysis of the Concepts of Pollution and Taboo*. London: Ark Paperbacks, 1985 [1966].

Eliot, George. *Middlemarch*. London: William Blackwood and Sons, 1874.

Fukuyama, Francis. *The End of History and the Last Man*. New York: Macmillan, 1992.

McCarthy, Tom. *Remainder*. London: Alma Books, 2007.

O'Neill, Joseph. *Netherland*. New York: Pantheon, 2008.

Rushdie, Salman. *Midnight's Children*. Toronto: Vintage, 1997 [1981].

Said, Edward. *Culture and Imperialism*. New York: Vintage, 1994.

Smith, Zadie. 'Mirrored Box'. *The May Anthology of Oxford and Cambridge Short Stories 1995*. Ruth Scurr and Chris Taylor (eds). Oxford and Cambridge: Varsity and Cherwell, 1995, 125–41.

—'The Newspaper Man'. *The May Anthology of Oxford and Cambridge Short Stories 1996*. Nick Laird and Toby Smith (eds). Oxford and Cambridge: Varsity and Cherwell, 1996, 7–33.

—'Mrs Begum's Son and the Private Tutor'. *The May Anthology of Oxford and Cambridge Short Stories 1997*. Martha Kelly (ed.). Oxford and Cambridge: Varsity and Cherwell, 1997, 89–113.

—'Picnic, Lightning'. *The May Anthology of Oxford and Cambridge Short Stories 1997*. Martha Kelly (ed.). Oxford and Cambridge: Varsity and Cherwell, 1997, 115–22.

—*White Teeth*. London: Penguin, 2001 [2000].

—*The Autograph Man*. London: Hamish Hamilton, 2002.

—'The Trials of Finch'. *The New Yorker*. 23 and 30 December 2002, 116–23.

—'Hanwell in Hell'. In *Martha and Hanwell*. London: Penguin Books, 2005, 25–49.

—'Martha, Martha'. In *Martha and Hanwell*. London: Penguin Books, 2005, 1–24.

—*On Beauty*. London: Hamish Hamilton, 2005.

—'The Girl with Bangs'. *The Best of McSweeney's Vol. 1*. Dave Eggers (ed.). Penguin Books, 2005, 79–87.

—'How to Fail Better'. *The New Yorker*. New York. 30 October 2006 (audiobook).

—'Hanwell Senior'. *The New Yorker* Online. 14 September 2007. http://www.newyorker.com/archive/2004/09/27/040927fi_fiction (accessed 29 January 2013).

—'Two Directions for the Novel'. *Changing My Mind: Occasional Essays*. Smith, Zadie. London: Hamish Hamilton, 2009, 71–96.

—'Accidental Hero' in *Changing My Mind: Occasional Essays*. London: Penguin Books, 2011, 232–8.

—'Dead Man Laughing' in *Changing My Mind: Occasional Essays*. London: Penguin Books, 2011, 239–54.

—*NW*. London: Hamish Hamilton, 2012.

1

'The Gift that Keeps on Giving': Zadie Smith's *White Teeth* and the Posthuman

Brad Buchanan

By the end of the nineteenth century, the discourses of science, archaeology, anthropology and psychology had combined to produce a strong cultural confidence (at least in the West) in the capacity of educated people to understand human beings' shared evolutionary history and inner lives, as well as to understand the ways in which their religious practices may have obscured the common human nature shared by all, even supposedly primitive peoples. This confidence emboldened thinkers such as Sigmund Freud, whose credentials as one of the twentieth century's most important humanists rest in large part on his theory of the Oedipus complex, to formulate descriptions of human nature that proved to be highly influential for much of the past century. However, these descriptions have broken down in recent years in part because of a new 'posthuman' movement in science, cybernetics and cultural theory, and literature has registered this breakdown in many ways. As explored below, Zadie Smith's novel *White Teeth* reflects much of this history; it pays tribute to Freud and his mythical hero, but also uses Oedipal tropes to provide a critique of an overly complacent humanism. Thus, while Smith has a great deal in common with other notable theorists and critics of the 'posthuman' such as Francis Fukuyama and N. Katherine Hayles, she also manages to connect some of the apparently innovative tropes of the 'posthuman' (such as environmental activism or genetic engineering) to the enduring paradoxes and self-critical movements of humanism itself.

Criticism of *White Teeth* has been dominated by a focus on post-colonial issues, in particular the concept of hybridity, and thus the novel's remarkable and explicit invocation of Fukuyama's examination of liberal democracy and its humanistic underpinnings has gone largely unnoticed. Relatively few critics have written about Smith's interest in genetic engineering and the threats it poses to the liberal humanist agenda that Smith is frequently (and in general implicitly) presumed to share with E. M. Forster, and even those writers who have focused on this topic tend to situate such concerns within the context of theories of racial identity and difference rather than look at an overtly (or even covertly) 'posthuman' side to her engagement with such scientific innovations. One example of this understandable tendency is Ashley Dawson's perceptive essay, 'Genetics, Biotechnology, and the Future of "Race" in Zadie Smith's *White Teeth*' published in Dawson's *Mongrel Nation: Diasporic Culture and the Making of Postcolonial Britain*, which discusses Smith's novel in the context of real-world developments such as the Human Genome Project. Dawson goes on, however, to relate the novel's discussion of such scientific advances to theorists of race such as Paul Gilroy and Robert Young, and only mentions Fukuyama in the context of a discussion of supposed 'cures' for homosexuality via the selection of genetic traits. Dawson's piece is persuasive, as far as it goes, but there remains a significant gap in Smith criticism as regards the 'posthuman' question. It is thus timely and appropriate to raise awareness of Smith's dialogue with theorists of the 'posthuman' in general, and with Fukuyama in particular; thus this essay will explore the richness of Smith's intellectual engagement with the (post) humanist tradition in *White Teeth* and her persistent use of the Oedipus trope in service of that engagement.

Smith has not completely abandoned the Freudian humanist version of Oedipus, as is seen when her narrator describes the Chalfen family in *White Teeth* as follows: 'The children had their oedipal complexes early and in the right order, they were all fiercely heterosexual, they adored their mother and admired their father and, unusually, this feeling only increased as they reached adolescence' (261). To have already 'had' one's 'oedipus complex' implies that one has achieved a comfortable identification with one's father, but at least one Chalfen boy still harbours significant animosity towards his father, Marcus. Joshua Chalfen is in desperate Oedipal rebellion against the smug confidence of 'Chalfenism'. his tight-knit family's self-serving ethos. Joshua sees his father's genetic experiments with mice as the crux of his family's mistakenly anthropocentric worldview, and subsequently he joins an animal rights group.

Smith moves the Oedipal theme out of Freudian waters, however, when Iqbal exhibits highly self-conscious and intellectual Oedipal traits. Exasperated by his son Millat, who has temporarily blinded himself to his surroundings with a video game that wraps itself around his head, Samad forces the video protagonist to die. Millat denounces this symbolic reversal of Oedipal roles, shouting, '"YOU KILLED ME WHILE I WAS WINNING!"' (124). At this, Samad gives his most explicit imitation of Oedipus:

Samad closed his eyes and forced his eyeballs to roll up as far as possible in his head, in the hope that his brain might impact upon them, a self-blinding, if he could achieve it, on a par with that other victim of Western corruption: Oedipus. Think: I want another woman. Think: I've killed my son. I swear. I eat bacon. I regularly slap the salami. I drink Guinness. (124)

Samad's guilt overwhelms his anger at his son, and he links his crimes with those of Oedipus. Yet on the surface this parallel is puzzling; whereas Samad feels he has been tempted by loose Western morals, Oedipus is hardly a 'victim of Western corruption'. Smith here seems to refer to the fact that many see Oedipus as the self-confident hero of Western rationalism and humanism and, in particular to Nietzsche's view, that Oedipus's excessive faith in his rationality begat the madness that led him to blind himself.

Through the unexpectedly Oedipal figure of Samad Iqbal, Smith reminds us that Freud's theory of the Oedipus complex has had two distinct and possibly mutually destructive effects: it has founded a new branch of humanistic inquiry, and it has suggested that this new mode of inquiry will reveal unacceptable truths about ourselves if one takes it seriously. There have been many critiques of Freud (including those by Deleuze and Guattari and Jacques Lacan), but very few have noted that the contradictions inherent in his thought are in fact endemic to humanism itself which is always an effort to push our knowledge of ourselves to (and past) all rational limits and thus to contradict or even destroy itself. Thus Freud's choice of Oedipus as the exemplar of universal human identity is fraught with telling irony, since Oedipus saw himself in precisely this same light before he learned that he had broken two of the most basic laws of human civilization (the prohibitions against incest and parricide). Thus although Freud defined the modern humanistic intellectual project by his example, he offered an unwitting warning about the consequences of humanism: an Oedipal rupture of the laws of humanity.

Another suggestive Oedipal character in *White Teeth* who calls humanism into question is Dr Marc-Pierre Perret, who has worked 'in a scientific capacity for the Nazis since before the war' (90). Perret worked on 'the sterilization policy' and 'the euthanasia policy' and was 'one of the very loyal' (90); thus he parallels Josef Mengele, the sadistic mastermind of Nazi experiments. Yet the mythic resonance with which Smith imbues Perret suggests that he is more than an evil Nazi doctor. Perret suffers from 'diabetic retinopathy', which, as he says, means that 'when I do not receive insulin I excrete blood [...] [t]hrough my eyes' (97). The image of bleeding eyes inevitably recalls Oedipus's bloody eye sockets at the end of *Oedipus Tyrannus*. Moreover, known as 'Dr. Sick' in the Greek village of his self-exile, Perret evokes Oedipus, the man who sets out to cure the Theban plague only to find that he is its cause and chief symptom. When Perret pleads with Archie Jones for his life, he explicitly mentions Oedipus as an ambiguous figure: '"I may yet redeem myself in your eyes ... or you may be mistaken – your decision may come back to you as Oedipus's returned to him, horrible and mutilated!' (445). Implicit in this warning is Perret's own self-comparison to Oedipus; he has seen his decision to work with the Nazis become 'horrible and mutilated'. Perret bases his appeal on his own individual humanity: 'I am a man [...] I breathe and bleed as you do' (444), and he has some admirable human qualities, yet he also invokes the search for 'human perfection' as something worth pursuing, even though it is ultimately only 'those worth saving' who might benefit from it (446). Again, we have a humanist full of contradictions and unacceptable insights; indeed Archie Jones implores Dr Perret to 'stop talking' (446) in order that Archie may finally decide what to do with him.

The very title *White Teeth* suggests Smith's ambivalent engagement, on a certain level, with the problem of what unites human beings (the unvarying whiteness of their teeth, as opposed to the varying colours of their skin). Yet the context of this phrase as it is placed within the narrative immediately makes such a humanist agenda problematic: it is used by J. P. Hamilton, a racist Englishman who reminisces: 'when I was in the Congo, the only way I could identify the nigger was by the whiteness of his teeth' (144). On a broader level, Smith's novel repeats this complex invocation, and refutation, of humanistic certitudes: its plot centres on the problem of defining a universal human nature in an age when technology threatens to usher in a new era of so-called 'posthuman' beings and values, as the Fukuyama-inspired title of one chapter 'The End of History Versus the Last Man', suggests. In order to try and unpack some of the thornier paradoxes surrounding humanism in Smith's novel, one must examine its relationship to Fukuyama's 1992 book *The End of History and the Last Man*.

This work famously argues that liberal democracy is the final and optimal stage in human development, and that it thus offers the prospect of 'the end of History' as well as the dissolution (real or projected) of a certain vision of humanism that makes 'History' as Fukuyama defines it possible. Fukuyama accepts what he calls 'the Hegelian-Marxist thesis' that 'history has proceeded dialectically, or through a process of contradiction' whereby 'a certain form of socio-political organization arises in some part of the world, but contains an internal contradiction which over time leads to its own undermining and replacement by a more successful one' (136). He notes that 'Hegel had defined history as the progress of man to higher levels of rationality and freedom' and adds that 'this process had a logical terminal point in the achievement of absolute self-consciousness' (64). In political terms, this 'logical terminal point' is liberal democracy, since, in Fukuyama's words, 'outside the Islamic world, there appears to be a general consensus that accepts liberal democracy's claims to be the most rational form of government' (211). Of course, in *White Teeth* Smith will focus on the one exception Fukuyama cites here through her portrayal of the Islamist group KEVIN, no doubt in part to interrogate Fukuyama's sweeping conclusions, but there is little in any of her work to suggest that she prefers any other form of government to liberal democracy.

In any event, it is clear that Fukuyama's Hegelian view of 'History' is dependent on a humanistic confidence in the universal significance and value of certain underlying principles that drive its 'evolution'. Yet once humanism has achieved universal acceptance, then this 'History' loses its driving purpose, since at that point, in Fukuyama's words, 'there would be no further progress in the development of underlying principles and institutions, because all of the really big questions had been settled' (xii). More unsettling still, this condition of consensus and stability paradoxically robs human beings of the very essence of their humanity, in Fukuyama's view. Fukuyama writes that according to Hegel, beyond the impulse for survival 'Man differs fundamentally from the animals, however, because in addition he desires the desire of other men, that is, he wants to be "recognized". [...] In particular [...] as a human being [...] with a certain worth or dignity' (xvi). Liberal democracy was (and is) the only form of government that ensures that this necessary universal recognition has a political manifestation, but Fukuyama is Nietzschean enough to find this problematic:

> Nietzsche believed that modern democracy represented not the self-mastery of former slaves, but the unconditional victory of the slave and a kind of slavish morality. The typical citizen of a liberal democracy was a 'last man' who, schooled by the founders of modern liberalism, gave up prideful belief in his or her superior worth in favor of comfortable self-preservation. (xxii)

Smith's *White Teeth* may be said to be full of these 'last men'; witness the description of Clara's first boyfriend, Ryan Topps, who is dubbed 'The Last Man on Earth' by girls who wonder if they would find themselves able to sleep with him if he truly were what the name implied (24). This dubious title is eventually transferred to Archie Jones, an equally unattractive figure in the eyes of most young women (he is, after all, a much older man with a limp and a rather drab personality), when he marries Clara after a New Year's Eve party (38). Joshua Chalfen, another unprepossessing male, inherits the mantle later in the book when Joely refers to him as likely to be 'the last man standing' (400) after the long-awaited confrontation between FATE and his father. For all their flaws, however, these men (or boys) do not seem to fit the Nietzschean stereotype of the 'last man' – for one thing the novel begins with Archie Jones's refusal of 'comfortable self-preservation' though a suicidal impulse.

Aside from the implied cowardice of the 'last man', this figure also represents a move away from the essentially human drive for recognition, as Fukuyama defines it: 'The last man had no desire to be recognized as greater than others, and without such desire no excellence or achievement was possible. Content with his happiness and unable to feel any sense of shame for being unable to rise above those wants, the last man ceased to be human' (xxii). Echoing Nietzsche's concerns, Fukuyama asks: 'Is not the man who is completely satisfied by nothing more than universal and equal recognition something less than a full human being. [...] Is there not a side of the human personality that deliberately seeks out struggle, danger, risk, and daring, and will this side not remain unfulfilled by the "peace and prosperity" of contemporary liberal democracy?' (xxiii). Fukuyama's rhetorical questions can be absorbed into a larger narrative about humanism itself: once humanism triumphs in a certain sphere (i.e. once the world has largely embraced liberal democracy and political freedom, for instance), it turns inevitably on itself, sees a former consensus as illusory, and begins a new self-critique.

In Stephen Yarbrough's words (taken from his book *Deliberate Criticism: Towards a Postmodern Humanism*), 'humanism [...] emerges' when 'critical practice reaches the point where it recognizes that what it is opposing is the product of its own practice' (19). For Yarbrough, humanism 'can bring itself to the point of self-recognition and therefore can exercise a will capable of self-negation' (19). In this regard, the 'end of history' as Fukuyama imagines it is equivalent to the 'posthuman' situation; indeed, as Fukuyama himself asks, 'how do we know that an apparent lack of "contradictions" in the apparently victorious social system – here, liberal democracy – is not illusory, and that further progress of time will not reveal new contradictions requiring a further stage of human historical evolution?' (137). These are uncomfortable ideas for Fukuyama, however; as one can see in his later book *Our Posthuman Future: Consequences of the Biotechnology Revolution* (published in 2002), where he laments the 'posthuman' impulse to question human nature, and argues that 'Human nature exists, is a meaningful concept, and has provided a stable continuity to our experience as a species' (*Future* 7).

In *Our Posthuman Future*, a work that appeared too late to influence Smith's *White Teeth* (which appeared in 2000) but which shares many themes with the novel, Fukuyama examines the role of science, especially genetics, in forcing a rethink of conceptions of the human. However, this is not an entirely new topic for Fukuyama; indeed, in *The End of History*, he discusses his opinion that 'Modern natural science has provided us with a Mechanism whose progressive unfolding gives both adirectionality and a coherence to human history over the past several centuries' (126). Science is a central factor in humanistic self-under-standing, yet it has had some deleterious moral effects on humanism, and in Fukuyama's view:

> The entire thrust of modern natural science and philosophy since the time of Kant and Hegel has been to deny the possibility of autonomous moral choice, and to understand human behavior entirely in terms of sub-human and sub-rational impulses. [...] According to Darwin, man

literally evolved from the subhuman; more and more of what he was understandable in terms of biology and biochemistry. (297)

Science increases human self-awareness, but it also allows humans to alter their identity in ways that may, from a certain point of view, compromise some formerly accepted or 'normal' human qualities. Advances in genetics are perhaps the single most salient example of this paradox, hence Smith's and Fukuyama's shared interest in them.

The plot of the final chapters of Smith's novel centres on the unveiling of FutureMouse©, a version of OncoMouse™, a creature used for cancer research by Du Pont & Co and discussed in Donna Haraway's book *Modest_Witness@Second_Millenium.FemaleMan©_Meets_OncoMouse™: Feminism and Technoscience*. Smith's cloned mouse has been genetically marked for an early death by the apparently well-meaning but nevertheless cruel medical research undertaken by the former Nazi Dr Benjamin Perret and his partner, Marcus Chalfen. In these chapters the reader is also privy to the plots and conversations of various radical groups who have one thing in common: they all deny that human beings are either the most important beings or the only source of intelligence in the universe. FATE (an animal-rights group), KEVIN (an extremist Islamic movement) and the Jehovah's Witnesses all converge on the FutureMouse© experiment because, in their eyes, it represents the hubristic human wish to dominate the universe and control our own 'good genes' as it were. As Brother Shukrullah says, scientists and humanists wish to convince others that 'it is human intellect and not Allah that is omnipotent, unlimited, all-powerful' (393).

Although her critique of human and humanist hubris is important, Smith's sense of irony makes these anti-humanistic movements seem either hypocritical or hopelessly naïve; the hypocrisy of KEVIN members who persist in smoking marijuana or having illicit sex is noted casually but repeatedly, while the foolish, all-too-human calculations of the date of the apocalypse by the (intensely sexist) Jehovah's Witnesses is plainly ridiculous. Even the apparently uncompromising animal rights activists need what Smith's narrator calls 'an originating myth that explained succinctly what people could and should be' (395) a myth that has more to do with the sexual appeal of the female half of the group's founding duo than with anything about animals. Smith suggests that such groups simply wish to escape from the human world as they have previously experienced it and establish, in essence, their own activist authority in a new sphere, regardless of the real nature of the cause.

Through the chaotic climax of her novel, Smith seems to question Fukuyama's assertion that science undermines the possibility of making autonomous moral choices; Archie Jones's final act in *White Teeth* is to save Marcus Chalfen from terrorists, which certainly appears to be an autonomous and moral choice. Moreover, the hand-wringing tone of Fukuyama's polemical writings about science in *The End of History* does not seem to be present in Smith's *White Teeth*; instead, one might see more affinities between Smith and the neo-Hegelian Alexandre Kojève, whose far more equable and open-ended view of this situation is quoted by Fukuyama:

> The disappearance of Man at the end of History [...] is not a cosmic catastrophe: the natural World remains what it has been from all eternity. And therefore, it is not a biological catastrophe either: Man remains alive as animal in *harmony* with Nature or given Being. What disappears is Man properly so-called [...] the Subject opposed to the Object. (310–11)

This disappearing act is arguably echoed in *White Teeth* by the dramatic escape of the FutureMouse©, unwittingly freed by Archie, through an air vent. A genetically altered mouse whose fate is encoded in its body is arguably a witty metaphor for human nature (see the question 'are you a man or a mouse?'), which, thoroughly denatured by science but now without the old humanistic narratives of 'Man' to fall back on, rejoins the animal kingdom, in a certain fashion. As if to reinforce this parallel between the mouse's situation and the lot of human beings, Archie even calls the escaping mouse his 'son' (448), thus inviting a whole constellation of Oedipal and post-humanistic readings of the novel.

Because of Smith's interest in exploring the paradoxical aspects of the wish to improve human lives by tampering with the very genes that are the very basis of one's biological identity, her work has a clear affinity with a set of ideas that many have come to call 'posthumanism'. It also affords an opportunity to reflect on some of the territory shared by the 'posthuman' and the humanist tradition it supposedly supplants, as well as to note some tensions or contradictions between different versions of the 'posthuman' itself. In her crucial work *How We Became Posthuman* N. Katherine Hayles, the most celebrated theorist, historian and spokesperson of the 'posthuman', refuses to provide what she terms a 'prescriptive' definition of 'posthumanism', but she nevertheless argues that in some forms, posthumanism assumes that 'informational pattern' is more important than 'material instantiation', and thus that 'embodiment is ... an accident of history rather than an inevitability of life'; she also notes that other versions of posthumanism consider that 'consciousness' is merely 'an epiphenomenon, an evolutionary upstart' (2–3). What these versions of posthumanism have in common is that they both assume a separation between mind and body. This separation, however, is not readily apparent in another 'posthumanist' view articulated by Hayles, namely the description of 'human being' as something that can be 'seamlessly articulated with intelligent machines' so that 'there are no essential differences or absolute demarcations between bodily existence and computer simulation, cybernetic mechanism and biological organism, robot teleology and human goals' (3). This final, and for Hayles, 'most important' kind of posthumanism posits a 'material-informational entity whose boundaries undergo continuous construction and reconstruction' (3).

Such a concept is certainly suggestive, but hardly provides sufficient grounds for disentangling posthumanism from its humanist predecessor. Indeed, Hayles herself suggests that the cultural, technological and intellectual 'changes' leading to the replacement of 'the human' by 'the posthuman' were 'never complete transformations or sharp breaks' and that therefore '"human" and "posthuman" coexist in shifting configurations that vary with historically specific contexts' (6). For instance, Hayles argues that, at its inception, 'cybernetics was a means to extend liberal humanism, not subvert it. The point was less to show that man was a machine than to demonstrate that a machine could function like a man' (7). Thus Hayles notes that 'many attributes of the liberal humanist subject, especially ... agency, continue to be valued in the face of the posthuman' (279). There is an explicitly 'performative' dimension to Hayles's definition of posthumanism, whereby, as she put it, 'people become posthuman because they think they are posthuman' (6).

According to Hayles, 'posthumanism' differs from traditional humanism mainly in refusing to see the human subject as 'an autonomous self with unambiguous boundaries' (290). This refusal certainly seems entirely characteristic of Smith's novel, where many characters are linked through Oedipal tropes (as has been demonstrated above) and manipulated by forces beyond their control (rather like the unfortunate FutureMouse©). Yet it is hard to imagine Freudian humanism, for instance, excluding the interrogation of an individual subject's autonomy or boundaries (the unconscious undermines both). Oddly enough, Hayles ignores the biological basis of humanism as posited by psychoanalysis, and only mentions Freud once in her famous book *How We Became Posthuman*. Although Hayles asserts that 'posthuman' texts 'reveal the fragility of consciousness' in a way that is 'distinctively different from ... Freud' she does not adequately explain how these differences occur or why they matter (279). Indeed, in Hayles's terms, Freud might well be made to fit quite comfortably into the 'posthuman' tradition, if Hayles is right that 'the posthuman is likely to be seen as antihuman because it envision the conscious mind as a small subsystem running its program of self-construction and self-assurance while remaining ignorant of the actual dynamics of complex systems' (286). This sounds rather like Freud discussing the conscious, supposedly rational mind and its attempts to repress the unconscious. Hayles reminds us that the traditional 'liberal humanist' worldview supposes that 'conscious agency is the essence of human identity' (288), yet if ever anyone systematically questioned this supposition, it was Freud, though Hayles credits only the 'posthuman view' for recognizing that 'conscious agency has never been 'in control' (288).

It is tempting to conclude that the 'posthuman' is an empty, negative and deliberately meaningless category concocted to disguise or elude the basic paradoxes of humanism, or, worse still, to prolong the humanist moment by pretending it has been eclipsed by history or by intellectual fiat. Yet there is something important in the sense of belatedness that the term 'posthuman' offers that may seem relevant to humanism as a whole. For instance, one should recognize the belated, recuperative nature of the Renaissance humanist project delineated by J. A. Symonds, who deems humanism to be 'an attempt to find the point of unity for all that had been thought and done by man, within the mind restored to consciousness of its own sovereign faculty' (52). Thus Renaissance humanism, which is frequently seen as the most dynamic and enduring version of humanism in the Western world, is thus in a sense already a kind of 'posthumanism' looking back on a classical vision of humanity's sovereignty. One might also adduce Michel Foucault's claim, articulated in *The Order of Things*, that 'man' has 'grown old so quickly that it has been only too easy to imagine that it had been waiting for thousands of years in the darkness for that moment ... in which he would finally be known' (308), and his conclusion that 'it is no longer possible to think in our day other than in the void left by man's disappearance' (342). Yet Foucault himself has not been immune from the charge that his own position has been compromised by its undeclared humanistic agenda. Like Freud, Foucault offers theories of desire and power that have a potentially universal application. Thus for Michael Hardt and Antonio Negri, Foucault's worldview is essentially 'an antihumanist (or posthuman) humanism', which according to Hardt and Negri's account, partakes of that which it is intending to critique (91–2).

The example of Foucault and his subsequent critics points to one of the ironies of intellectual history: one can only (or only wish to) recognize humanism in retrospect, when one is already inclined to dismiss it as uninteresting, received wisdom or reject it as a tainted inheritance. Steven Yarbrough touches on this paradox when he notes that, 'humanism has seldom been the mainstream of thought in the West but has usually seemed ... outrageous at the time it appears, though it is often judged later to have been representative' (18). Another way of looking at this would be to say that humanism seems to possess a version of what Freud called 'the death drive'. After all, humanism is not so much a stable set of universal concepts as a commitment to finding new concepts that might be universal, and in *Beyond the Pleasure Principle* Freud himself shifted his emphasis away from the erotic trope of Oedipal desire to the desire for death. Humanism itself must always be destroying itself in a search for a new image, a new way of understanding what history has shown us that we are. Thus even remarkably persuasive ideas, such as Freud's claims about the universal nature of the Oedipus complex, must be annihilated in order to make way for new modes of self-understanding (or self-misunderstanding). Shoshana Felman has articulated this myth-seeking, self-transcending aspect of humanism as an aspect of science itself: 'only when this (mythical, narrative) movement of "going beyond" stops, does science stop' (1051). Following Lacan's lead, Felman recognizes that Oedipus is crucial to what she refers to as the 'death-instinct of psychoanalysis itself' (1043). Yet this 'death-instinct' is present in any humanistic discourse, which must seek (and exceed) its own limits in order to live up to its task.

Felman also links science to myth in a provocative way that reminds us of the need to question science's claims to truthfulness and rationality: 'Only when the myth is not acknowledged, is *believed to be a science*, does the myth prevail at the expense of science. [...] There is no 'beyond' to myth – science is always, in one way or another, a new (generative) myth' (1051). If humanism itself may be said to be a kind of myth or, at the very least, to have as much in common with myths as with science, then we must acknowledge that any rejection or antithetical sequel to it (such as some would have posthumanism become) is also a myth. If Levi-Strauss is right in saying that each new interpretation or version of the Oedipus myth, however revolutionary, becomes another aspect of the original myth itself, then the same may be said of humanism. In this sense, humanism, being always already posthumanist, is in the condition of Oedipus at Colonus, in Shoshana Felman's words in 'Beyond Oedipus' a place where Oedipus 'assumes his own *relation* to the discourse of the Other' and thus 'awaits – and indeed *assumes* – his death' (1028). Yet the awaited death of humanism never quite arrives, as Felman herself acknowledges. Felman puts it as follows: 'while psychoanalysts may take Freud at his word, believe, in other words, that [...] in the meaning of Freud's story of desire, *the tale is ended* – Lacan is there to tell us [...] nothing other than this ultimate discovery, this ultimate enigma: that the tale has, in effect, *no end*' (1037).

Such musings may appear to have taken us far away from Smith and her concerns in *White Teeth*, but that impression is deceptive. Like Felman, Smith has noticed and comment on the drive for narrative that has arguably kept Oedipus at the forefront of postmodern texts, perhaps in part because of Roland Barthes, who in *The Pleasure of the Text* has described the Oedipus myth as a paradigmatic narrative: 'Doesn't every narrative lead back to Oedipus? Isn't storytelling always a way of searching for one's origin, speaking one's conflicts with the Law, entering into the dialectic of tenderness and hatred?' (47). Barthes also complains that 'Today we dismiss Oedipus and narrative at one and the same time: we no longer love, we no longer fear, we no longer narrate. As fiction, Oedipus was at least good for something; to make good novels, to tell good stories' (47). As if to reinforce Barthes' point here, Smith makes sure that readers will note that *White Teeth* is structured around the same principle as Sophocles' Oedipus Tyrannus, which is anagnorisis, or recognition; for instance a character named 'Mad Mary' looks at Samad with '*recognition*' [Smith's italics] during his obsessive affair with Poppy-Burt-Jones: 'She had spotted the madman in him' (149). The final, and arguably the most telling, recognition in the book occurs when Iqbal realizes that the events of his and Archie's lives will make a good narrative: 'He gets to the fundamental truth of it, the anagnorisis: "*This incident alone will keep us two old boys going for the next forty years.*" It is the story to end all stories. It is the gift that keeps on giving' (441).

If one can share Smith's optimism about the ongoing value of narrative, one might see Oedipus's tale as exactly this kind of never-ending 'gift' that enables us to look at 'past, present and future' simultaneously, recognizing that one need no longer feel trapped by the old, over-determined definitions of humanity that dominated the twentieth century, since humans can change their natures as easily and suddenly as the scientists in Smith's novel can alter the genetic identities of the doomed mice they experiment on. Perhaps even Oedipus has a new face to wear for the new millennium, having escaped, like the Smith's genetically altered mouse (whom Archie Jones calls his 'son') from the fatal cage built by history and science. No doubt one too should feel fortunate to have escaped from the need to accept or reject the Freudian theory about Oedipus as either true or untrue, and to have reached a stage when one can treat it simply as one narrative among many others, a narrative about the need for narratives. The same can also perhaps be said of humanism, which purports to 'end all stories' (i.e. to debunk all fictions centred on superhuman deities) and ends up being just another 'story' in its own right. Yet this loss of authority is perhaps also a blessing, since this new, decentred or indeterminate 'humanism' is a 'gift' that will never stay still long enough to be fully assimilated or transcended. It 'keeps on giving' in the sense that it adapts itself to each new historical or technological development to pose the question of human identity and universality at every turn. Thus one might say that humanism is both a 'story to end all stories' containing in itself a drive for its own obsolescence, and a 'gift that keeps on giving' continually renewing itself, even in such apparently oppositional forms as posthumanism.

Bibliography

Barthes, Roland. *The Pleasure of the Text.* Trans. Richard Miller. New York: Hill and Wang, 1975.

Dawson, Ashley. *Mongrel Nation: Diasporic Culture and the Making of Postcolonial Britain.* Ann Arbor, MI: The University of Michigan Press, 2007.

Deleuze, Gilles and Felix Guattari. *The Anti-Oedipus: Capitalism and Schizophrenia.* Trans. Robert Hurley. New York: Viking, 1977.

Felman, Shoshana. 'Beyond Oedipus: The Specimen Story of Psychoanalysis'. *Lacan and Narration: The Psychoanalytic Difference in Narrative Theory.* Robert Con Davis (ed.). Baltimore: Johns Hopkins University Press, 1983, 1021–53.

Foucault, Michel. *The Order of Things.* Trans. Anonymous. New York: Vintage Books, 1973.

Fukuyama, Francis. *The End of History and the Last Man.* New York: Macmillan, 1992.

—*Our Posthuman Future: Consequences of the Biotechnology Revolution.* London: Profile Books, 2002.

Hardt, Michael and Antonio Negri, *Empire*. Cambridge, MA: Harvard University Press, 2000.

Hayles, N. Katherine. *How We Became Posthuman: Virtual Bodies in Cybernetics, Literature and Informatics*. Chicago, IL: University of Chicago Press, 1999.

Smith, Zadie. *White Teeth*. New York: Vintage, 2000.

Symonds, J. A. *The Renaissance in Italy: The Revival of Learning* Vol. II. London: Smith, Elder & Co., 1877.

Yarbrough, Stephen R. *Deliberate Criticism: Towards a Postmodern Humanism*. Athens, GA: University of Georgia Press, 1992.

2

White Teeth Reconsidered: Narrative Deception and Uncomfortable Truths

Ulrike Tancke

Almost ten years after its initial publication, Zadie Smith's debut novel *White Teeth* continues to elicit controversy, with the debate oscillating between enthusiastic appraisal and outright dismissal. When *White Teeth* was released in 2000, the novel garnered rave reviews, hailing the author – then only 24 years old – as, in Stephanie Merrit's words, 'the first publishing sensation of the millennium'. This enthusiasm was, to some extent, due to Smith's age, ethnicity and background: 'She's young, black, British', as the full title of the same review points out – a selection of adjectives denoting a welcome degree of sexy exoticism, safely hemmed in by the reassuring waiver of Britishness. If Zadie Smith herself quickly developed into a publishing phenomenon, her novel seemed to tie in with the prevailing, cheerfully positive vision of multicultural Britain in the early Blair years. For Merrit the novel boasts '[an] imaginative element [...] [that] extends to the way in which race relations are portrayed in the book. Smith offers a very optimistic vision: prejudice exists, but tolerance appears in equal measure, and racist violence is only mentioned briefly and at second hand'. Greeted with such an enthusiastic reception, *White Teeth* almost instantly became canonical, as an epochal novel celebrating the heterogeneity of British urban society around the millennium.

More recently, however, a decidedly critical reception of the novel has gained ground, which dismisses *White Teeth* for what is seen as its facile take on the contemporary multicultural reality. What is more, it is becoming *de rigeur* in academic circles to ostracize the novel precisely because of the marketing hype it has engendered and its perceived exploitation of exoticism. Bertold Schoene, for instance, argues along these lines, as he bemoans, with a thinly-veiled nod towards *White Teeth*,

> a ceaseless popular craving for the next new thing, causing the market to be inundated by an ever-growing number of debut novels by Creative Writing graduates commissioned by literary agents whilst still in the process of being written. [...] In my view, they are best described as novels of no consequence, devoid of truth, beauty and community. (184–5)

Schoene's emphasis on what he perceives as the failure to express a sense of 'community' in novels like *White Teeth* ties in with the critique of its alleged seriousness of approach. Indeed, the novel has been criticized for its humorous portrayal of serious social concerns, i.e. the very qualities which were lauded by reviewers have also been read as constituting an ethical failure at the heart of the novel.

Rather than siding with either of these views – the celebratory or the critical one – my aim in this essay is to re-evaluate *White Teeth*'s pivotal yet ambiguous position in literary studies. It seems high time to rid the novel of the inflated critical discourse that has developed around it, and instead to focus on the text itself – which, at a closer look, warrants neither of these views to an unqualified extent. I agree with Jonathan Sell, who deplores the 'misrepresentations and expropriations to which [the novel] has been subjected at the hands of critics, academics, social collectives and political groupings, [so] much ... so that the novel's own undistorted voice is barely heard amid all the hysteria it almost certainly had no wish to provoke'. Extending Sell's point, I will argue that the novel's reception – favourable and otherwise – is conditioned by the narrative mechanisms by which it operates, and that it is necessary to disclose these strategies in order to arrive at an adequate appreciation of its key concerns.

In terms of content, *White Teeth* is set up as a family saga chronicling the lives of a set of London families of English, Caribbean, Bengali and Jewish-British origins, and centring on the friendship between Archie Jones, a white British man married to Clara, a black Caribbean woman, and Samad Iqbal, originally from Bangladesh. Although this ethnically diverse and heterogeneous character cast might invite associations with the playful hybridity fetishized by certain strands of postcolonial criticism, the underlying message is diametrically opposed to this stance, as it centres on the characters' fates as first- and second-generation immigrants in Britain, and on the painful effects of ethnic mixing and the blurring of racial and cultural boundaries.

While its use of humour and comedic elements has been variously noted, the narrative method and perspective employed in *White Teeth* have received comparatively little critical attention to date. To a large extent, the critical commentary on Smith's use of narrative strategy and perspective that does exist has been bound up with the dismissive reaction to the novel at the negative end of the critical spectrum. James Wood in particular accuses *White Teeth* of being unable to present sufficiently nuanced characters with a believable degree of interiority. In a review in *The New Republic* Wood speaks of a 'crisis of character' as, in his view, the novel reduces its figures to mere 'caricature' (42). According to his view expressed in *The Irresponsible Self: On Laughter and the Novel* (2004) Smith is guilty of pursuing what he calls 'hysterical realism', a form of writing which promotes 'a culture of permanent storytelling' and pursues 'vitality at all costs' (178), thereby sacrificing substance for the sake of 'shiny externality' (183). Moreover, in his *New Republic* review Wood claims that the voice of the narrator consistently cancels out that of the characters; she 'not only speaks over her character[s], she reduces [them], obliterates [them]' (45).

Paul Dawson takes up on this assessment when he groups *White Teeth* with a set of recent literary works which, to him, signal a return to the allegedly outmoded principle of authorial omniscience, boasting 'an all-knowing, heterodiegetic narrator who addresses the reader directly, offers intrusive commentary on the events being narrated, provides access to the consciousness of characters, and generally asserts a palpable presence within the fictional world' (143). Dawson specifies this twenty-first-century variant of authorial omniscience as a term 'best used to describe a certain type of narrative in which a heterodiegetic narrator, by virtue of being an authorial proxy, functions as an extradiegetic character, setting up a communicative rapport with the reader in order to rhetorically highlight the value of the narrative to a broader extraliterary public sphere' (149). In the case of *White Teeth*, Dawson notes that we are dealing with what he calls a 'pyrotechnic storyteller' (153), a somewhat facetious coinage which denotes a 'typically humorous or satirical [narrator], [who] relies less on moral introspection or historical research than on a flourishing and expansive narrative voice, a garrulous conversational tone, to assert control over the events being narrated' (153). Dawson's assessment dovetails with Wood's in that he similarly notes that this narratorial stance comes at the cost of the characters and their individual, independent perspective taking second place.

However, such a categorization of *White Teeth* as a novel characterized by authorial omniscience does not fully do justice to the text. For one thing, a more comprehensive account of its narrative strategies ought to acknowledge that Smith, as Philip Tew says, 'combines omniscient narration with an extensive use of free indirect discourse' (49) and mirrors what Peter Childs explains are the 'vocabulary and speech-mannerisms of her characters [...] to show events from their perspective' (201), which Tew also observes (49). Moreover, as Tew correctly comments, the very question of whether the text allocates primacy to the narrator at the expense of the characters is highly reductive and misses the novel's central point, its critique of fashionable multicultural discourse and the multicultural reality. Tew points out that, even if Smith occasionally 'undermin[es] her characters, [she] does so to cultural shibboleths such as liberalism, political correctness and multiculturalism' (49–50).

I take this last observation as the starting point for my own argument, as it essentially contains the novel's ethical impetus, which does not lie, I believe, in its preference for authoritative commentary at the expense of individualized perspective. Rather than boasting a dubious practice on Smith's part of 'undermining' her characters, the narratorial comments are strategically employed in the narrative to convey a complex and ideologically challenging message, which asks readers to critically assess one's own, commonly held beliefs and widely accepted convictions. The novel's ubiquitously ironic and comical tone further complicates this narrative mechanism, as it appears to be at odds with *White Teeth*'s more poignant and profound commentary on the multicultural reality. It establishes a strategy that puts to the test the reader's critical credentials: I argue that it functions as a mechanism of narrative *deception*, in that it misleads the readers about the narrative's underlying rationale. What is more, it even makes them complicit in this deception, as they are, to some extent inevitably, taken in by the text's surface humour. In other words, the text seems to pursue a different agenda than the one it ostensibly promotes, and to allow or even invite readers to fall prey to these very mechanisms. However, such tactics should not be dismissed as ethically questionable, to the extent that the novel could be accused of veiling a serious message for the sake of a few cheap laughs. Underneath its surface comedy, *White Teeth* presents uncomfortable truths not just about British multicultural society, but also about the human condition at large, and the narrative voice is at the core of this strategy – a disturbing dimension that ultimately demands of readers that they should question their own individual ways of reading.

The seriousness of the issues in which *White Teeth* deals is hinted at when the narrative voice coins the phrase 'original trauma' (161) to capture the effects of the experience of migration and settlement in Britain – a clear indication of the poignancy at the core of the novel's vision. The passage in which this expression occurs is exemplary of the way in which the narrative consciously and consistently mixes ironic commentary and comical interludes with highly disturbing observations. For instance, when Samad and Alsana's twin sons Magid and Millat, and Archie and Clara's daughter Irie are on their way to see Mr Hamilton, a World War II veteran to whom they are supposed bring Harvest Festival gifts as part of a school project, the narrator subtly mocks the intermingling of cultures and histories that the encounter implies. The commentary on the scene, however, charts a gradual progression from the ironic to the serious:

> Unbeknownst to all involved, ancient ley-lines run underneath these two journeys [Irie's and Magid and Millat's] – or, to put it in the modern parlance, this is a rerun. We have been here before. This is like watching

TV in Bombay or Kingston or Dhaka, watching the same old British
sitcoms spewed out to the old colonies in one tedious, eternal loop.
Because immigrants have always been particularly prone to repetition –
it's something to do with that experience of moving from West to East
or East to West or from island to island. Even when you arrive, you're
still going back and forth; your children are going round and round.
There's no proper term for it – *original sin* seems too harsh; maybe
original trauma would be better. A trauma is something one repeats and
repeats ... [Immigrants] can't help but re-enact the dash they once made
from one land to another, from one faith to another, from one mother
country into the pale, freckled arms of an imperial sovereign. (161;
original emphasis)

The narrative strategy employed in the passage is characteristic of the
novel as a whole: it is in large parts written in a light-hearted, ironic and
subtly mocking tone, but at the same time offset with an underlying layer
of serious, even poignant commentary. What this passage traces, in effect,
is a rapid trajectory from seemingly carefree and trivial references to global
popular culture, to a painfully serious observation. With its invocation
of the idea of 'original trauma', the text conceptualizes migration as an
experience that constitutes a fundamental shattering of identity and a threat
to selfhood. Trauma can be broadly defined as an experience that is as
Radstone describes it 'elusive and impossible to grasp', and that 'elude[s]
sense making and the assignment of meaning [and that hence] cannot be
integrated into memory, but neither can [...] be forgotten' (117). Trauma
constitutes a fundamental threat to identity: according to Brison it 'undoes
the self by breaking the ongoing narrative, severing the connections among
remembered past, lived present, and anticipated future' (41). This sense
of the traumatic permeates the novel, and the characters' experiences
must be read as an effect of their 'original trauma' of not belonging, and
being torn between conflicting origins and their respective demands and
impulses. Although the passage is consistently written from the narrator's
point of view, without explicitly acknowledging the individual characters'
perspectives on the matter, it is precisely through the powerful gesture
of authorial omniscience that the reader is invited, if not convinced, to
read the characters' experiences through the lens of violence and trauma.
Moreover, at the level of the plot it sets the tone for the following course
of events, as Mr Hamilton turns out to be a kind of old-school prejudiced
imperialist who remembers when he was in placed in the Congo with the
army how 'the only way I could identify the nigger was by the whiteness
of his teeth' (171), and at this point the visit morphs into an emblematic
encounter with the ever-present spectre of racism.

This urges the question, of course, to what extent the ironic tone of the
passage is a deliberate tactics of misleading the reader, of drawing attention
away from the seriousness of the issues at stake. James Wood argues along

these lines when he claims in his review of the novel that *White Teeth*'s 'mode of narration seems to be almost incompatible with tragedy or anguish' (41) and that the novel therefore 'lacks moral seriousness' (43). My reading, however, turns this argument on its head, as it examines how Smith's strategy instigates a complex and nuanced approach by which 'tragedy and anguish' are seemingly neutralized but, at a closer look, attract careful scrutiny and honest appreciation. By using the strategy of indirect focusing exemplified in the above passage – that is, using surface comedy to highlight a profound poignancy – the readers' credentials are deliberately tested and their unacknowledged penchant for easy answers and comic resolution is exposed.

This strategy of implicitly drawing attention to what is initially submerged can be traced in an exemplary fashion in one of the most oft-quoted passages from the novel, which outlines the immigrant condition in late twentieth-century Britain:

> This has been the century of strangers, brown, yellow and white. This has been the century of the great immigrant experiment. It is only this late in the day that you can walk into a playground and find Isaac Leung by the fish pond, Danny Rahman in the football cage, Quang O'Rourke bouncing a basketball, and Irie Jones humming a tune. Children with first and last names on a direct collision course. Names that secrete within them mass exodus, cramped boats and planes, cold arrivals, medical checks. (326)

Far from being a 'needless little lecture', as James Wood dubs it (44), the passage is highly significant insofar as, beneath its veneer of irony and wordplay, it conveys a deeply serious message. It juxtaposes two fundamentally distinct worlds, the seemingly carefree atmosphere of a London school playground, and the harshness that makes up the typical fate of the most diverse immigrants. The setting itself is highly ambiguous: while the playground is a quasi-external, open space free of classroom constraints, it is also constantly monitored and presumably fenced off. In spite of this ambiguity, the reader is all too easily deluded by the initial sense of playfulness that the scene engenders and made to believe that this is all somehow 'fun', the result of a large-scale 'experiment'. This turn of phrase sets the tone for the remainder of the passage, somewhat mellowing in advance the harsh reality evoked in the following sentences. Indeed, a reading in terms of the celebratory nature of multicultural life is proved wrong by the narrative voice itself, as is highlighted by the following lines, which explicitly evoke the persistent reality of racism:

> Yet despite all the mixing up, despite the fact that we have finally slipped into each other's lives with reasonable comfort […] [t]here are still young white men who are *angry* about that; who will roll out at closing time

into the poorly lit streets with a kitchen knife wrapped in a tight fist. (327) [original emphasis]

In the face of narratorial remarks of this kind, it is hard to understand why many critics have fallen prey to the politically correct, jargonistic celebration of multiculturalism that the novel may seem to invoke, but is effectively at pains to disavow, an issue discussed for instance by Peter Childs (210). The fault lines and limitations of the multicultural ideal are all too obviously exposed by a reality in which difference does matter and sameness is sometimes violently pursued. What is more, apart from the threat of racist violence, difference has detrimental implications for the migrant in yet another respect: 'it makes an immigrant laugh to hear the fears of the nationalist, scared of infection, penetration, miscegenation, when this is small fry, *peanuts*, compared to what the immigrant fears – dissolution, *disappearance*' (327) [original emphasis]. This is a far cry from fashionable conceptualizations of hybrid multicultural identities, and it casts doubt on readings of the novel such as Schäfer's which understand it as 'offer[ing] a surprisingly affirmative approach to the complicated multiplicity of postcolonial subjectivity' (109). Elaine Childs rightly observes that 'hybridity itself is less a utopia than a source of anxiety for many of *White Teeth*'s characters' (8). Instead, they are persistently engaged in a quest to establish their roots, a quest which is inherently irresolvable and painful to boot, and which for that very reason does not allow for a facile acceptance of multiplicity.

The traumatic nature of the experience of migration lies in the fundamental threat to identity and selfhood it entails, both literally and metaphorically. What this passage reiterates, then, is the novel's characteristic strategy of employing dual layers of narrative – surface comedy or irony coupled with a profoundly serious 'deep' underlying level which surfaces. While the comedic stance may be the most immediately recognizable and most readily appealing, it is the second narrative layer which conveys the novel's more significant and potentially far more disturbing points. The fact that this kind of commentary is offered via a third-person narrator's authoritative intervention does not diminish the characters' credibility, but rather gives a voice to their experience that may otherwise not be heard, cultural externalities that frame their lives.

This narrative duality is ubiquitous in the novel. It is also discernible in those passages in which the omniscient narrator retreats in favour of the characters' internal perspective. This mechanism can be traced, for instance, in the depiction of Millat, who lives out his sense of unbelonging in a particularly destructive fashion. As a teenager, he gets involved in a succession of street gangs that eventually morph into a radical Islamic organization. Admittedly, this fundamentalist group is pictured as a silly project of bored and disillusioned adolescents of less than dogmatic Muslim faith and lacks a sound ideological footing; their 'acronym problem'

(295) of *Keepers of the Eternal and Victorious Islamic Nation*, or KEVIN is symptomatic. In fact, several critics have taken issue with this comic portrayal of a group that signifies, essentially, a terrorist threat and a rejection of universal human rights. Susie Thomas, for instance, argues with historical hindsight that with regard to the coordinated bomb attacks by Islamic fundamentalists on the London transport system on 7 July 2005:

> 7/7 has exposed the fatuousness of Smith's cute celebration of cultural hybridity: [...] now that KEVIN has come to King's Cross with his backpack, Smith's insight and understanding of contemporary issues seems hopelessly inadequate. (6)

While one might, of course, hold the opinion that to portray an extremist group in anything but a serious light is insensitive or shows a lack of good taste, the verdict in readings such as Thomas's seems to me to miss the crucial point of the novel. After all, the ironic overtones that are undoubtedly present in Smith's treatment of KEVIN are only one side of the coin – on the other hand, the violent and aggressive dimensions of Millat's activism are strongly palpable, not least in the final scene of the novel, in which they stage an armed assault on the launch of Marcus Chalfen's genetically modified Future Mouse. For all the mockery that its depiction abounds with, KEVIN does propound fundamentalist ideas of violently upholding cultural difference. It is a helpless counter-reaction, fuelled by a diffuse anger, to the sense of alienation Millat and his peers experience in a society that responds to ethnic difference with blunt and discriminatory categorizations:

> He knew that he, Millat, was a Paki no matter where he came from; that he smelt of curry; had no sexual identity; took other people's jobs; or had no job and bummed off the state; or gave all the jobs to his relatives; that he could be a dentist or a shop-owner or a curry-shifter, but not a footballer or a film-maker; that he should go back to his own country; or stay here and earn his bloody keep; [...] that no one who looked like Millat, or spoke like Millat, or felt like Millat, was ever on the news unless they had recently been murdered. In short, he knew he had no face in this country, no voice in the country [...]. (233–4)

This passage is clearly designed to offer Millat's point of view. Ironically, the rambling tirade of allusions to low-key racism aptly demonstrates that Millat, indeed, has 'no voice': the narrative constantly veers between Millat's free indirect discourse and unmarked quotations of stereotypical racist commentary. In other words, all Millat can do to express his sense of self is cite populist formulae that ostracize him – or, indeed, take recourse to violence. As John McLeod observes, 'in episodes such as these, there is an attempt to render a distinctly poignant and solemn articulation of the pain of being '"different" in London, and the dangerous consequences this may create' (42). If the comical portrayal of Millat's group appears to predominate, this can be taken as yet another example of our habit to read selectively and to delude ourselves about the poignancy with which the novel treats the issues it deals in.

This poignancy is also present in the novel's portrayal of mixed-race Irie, who reacts to her sense of alienation with aggression, in her case directed against herself. Again, the text clearly offers us Irie's perspective, dotted with broader cultural references inserted by the narrator. Examining herself in the mirror, she finds that her voluptuous figure, inherited from her grandmother, does not conform to European ideals of beauty:

> The European proportions of Clara's figure had skipped a generation, and she [Irie] was landed instead with Hortense's substantial Jamaican frame, loaded with pineapples, mangoes and guavas [...] ledges genetically designed with another country in mind, another climate. (265–6)

It is significant that the narrator's commentary focuses on the fact that these features are inherited, that is, they cannot be changed at will. As Irie painfully realizes, a significant part of who she is – her body – is something she was born with, inherited genetically. Her attempts to change her appearance fail miserably and only highlight the futility of her endeavours. By extension, Irie's Caribbean roots, which her shape points to, are equally irremovable, beyond the scope of individual self-fashioning. Because she is unable to transcend the corporeal constraints to which her body subjects her, Irie feels disconnected from England, her country of birth. What is more, it is almost as if her difference has prevented her individuation and thwarted her sense of self. In a painful reversal of the Lacanian mirror, she fails to be recognized by her 'other': 'There was England, a gigantic mirror, and there was Irie, without reflection. A stranger in a stranger land' (266).

Moreover, Irie's self-alienation also has a disturbing dimension that forbids reading her as a mere victim of hegemonic (white) ideals of beauty. Earlier in the novel she is shown to fiercely cling to any scrap of information on her origin on which she can lay her hands. Staying with her grandmother Hortense during a brief stint of adolescent rebellion Irie discovers fragments concerning the Jamaican branch of her family, becoming obsessed with 'the secrets that had been hoarded for so long' (399) and dedicates herself to unearthing the hidden recesses of the past:

> She laid claim to the past – her version of the past – aggressively, as if retrieving misdirected mail. So *this* was where she came from. This all *belonged* to her, her birthright, like a pair of pearl earrings or a post office bond. X marks the spot, and Irie put an X on everything she found, collecting bits and bobs (birth certificates, maps, army reports, news articles) and storing them under the sofa, so that as if by osmosis the

richness of them would pass through the fabric while she was sleeping
and seep right into her. (400; original emphasis)

Importantly, Irie is not portrayed as the stereotypical postcolonial subject,
condemned to marginalization. Rather, her gestures of 'la[ying] claim
to the past' are suffused with images of mastery: it is 'her version of the
past' that her research conjures up, and her marking of texts and objects
smacks of a positively 'colonialist' act of taking possession. The text itself
is aware of these implications: two pages onwards, the narrator comments
that 'Jamaica appeared to Irie as if it were newly made. Like Columbus
himself, just by discovering it she had brought it into existence' (402).
Again, one is dealing with an omniscient narrator who is offering the reader
insights into Irie's psyche, and these narratorial commentaries contain
the essence of the novel's message. More importantly, they jar with the
reader's common expectations of the postcolonial subject's victim status
and clear-cut oppressor–perpetrator dichotomies. Instead, the text suggests
that the search for roots is both a universal human need and a profoundly
disturbing endeavour expressive of a desire for power and dominance – a
condition that locks people into a cycle of violence and pain from which
they seem unable to escape.

Evidently, then, *White Teeth* highlights the painful underbelly of migration
and cultural mixing. Far from offering an 'undemanding multiculturalism',
as Susie Thomas claims (6), it demands that its reader look beneath the
veneer of light-hearted comedy that a cursory reading might foreground.
Moreover, it is those passages which clearly render the point of view of one
of the novel's characters that candidly expose its critique of widespread
multiculturalist ideals. A selective reading that fails to take note of the less
optimistic, if not outright brutal and violent facets of *White Teeth* surely
falls short of aptly recognizing the novel's agenda. Beyond its commentary
on contemporary multiculturalism, what *White Teeth* promotes is a set of
unsettling truths: the inescapability of roots and history in human lives,
the impact of biology and the body on our sense of self, and the violence
intrinsic to human affairs. This also explains, I believe, why so many
readers and critics apparently fall prey to misreadings that consistently
ignore the disturbing flip side of multicultural coexistence. After all, what
White Teeth invites one to appreciate are those elements of a shared human
condition that people so often prefer to ignore. The narrative perspective
replicates this mechanism with its veneer of surface comedy, at the same
time as it draws attention to these unacknowledged realities. In this sense,
the narrative omniscience that pervades the text is the key to communicating the novel's message. The narrator does not, however, function as a
moralizing manipulator whose dominance drives home a particular point
and serves to silence alternative worldviews. Rather, the narrative voice
brings to the surface the poignant experiences, emotional dilemmas and
violent potentials that the characters' actions imply. In so doing, it alerts

readers to those dimensions of the text which they would mostly prefer to overlook and thereby makes each one complicit in the very interpretive ventures the novel seeks to expose as insufficient. The narative's emphasis on the palpably material impact of history, on violence and the body jars with contemporary fantasies of playful hybridity and autonomous self-fashioning. The narrative perspective this realizes a meta-critical impetus, by which the novel exposes individual ways of reading: people tend to read into a text what they prefer or want to read; that is, they all too easily ignore those aspects of a text that contradict their own professed agendas.

Bibliography

Brison, Susan J. 'Trauma Narratives and the Remaking of the Self'. In *Acts of Memory: Cultural Recall in the Present*. Mieke Bal, Jonathan Crewe and Leo Spitzer (eds). Hanover and London: University Press of New England, 1999, 39–54.

Childs, Elaine. 'Insular Utopias and Religious Neuroses: Hybridity Anxiety in Zadie Smith's *White Teeth*'. *Proteus* 23 (2006): 7–12.

Childs, Peter. *Contemporary Novelists: British Fiction Since 1970*. Houndmills: Palgrave Macmillan, 2005.

Dawson, Paul. 'The Return of Omniscience in Contemporary Fiction'. *Narrative* 17.2 (2009): 143–61.

McLeod, John. 'Revisiting Postcolonial London'. *The European English Messenger*. 14 (2005): 39–46.

Merrit, Stephanie. 'She's young, black, British – and the first publishing sensation of the millennium'. *The Observer* 16 January 2000: http://www.guardian.co.uk/books/ 2000/jan/16/fiction.zadiesmith (accessed 29 September 2009). N. Pag.

Radstone, Susannah. 'The War of the Fathers: Trauma, Fantasy, and September 11'. In *Trauma at Home. After 9/11*. Judith Greenberg (ed.). Lincoln and London: University of Nebraska Press, 2003, 117–23.

Schäfer, Stefanie. '"Looking back, you do not find what you left behind': Postcolonial Subjectivity and the Role of Memory in White Teeth and The Inheritance of Loss'. In *Hello, I Say, It's Me': Contemporary Reconstructions of Self and Subjectivity*. Jan D. Kucharzewski, Stefanie Schäfer and Lutz Schowalter (eds). Trier: Wissenschaftlicher Verlag Trier, 2009, 107–27.

Schoene, Berthold. *The Cosmopolitan Novel*. Edinburgh: Edinburgh University Press, 2009.

Sell, Jonathan P. A. 'White Teeth'. *The Literary Encyclopedia*, 23 April 2008: http://www.litencyc.com/php/sworks.php?rec=true&UID=8775 (accessed 9 June 2010). N. Pag.

Smith, Zadie. *White Teeth*. London: Penguin, 2001 [2000].

Tew, Philip. *Zadie Smith*. Houndmills: Palgrave Macmillan, 2010.

Thomas, Susie. 'Zadie Smith's False Teeth: The Marketing of Multiculturalism'. *Literary London: Interdisciplinary Studies in the Representation of London* 4: 1 (2006): http://www.literarylondon.org/london-journal/march2006/thomas. html (accessed 29 September 2009).

Wood, James. 'Human, All Too Inhuman: The Smallness of the "Big" Novel. *White Teeth* by Zadie Smith'. *The New Republic* 223.4 (2000): 41–5.

—*The Irresponsible Self: On Laughter and the Novel*. New York: Farrar, Straus and Giroux, 2004.

3

Body Larceny: Somatic Seizure and Control in *White Teeth*

Joanna O'Leary

Following the 2000 publication of *White Teeth*, most scholars and reviewers focused largely on the novel's model of multiculturalism. 'The reading of *White Teeth*', Katarzyna Jakubiak has noted, 'as an "optimistic", at times even "utopian" view of race relations, unites critics regardless of their geographic location' (202). Issues of national identity in the text have equally engendered robust discussions of its representations of *hybridity*. In *The Contemporary British Novel* Philip Tew has argued that this idea's 'complex and adaptive sense of always contending cultures and individualities can bring about a reading of a new Britishness that absorbs much of the old', and notably writes that 'this consciousness is active in the literary scene, part of a renewed radicalization of the novel [...]perhaps best epitomized by the huge success and popularity of Zadie Smith's *White Teeth*' (xii). Likewise, for Raphael Dalleo, the novel sustains variously a 'critique of hybridity discourse' (100).

Such scholarly emphasis on the novel's apparently rosy view of ethnic heterogeneity, however, can distract us from its exploration of the desirability of general human, rather than specific racial, perfection. Set against a backdrop of genetic manipulation, *White Teeth* continually confronts the reader with questions concerning whether an ideal body form exists, and the moral issues of manipulating other (non-ideal) bodies. The parental (P_1) generation subscribe to certain ideas of bodily perfection for their own children while they themselves inhabit bodies that have degenerated, eroded, expanded, or even permanently malfunctioned. The tension that arises when their imperfections are placed in the context of a scientific society that seems to promote striving ceaselessly towards an unattainable ideal leaves the reader wondering if power over the body is assumed but never realized. While all the characters in *White Teeth* wrestle with issues of somatic manipulation, perhaps the most compelling is Samad Iqbal's struggle to control both his body as well those of his sons and wife.

The body desired vs. the body occupied

The body of the young Samad Iqbal is already significantly marked; to Archie he bitterly recollects how on the third day of serving in Italy, a 'bastard fool' shot through his wrist, leaving him with a dead, grey hand (76). Unlike other characters in the novel whose bodies are changed by accident, trauma or age, Samad aggressively insists that his intimates and the world should continually recognize and remember this injury. However given the option to have the hand removed, Samad claims he 'wouldn't have it amputated' because he wishes to meet his maker in one piece: 'Every bit of my body comes from Allah. Every bit will return to him' (76).

He may have been better off without the dead hand, however, for in the 30-plus years following his accident, it will alternately haunt and invigorate him. At the conclusion of the war, the younger Samad despairs over the hand and other signs of bodily deterioration:

> He saw his reflection this evening, and it was ugly. He saw where he was
> – at the farewell party for the end of Europe – and he *longed* for the East.
> He looked down at his useless hand with its five useless appendages; at
> his skin, burned to a chocolate-brown by the sun; he saw into his brain,
> made stupid by stupid conversation and the dull stimuli of death, and
> longed for the man he once was; erudite, light-skinned Samad Miah. (94)

Proclaiming himself 'worse for the wear', Samad mourns the death of a greater self and a better body. Once 'the warm color of baked bread', his skin is now overcooked, 'burned to a chocolate-brown by the sun' (94, 71). He perceives that his sharper, educated younger self has been replaced by someone slower who has been rendered 'out of sorts' by the dull, unrefined world of war. This weathered body is the one that the reader associates with Samad because it is the only one the reader really knows; the 'erudite, light-skinned Samad Miah' exists only as aspiration and nostalgic ideal. For that reason, the character of Samad becomes the novel's most profound representation of the gap between the body inhabited and the body desired. His continual rejection of his body prompts even more questions concerning whether in spurning his body, Samad automatically rejects himself, and whether one can pick and choose which somatic changes to comply with and which to reject.

While satisfactorily resolving these questions lies beyond the scope of this essay, considering the particular case of Samad in light of ongoing discourse concerning the body facilitates a more informed understanding of his somatic issues. In 'Time Binds, or Erotohistoriography', Elizabeth Freeman discusses the idea of incorporation, initially described by critics Nicolas Abraham and Maria Torok, which according to Freeman's summary 'is the pathological form of a process they call introjection, where the lost object serves as a means for the subject to rework its originary erotic autonomy' (63–4). Interestingly in terms of Samad, Abraham and Torok actually specify that ion such contexts 'fantasy is essentially narcissistic, it tends to transform the world rather than inflict injury on the subject' (125). Samad cannot forgive the world for injuring him. Freeman references this process in an argument for the sort of 'time binding' that affects queer persons and groups; she defines 'binding' as a 'model of dispersed by insistently carnal continuity' and figures it as a sort of predicament faced by queers, who cannot guarantee the succession of queers. 'Binds' are also 'attachments' formed 'against spatial and temporal boundaries' (61). Despite the specificity of Freeman's terminology and analysis, such concepts are nevertheless helpful in comprehending and charting the development (or anti-development) of Samad. The effective loss of Samad's right hand plunges him into what Maria Torok describes as follows precisely not in terms of an unshakeable obsession with the lost object since:

> The illness of mourning [melancholia] does not result, as might appear, from the affliction caused by the objectal loss itself, but rather from the feeling of irreparable crime: the crime of having been overcome with desire, of having been surprised by an overflow of libido at the least appropriate moment, when it would behoove us to be grieved in despair. (110)

The particular significance of Samad's *right* hand lends itself to categorization as a fitting symbol of loss in Torok and Freeman's discussion. If in possession of two fully functional hands, Samad would have been free to engage in mainstream, right-handed male masturbation. His injury, combined with his 'marriage to the small-palmed, weak-wristed, and uninterested Alsana', necessitate using his one and only functional appendage to engage in satisfying but religiously troubling masturbation (115). Although Samad overtly mourns that the loss of the right hand means 'more blood and sticky guilt on [his] one good hand', his conscious grief may be masking discomfort over the 'overflow of libido' he felt upon realizing for what the remaining hand, by process of elimination, must be responsible (127). As Freeman points out, Freud argues that 'subjectivity begins when the libido invests in an uncomfortable bodily sensation by means of which it doubles back upon itself to delineate body parts as such' (61). Therefore, Samad comes into being and is in a way reborn, when he subconsciously associates the cumbersome dead hand with sexual drive.

In constantly looking back to a better self as well as telling and retelling the story of Mangal Pande, Samad can be considered 'bound' temporally in Freeman's sense because Samad's continual regression cannot help but disallow a whole-hearted progression. Although as Freeman points out, 'even as it suggests connectivity, "binds", also names a certain fixity in time, a state of being timebound, belated, incompletely developed, left behind or not there yet, going nowhere' (61). And 'going nowhere', as Freeman points out, has 'everything to do with sex' because binding implies a 'containment of otherwise freely circulating libidinal energies' (61). One may reasonably assume that Samad's self-hatred climaxes when in 1945 he concludes to Archie, 'I have been thinking that I am buggered, Lieutenant Jones. I see no future' (94). For a 'cripple' whose 'faith is crippled' there seems to be no choice: 'If I were to pull this trigger, what will I leave behind? An Indian, a turncoat English Indian with a limp wrist like a faggot and no medals that they can ship home with me' (95). Because the future is as good as death, there might as well not be one; thus, Samad's only option for life is the past, an uncomplicated place where he is a heterosexual good Muslim with two hands, light skin and no shame.

Bound ceaselessly to what Graham Huggan describes as the migrant's 'ever-present burden of the past' (760), Samad Iqbal attempts to release what might have been 'otherwise freely circulating energies' first by some vigorous left-handed masturbation and then by an ineffectual, guilt-ridden affair with Poppy Burt-Jones. The masturbation outlet provokes mixed feelings: 'Those two months, between seeing the pretty redhaired music teacher once and seeing her again, were the longest, stickiest, smelliest, guiltiest of Samad's life' (117); and the affair, as Shiva Bhagwati predicts, 'never works' (122). What appears instead is a more viable vessel for his sexual energies: his children.

The expectant child

Initially, Samad Iqbal invests everything in his sons Millat and Magid because through them he can accomplish all that his 'buggery' hand prevented. Although many scholars have posited the idea of the child as a vehicle for parental aspirations was especially popular in the nineteenth century, as critic James Kincaid has pointed out, 'this great image of erotic passion in the *modern* Anglo-American imagination is put together out of childhood and emptiness' (12). Kincaid's study *Child-Loving* primarily concerns itself with the implications of the figure of the ideal child on American culture, but his critique speaks more broadly of a general Western conception:

> Childhood can be made a wonderfully hollow category, able to be filled up with anyone's overflowing emotions, not least overflowing passion. Into this vacuum, then, strong desire can leap, calling itself

pure and calling what it finds not pedophilia but tragic romance. Two little children stand at the center of our erotic figurings, and they do so precisely because they are so pure. (12)

While Kincaid does not refer specifically of the two Iqbal boys in this passage, his conclusions are eerily relevant when considering Samad's infatuation with both children early in the novel. The birth of his sons signals not just a reorientation in focus from himself and his own troubles to the potential of his own progeny, but also engenders a grander overhaul of Samad's entire worldview:

Children. Samad caught children like a disease. Yes, he had sired two of them willingly – as willingly as a man can – but he had not bargained for this other thing. This thing that no one tells you about. This thing of *knowing* children. (105)

This 'thing' that no one told Samad is the degree to which children as an idea come to dominate your entire existence once you become a parent. It is not just Millat and Magid who have hijacked their father's life, but also the ideal they represent. In that way, all children have become Samad's children, and for that reason, he finds himself a 'parent-governor', the inevitable leader and protector of the child community and what it represents: generally, the future; personally, the achievement of his unmet goals. Although at first Samad is 'turning up at weekly school council meetings, organizing concerts, discussing plans for a new music department, donating funds for the rejuvenation of the water fountains', his attention to reforming the twins' educational environment wanes when it becomes clear his efforts have not so much as changed the school's pedagogical techniques as they have drawn him into a dead-end extra-marital affair (105).

It is in the midst of this relationship with Poppy Burt-Jones that Samad realizes the futility of trying to overhaul the entire British educational system and to block the cultural forces that are negatively affecting his sons. During his forays with Poppy, Magid and Millat begin to haunt him: 'I see the twins whenever I am with her – like apparitions! Even when we are ... I see them there. Smiling there' (157). Their appearance even during intercourse reminds Samad of his own moral degeneration, and subsequently suggests to him his ineligibility for parenthood: 'I looked at my boys Archie [...] I kept thinking: how can I teach my boys anything, how can I show them the straight road when I have lost my own bearings' (158). The grinning specters of Magid and Millat, seemingly mocking their father's weakness and incompetence, are sufficient provocation for him to take drastic action. Samad fells impelled to ask himself: '*What kind of a world do I want my children to grow up in?*' (158). Although Smith's novel is comic, as Tew points out in *Zadie Smith* (2010) 'the characters laugh very little. They do not share humour among themselves' (48) and this evidently includes Samad concerning his transgressions. As he feels himself 'hellbound', the only redemption possible is through saving [his] sons by removing one or both to the place of his direct (and their indirect) origin. In Bangladesh, Samad decides 'Roots were what saved, the ropes one throws out to rescue drowning men, to Save Their Souls' and imagines his children will acquire 'roots on shore, deep roots that no storm or gale could displace' (161). He can prevent Mickey Abdul's glib conclusion of 'We're all English now, mate' (160) from ever applying to Magid and Millat if he can only remake them by substituting East for West in the origin of their identity.

Ironically, as Phyllis Lassner notes, 'consequence' is more elusive' for Samad, especially given that 'both sons defy his plotting' (196). Nevertheless, via this geographical transplantation, Samad not only intends for his children to save themselves as well as him, but also he wishes to effect progress he was unable to inspire. For along with acting as vessels of their father's desire, Magid and Millat also serve as arbiters of futurity in a manner distinctly more significant than other child characters in *White Teeth* such as Irie Jones or Josh Chalfen. Lee Edelman, in honing in on the figure of the child in his discussion of reproductive futurity, specifically examines what he calls 'the pervasive invocation of the Child as the emblem of futurity's unquestioned value [...]' (4). Edelman questions the extent to which the figure of the Child has been elevated such that it becomes an untouchable symbol of temporal progression. Although Edelman's study more explicitly concerns how the queer population has exempted itself from a future by resisting normative reproductive practices, his thoughts on Western society's over-indulgence of the child figure in part explains why Samad focuses blindly on their development.

Indeed, the novel privileges Magid and Millat, rather than other child characters, with a special responsibility to temporal progression in its attempts to explore the power of heredity. As identical genetic copies, the twins are the ideal case study for examining the nature–nurture effect as well as contemplating the utility and desirability of somatic control. Samad's splitting of the twins effectively becomes an unplanned experiment on the influence of environment on growth and development and throughout the novel one looks forward to comparing the results when both twins finally emerge from their respective geographical 'wombs' of Bangladesh and England. Their parallel maturation is far from conclusive evidence that Samad's initiative in removing one to Bangladesh was at all successful (mostly because his own specific goals for them are ambiguous), and it is not the concern of this essay to explore fully the novel's treatment of genetic versus environmental determinism. More important, perhaps, is to note that even though only Magid is sent away, both children reject serving as the vehicles for their father's desire and yet at the same time cannot escape somatic corrosion from external forces.

The obsession with the child figure Edelman outlines and that which is exemplified by Samad lays the groundwork for other, potentially more important questions about the child's capacity to resist being idealized, and exactly what impact this 'bad' child might have on conceptions of futurity. Kincaid addresses this issue to some extent when he argues: 'By insisting so loudly on the innocence, purity, and asexuality of the child, we have created a subversive echo: experience, corruption, and eroticism' (4–5). Because even as a young child Millat 'was the one more in need of moral direction', it is not surprising to Samad or the reader when he grows older he appears not live up to Samad's vision of him (163). 'He was arsey and mouthy, he had his fierce good looks squashed tightly inside him like a jack-in-the-box set to spring aged thirteen, at which pointed he graduated from leader of zit-faced boys to leader of women' (181). Although Samad bemoans the behaviour of 'the son he *could* see', it is not simply because Millat has become the son he did *not* want. In spurning his father's desires, Millat unconsciously strangely fulfils them by becoming an influential leader among his peers, an objectively attractive and sexually attractive boy, and a devoted, albeit militant, Muslim (180).

While his brother Magid initially appears to be ample proof of the success of Samad's removal and redemption plan, he, too, eventually disappoints Samad, by rejecting Islam entirely:

> That is the very reason I sent the child there – to understand that essentially we are weak, that we are not in control. What does Islam mean? [...] I surrender to God [...] This is not my life, this is his life. This life I call mine is his to do with what he will. (240)

Magid is pegged as a failed case even though he has exceeded his father's scholarly expectations; however, because this achievement predisposes him to developing a more nuanced approach to faith and religion than Samad, he eventually evolves beyond his father's vision. Samad does not see the irony in his admonishment of Magid for failing to see that 'we are not in control' when Samad attempts to do what he will with his son's life. It is not just Samad who suffers because his child falls short of his preconceived ideal:

> Still, there was much discussion [...] and not just Millat but *all* the children [...] *what was wrong with all the children*, what had gone wrong with these first descendants of the great ocean-crossing experiment? Didn't they have everything they could want? (182)

These 'first descendants', who have been fed 'regular meals', dressed in 'clean clothes from Marks 'n' Sparks', shaped by a 'top-notch education' and filled with the hopes and dreams of their parents fail to respond as intended to such environmental influences.

This resistance on the part of the children manifests itself in 'mascara in the evenings', 'marijuana and very baggy trousers', 'sex before marriage with a Chinese boy' and other deviant behaviours that continually change and mark the body such that it slips from the grasp of the parents and becomes more controlled and identified with the child (182). Samad's motivation for sending Magid so far away is in part an attempt to prevent or at least ignore the inevitable changes and alterations to Magid's body that reinforce Samad's ultimate inability to determine his son's future: 'Two sons. One invisible and perfect, frozen at the pleasant age of nine, static in a picture frame while the television underneath him spewed out all the shit of the eighties [...] above which mess the child rose untouchable and unstained' (180). Temporally freezing Magid such that he remains 'static' as everything but him changes is the only way Samad can hold onto the vision of his idealized son and continue to employ him to satisfy his own desires. Magid, 'A ghostly daguerreotype formed from the quicksilver of the father's imagination' is therefore removed before Samad witnesses his erosion, for 'Samad had long learned to worship what he could not see' (180).

The unavoidable changes to Magid's body that occur out of Samad's line of sight may threaten his presumed control and for that reason he tends to interpret these alterations as proof of his own vision. For example, when Magid writes home to report of his broken nose that, Clara reports, makes him look like 'a little aristocrat, like a little Englishman', thereby rendering him and Millat 'not so much like twins anymore', Samad welcomes this change. 'It is good that you see the difference between you two boys, Millat, now rather than later', proclaims Samad, who likes the idea of the broken nose because it aligns with the differentiation he himself has attempted to effect by imposing a physical separation between the two boys (180). Magid's body is now marked as to distinguish him not just from his twin but also from his peer group: 'Others may scoff, but you and I know that your brother will lead others out of the wilderness. He will be a leader of tribes. He is a natural *chief*' (180). Invoking the injury as evidentiary support of his son's future greatness, Samad attempts to take ownership over Magid's new, marked body by re-projecting specific expectations. His pronouncement directly leads his failure to reclaim Magid, for 'Millat laughed so hard at this' that 'he lost his footing, slipped on a washcloth, and broke his nose against the sink', thus rendering him once again physically identical to his brother (180).

Alsana in pain

Samad's efforts to 'freeze' Magid and control both the bodies of both his sons are undermined not only by the twins' natural growth and continual mutations in response to external forces, but also by his wife. Alsana's success in resisting Samad's attempts to control her body threaten his confidence by reminding him of his failure to own even that which was given explicitly to him. Indeed, even before she was a body that could be controlled, the absence that would become Alsana was already promised to Samad. Because her family was 'the very best people' with 'extremely good blood', Samad looked forward to the birth of his future wife who was supposed to (as is the 'propensity among their women') have 'really enormous melons' (83). The potential body of the not-yet-born 'Miss Begum' as well as the knowledge that she will be younger and 'easy' was enough to secure Samad's confidence in the match. Once married, Samad readily learns that he cannot hope to control Alsana 'who was prone to moments, even fits – yes, fits was not too strong a word – of rage' (51). When Samad infuriates her the writhing Alsana on occasion '[slammed her little fist on to the kitchen table' and even 'punched him full square in the stomach' to assert her ownership of her body and display its power (51, 52).

Alsana allows her husband to mark her body permanently just once, via the pregnancy with the twins, but then denies him access. Once impregnated, Alsana exercises full control over the (unborn) children, not even allowing Samad to accompany her to the ultrasound: 'He didn't see anything. He wasn't there. I am not letting him see things like that. A woman has to have the private things – a husband needn't be involved in body-business, in a lady's ... *parts*' (63). Designating the body a private realm to which only a privileged few have access empowers Alsana by giving her a material means of leveraging power in a relationship that is culturally predisposed to be patriarchal. Just as Alsana gives little of her body to Samad, she expects and desires the same from him. After Alsana asserts that 'not everybody wants to see into everybody else's sweaty, secret parts' (65), her 'Niece-of-Shame' responds 'How can you *bear* to live with somebody you don't know from Adam?' (65), a point rejected by her aunt since as Alsana insists it is this practice of bodily nondisclosure that enables Alsana to tolerate Samad to the extent that their marriage can endure:

> Yes, I was married to Samad Iqbal the same evening of the very day I met him. Yes, I didn't know him from Adam. But I liked him well enough [...] I thought he had a good face, a sweet voice, and his backside was high and well formed for a man of his age. Very good. Now, every time I learn something more about him, *I like him less*. So you see, we were better off the way we were. (66)

If the success of connubial relations depends on both parties' willingness to *not* possess, to *not* know the other's body, then one can understand why the Iqbal marriage is less than blissful.

Before Samad ships Magid off to Bangladesh, the point at which he transitions from attempting to control equally the bodies of wife and children to focusing almost all his energy on the body of Magid, he pre-empts Alsana's confrontation by attacking first: 'Look at you, look at the state of you! Look how *fat* you are!' [...] 'Look how you dress. Running shoes and a sari?' [...] 'We never see family anymore – I am ashamed to show you to them' (166).

Samad, with his 'buggery hand', pot-belly, and graying hair, is repulsed by how his wife has changed in response to temporal forces, cultural pressures and her own initiative to increase her body mass precisely because he has sanctioned none of these influences (75).

Keeping up with the Jones

When compared to the marriage of Alsana and Samad, the relationship between Archie Jones and Clara Bowden seems downright idyllic. The relative success of their marriage despite similar (and perhaps even greater) obstacles can be attributed to the absence of a desire in both partners to control each others' bodies and the body of their daughter. Like Samad, Archie's body is marked by war prior to meeting Clara, but because he is not openly fixated on the injury, neither is anyone else:

> Archie even had a bit of shrapnel in the leg for anyone who cared to see it – but nobody did. No one wanted to talk about *that* anymore. It was like club-foot, or a disfiguring mole. It was like nose hair. People looked away. (12)

While Samad does not question the importance of his history and willingly chains himself to the past, Archie decides early on that 'There was no relevance in the war – not in 1955, even less now in 1894. Nothing he did *then* mattered *now*' (12). His suicide crisis further reinforces this belief that what is passed is unimportant; after being saved early on New Year's day, Archie feels himself in a 'past-tense, future-perfect kind of mood' (15). After his epiphany 'A new Archie is about emerge', one that is all about futurity, focusing exclusively on '*maybe this, maybe that*' (15). Unlike Samad, Archie need not continually reject his body because he is interested not in what it did *not* help him achieve but rather in what it might bring. His subsequent relationship with Clara reaffirms the irrelevance (or the power) of his marked body for this woman 38 years his junior and 'the most beautiful thing he had ever seen' marries him after just six weeks (20). Even though Clara herself 'understood that Archibald Jones was no romantic hero' (40) what with 'the way his stomach hung pregnant over his belt', she decides, 'He was a *good* man. And *good* might not amount to much, *good* might not light up a life, but it is something' (41). She circumvents the problem of the present 'white, flabby' Archie during love-making by focusing on the image of 'young soldier Archie' and comforting herself the rest of the time with the knowledge that his inherent 'goodness' transcends his less desirable body.

Because Archie has 'No aims, no hopes, no ambitions' he, unlike Samad, does not require a vessel for his overflowing desires (41). Archie's passion for his wife suggests that he got all he ever wanted in Clara, and for that reason, the birth of his daughter Irie is an added bonus, not an opportunity to project his unfulfilled aspirations. His early enthusiasm about the unborn child revolves around the idea that she is product of both him and wife and not something whose fate he alone can determine: 'Her and me have a child, the genes mix up, and blue eyes! Miracle of nature!' (59). Archie revels in the fact that he was won the genetic lottery, implicitly accepting that following conception his involvement in the child's development will be limited.

Like Archie, Clara relinquishes control over her daughter's body, welcoming the fact that 'The European proportions of Clara's figure had skipped a generation, and she [Irie] was landed instead with Hortense's substantial Jamaican frame' (221). Though Irie is inclined to be 'obsessed' with her weight, and as a result, wears 'elaborate corsetry' to change her somatic appearance, Clara tries to persuade her against this self-rejection: 'What is Lord's name are you wearing? How can you breathe? Irie, my love, you're fine – you're just built like an honest-to-God Bowden – don't you know you're fine' (222). Convinced she is anything but 'fine', Irie later attempts a more violent manipulation of her body when she goes to P. K'.s Afro Hair 'intent upon transformation, intent upon fighting her genes' (227). But she soon realizes the inauthenticity of her mutated body with its unnaturally straight when she catches 'an unfortunate glimpse of herself in the scratch and stain of the hall mirror' and when she witnesses Samad and Alsana's argument over the changes in Magid. As Alsana pleads, 'You say we have no control, yet you always try to control everything! Let *go*, Samad Miah. Let the boy go', (241) Irie sees her own desires for somatic control exponentially magnified in Samad and understands the suffering that results from continually trying to lay claim over a resisting body. Although Samad ignores Alsana's warning, '*You have to let them make their own mistakes ...* ' Irie absorbs this advice as she 'stood, facing her own reflection, busy tearing out somebody else's hair with her bare hands' (241). While the immediate effect of this scene is Irie's appreciation of the folly of seeking total somatic control, this event also positions her to save and even redeem Samad later in the novel.

Irie and futurity

The return of Magid Mahfooz Murshed Mubtasim Iqbal 'shook the houses of Iqbal, Jones and Chalfen' by revealing how much a child can deviate from his parents' expectations (350). Alsana doesn't 'recognize him'; Joyce and Irie 'viewed the new arrival with equal suspicion'; and Samad views him as 'some clone [...] not an Iqbal' but (350). Magid has not just spurned Samad's attempts to control his development; he has rejected his father altogether and replaced him with Marcus Chalfen. It is Magid whom ironically Marcus wants to shape and nurture: 'Magid was a confidant, an apprentice and disciple, accompanying Marcus on trips, observing him in the laboratory. The golden child. The chosen one' (352). Magid becomes the vessel for Marcus' hopes already: 'Maybe he had begun to hope, begun to *believe*, that Magid would be a beacon for right-thinking Chalfenism even as it died a death here in the wilderness' (348). For like Samad, Marcus has been rejected by his chosen vehicle of desire:

> As far as Josh's decision went, Marcus felt as he did about all human decisions of this kind. One could neither agree nor disagree with them as *ideas*. There was no rhyme nor reason for so much of what people did. And in his present estrangement from Joshua he felt more powerless than ever. It hurt him that even his own son was not as Chalfenist as he'd hoped. (348)

Although Marcus similarly suffers from being 'powerless' over his son, he recovers far more quickly than Samad because he finds another body that consents to his control. Interestingly, Marcus also does not code Josh's behaviour as a son's rejection of the father but rather as one individual's unavoidable conflicts in ideas with another. As evidenced by his scientific work, Marcus is certainly open to manipulating a person's genetic make-up, thereby predisposing or inclining him to be or act a certain way, but he nevertheless recognizes that once formed, a human being resists complete control.

With no alternate vessel in which to place his remaining strong desires and expectations, Samad Iqbal flounders: 'His sons had failed him. The pain was excruciating. He shuffled through the restaurant with his eyes on the ground' (351). But Samad is primed for a release from this pain by one who has also greatly suffered from her lack of somatic control: Irie Jones. She enlightens Samad and Alsana as well as her own parents that a 'peaceful existence' is not unattainable. 'What a *joy*' their lives must be, proclaims Irie (herself rather unjoyfully) of the 'lucky motherfuckers"' who do not presume to control their children's destiny: 'They don't mind what their kids do in life as long as they're reasonably, you know, *healthy. Happy*. And every single fucking day is not this huge battle between who they are and who they should be, and what they were and what they will be' (426). Even though Samad does not respond directly to Irie's recommendations, his final interaction with Hortense suggests that he has given up his quest for somatic control. Dispatched by Archie during the FutureMouse press conference to see if Mrs. Bowden 'could possible reduce the noise somewhat ... ' Samad unexpectedly experiences a life-altering revelation in his encounter with his mother-in-law. Smith prepares the reader for this moment of truth in her visual presentation of Hortense Bowden, who sits with a 'banner between her knees that states, simply, **THE TIME IS AT HAND**-Rev. 1:3' (429). Although he 'feels his resolve', Samad:

> Finds himself, to his surprise, unwilling to silence her. Partly because he is tired. Partly because he is old. But mostly because he would do the same, though in a different name. He knows what it is to seek. He knows the dryness. He has felt the thirst you get in a strange land – horrible, persistent – the thirst that lasts your whole life. (439)

As Hortense sings, Samad allows himself to accept defeat. The comfort he receives in recognizing that he is not alone in his 'horrible, persistent thirst', that others experience an insatiable desire for somatic control, ultimately enables him to acquiesce despite the fact that wife and sons are not and will never be exact representations of his hopes and dreams. Samad may not stop desiring control over their bodies to combat his own perceived inadequacies, but his acknowledgement that this 'thirst' will 'last your whole life', frees him from any expectations of achieving any sort of lasting power.

Towards the very end of *White Teeth*, Smith writes, 'The end is simply the beginning of an even longer story' and the same prescription applies to this essay (448). Although this examination of body issues in novel is oriented around the Samad Iqbal because his 'buggery hand' looms over the narrative in a way that demands significant attention, the more overt despair Samad experiences as a result of his inability to effect his own somatic make-over by controlling others' bodies may overshadow other more subtle manifestations of body concerns. The 'complete lack of teeth in the top of [Clara Bowden's] mouth', for example, warrants similar analysis in the context of Freeman's theory of introjection. Similarly, the Chalfen's cheeky baby Oscar gestures towards the figure of the resistant child and thus demands critical contextualization within Kincaid and Edelman's scholarship.

White Teeth demonstrates that the age of scientific technology significantly complicates the practice of appropriating an external (often child's) body to act as a container for one's aspirations and expectations. Controlling and manipulating the expression of genes both before and after birth means not only that the body as vessel can be designed to specification but also that its fixity cannot be assured. If 'hereditary make-up' continues to become a more fluid concept, then theoretically a generation of bodies could eventually emerge that continually resists all classifications of race, gender, sexuality and class. A botched or undesirable somatic identity, such as in the case of Samad Iqbal, would no longer be an obstacle if one has the ability to endlessly reinvent and reconfigure the body. More than ever before 'ever-evolving' would be an accurate description of the physical, the emotional and the sexual. At such a point, the questions posed at the beginning of this essay concerning the ideal body and power over that ideal body, while still relevant, may be put aside in favour of asking why anyone would need to want such control at all.

Bibliography

Abraham, Nicolas and Maria Torok. 'Mourning or Melancholia: Introjection versus Incorporation'. *The Shell and the Kernel: Renewals of Psychoanalysis.* Vol. 1. Nicholas Rand (ed. and trans.). Chicago: University of Chicago Press, 1994, 125–38.

Dalleo, Raphael. 'Colonization in Reverse: *White Teeth* as Caribbean Novel'. *Zadie Smith: Critical Essays.* Tracey Lorraine Waters (ed.). New York: Peter Lang, 2008, 91–104.

Edelman, Lee. *No Future: Queer Theory and the Death Drive.* Durham, NC: Duke University Press, 2004.

Freeman, Elizabeth. 'Time Binds, or Erotohistoriography'. *Social Text* #84–85. Special Issue, *The New Queer Theory* (October 2005): 57–68.

Huggan, Graham: 'Is the "Post" in "Postsecular" the "Post" in "Postcolonial"?' *Modern Fiction Studies* (56:4) Winter 2010, 751–68, 837.

Jakubiak, Katarzyna. 'Simulated Marketing: The International Marketing of *White Teeth*'. *Zadie Smith: Critical Essays.* Tracey Lorraine Waters (ed.). New York: Peter Lang, 2008, 201–18.

Kincaid, James R. *Child-Loving: The Erotic Child and Victorian Culture.* New York: Routledge Press, 1992.

Lassner, Phyllis. *Colonial Strangers: Women Writing the End of British Empire.* New Brunswick: Rutgers University Press, 2004.

Smith, Zadie. *White Teeth.* New York: Vintage International, 2000.

Tew, Philip. *The Contemporary British Novel.* London: Continuum, 2004.

—*Zadie Smith*. London: Palgrave Macmillan, 2010.

Torok, Maria. 'The Illness of Mourning and the Fantasy of the Exquisite Corpse'. *The Shell and the Kernel: Renewals of Psychoanalysis.* Nicholas Abraham and Maria Torok, (eds and trans.). Nicholas Rand. Chicago: University of Chicago Press, 1994, 107–24.

4

Celebrity, Suburban Identity and Transatlantic Epiphanies: Reconsidering Zadie Smith's *The Autograph Man*

Philip Tew

Set initially in an imaginary multicultural suburb in northwest London, called somewhat ironically Mountjoy, Zadie Smith's second novel, *The Autograph Man* (2002) centres on a protagonist with Sino-Jewish parentage, Alex-Li Tandem. The novel is not usually regarded as being among her best work, and to many readers, even academic ones, certainly it represented a disappointment after the populist success and recognition of *White Teeth* (2000). Consider examples of the second novel's reception. Urszula Terentowicz-Fotyga suggests its relative unpopularity may have resulted from the belief its representation of multiculturalism was not as central to its aesthetic dynamics as it had been assumed by many to have been in Smith's first novel (although see Ulrike Tancke who in this volume problematizes such presuppositions). According to Terentowicz-Fotyga 'the second novel is organized around the theme of culture industry and the hyperreal experience of space. A fluid sense of identity in *The Autograph Man* is not so much an effect of migration and displacement as of problematic experience of reality' (57). Adam Mars-Jones decides that *The Autograph Man*'s promising narrative fails in other very specific ways:

> Smith has thought a lot about celebrity, and quotes 'the popular wise guy Walter Benjamin' at one point, defining aura as an effect of distance impervious to intimacy, but she's absolutely unable to reproduce it. Reading the first sentence into which she has slipped an invented celebrity is like tripping on the edge of a carpet.

[...]

The join is always obvious between the evoked and the invented. The grafts never take. Even the plotting goes haywire in the Kitty Alexander parts of the book, so that dogs cross the Atlantic undetected and unquarantined, and newspapers run obituaries without even the most amateurish verification of the fact of death. (N. Pag.)

Alex Clark concludes, 'the caperishness that marks its latter portions and that veers dangerously close to outright chaos, the more outlandish plot contrivances, some of the less funny jokes (two characters greeting each other as Kofi Annan and Boutros Boutros-Ghali for no apparent reason), we might well have done without' (N. Pag.). Michiko Kakutani notes positively 'the tension between the symbolic and the mundane' but complains overall that Smith's second novel remains 'a flat-footed, grudging performance. Dour where *White Teeth* was exuberant; abstract and pompous where *White Teeth* was brightly satiric; tight and preachy where *White Teeth* was expansive' (N. Pag.). James Wood dismisses Smith's adoption of an 'irrelevant intensity' that so characterizes many contemporary writers. Wood adds, 'The management of irony and sincerity – their proper apportioning, their containment and release – is the vexed issue of this novel, as of so many contemporary works' (N. Pag.) Even more damning for him is a central problem that Wood perceives in terms of how one might succeed in depicting a culture where symbol supersedes experience (and even reality), with Smith's novel being forced into being as superficial as the culture it purports to be satirizing:

And if Smith is really concerned about Alex's destiny, his wandering in the field of signs that is his career, then why does the novel so willingly indulge in just the sort of pop-culture vacancy that Alex tries to resist? Such vacancy is embedded deep in the texture of the prose.

[...]

Smith's reply might be that she is merely being a good novelist, seeing her characters as they would see themselves, and that in a world of signs nothing is authentic. But what then of Smith's smirking epigraphs, which belong to the novel rather than to the characters?

[...]

And if Smith is offering up her own novel as an example of the very corruption afflicting her characters, one would have to say that to poison a whole novel is a very lengthy way of making a point about a single modern germ. Besides, confession is not absolution. The identification of a problem is not necessarily a form of resistance to it, and may be only an easy complicity.

My reading is that Wood no more than half right in his attack, in that he ignores certain ways in which Smith attempts to undermine quite subtly certain shibboleths of contemporary intellectual culture, and also once Alex (as he is referred to in most of the text) is on board a flight to America a transformation is suggested, indicated albeit obliquely and ironically by Smith's reference to the influence of Martin Amis's *Money: A Suicide Note* (1984), and henceforth the underlying dynamics of Smith's novel do alter radically.

Despite such dismissals as outlined above, this present essay seeks to redeem at least certain aspects of Smith's novel, doing so by outlining the various ways in which such critics have undervalued the novel in terms of its the treatment of the everyday, of location and of its development in the American section of a radical concept of understanding oneself from another perspective informed by an epiphany concerning one's set of values. I will consider several key elements that serve to illuminate Smith's purpose in approaching celebrity culture through its personal inscription in the autograph, whose collection was already established as a fashion and cultural practice among upper class Europeans in the seventeenth and eighteenth centuries. Clearly important to the text is a sense of protagonist, Alex's relationship to the mundane dynamics of suburbia in which he exists. In this quotidian environment he has denied various suppressed fantasies that subtend the apparent normality of his life. Barely beneath the surface is his sublimated quest for inner meaning and personal identity. As with Smith's other novels a strong sense of familiarity grounds her narrative, but there is more than habituation that informs her concept of community that subtends her descriptions of people in suburbia. Location signifies and is reflected in people's consciousness. Eventfulness and action are also reflected in the myriad symbols that surround them, but in *The Autograph Man* Alex's life is literally awash with such points of reference, an oceanic swelling of the possibilities of meaning which are in excess of any individual's visceral understanding.

The very transatlantic setting (and its underlying culture) demonstrates a new dimension in Smith's work, a definite reaching beyond the local and familiar that will be repeated in the third novel, *On Beauty* (2005), a narrative that in 'Zadie Smith's *On Beauty*: Art and Transatlantic Antagonisms in the Anglo-American Academy' I describe as having a 'plot [that] revolves around certain intriguing and subtly inflected Anglo-American ideological oppositions and dichotomies related to art, beauty, and aesthetic meaning [...]' (219). Smith seeks to comprehend the novel as a genre by situating and contextualizing its primary elements. While reflecting on her fiction and writing practice in a 2012 interview in *The New Yorker* Smith positioned her writing in terms of characterizations that respond in complex ways to issues such as environment and upbringing:

I used to have this envious feeling towards the type of writer who never gives a second thought to whether their readers might not all be white and middle class and highly educated. That's the whole world to them. All their characters sound like the author and like each other and like the reader. It seemed to me you could write so much more cleanly and stylishly when you didn't have to try and think yourself into many places at the same time. Of course, it probably isn't easier – the grass always looks greener elsewhere. Anyway, in my situation, every time I write a sentence I'm thinking not only of the people I ended up in college with but my siblings, my family, my school friends, the people from my neighborhood. I've come to realize that this is an advantage, really: it keeps you on your toes. And it seems clear to me that these little varietals of voice and lifestyle (bad word, but I can't think of another) are fundamentally significant. They're not just decoration on top of a life; they're the filter through which we come to understand the world. To be born into money is ontologically different than to be born without it, for example. (N. Pag.)

This authorial ambition embraces a more complex notion of community than simply wishing to record a range of multicultural identities. Rather Smith seeks to position all of her characters in the wider complexities and variations of being that affect all social selves and our ontological understandings of them. Smith details such lives not just through their individual substance, but offers a series of indicators by which we chart our intersubjective relations. Amid the mundane and the everyday, the curious and eccentric nature of such intersecting suburban lives draws her interest. Alex is unusual, even eccentric as regards his profession, the philography indicated by the book's title. However in terms of any wider engagement her protagonist seems a failure. Reclusive at times, he suffers from a form of arrested development. He lacks vitality; he suffers from hypochondria just like his father, Li-Jin; Alex is marked by a traumatic loss when his father dies after collapsing when his son is 12, an event Alex partially suppresses, seemingly unable to reconcile himself with the reality of this death. The original trauma occurs when they attend a wrestling match between Big Daddy and Giant Haystacks, which description opens the novel. With friends Mark Rubinfine and Adam Jacobs Alex makes the acquaintance of Joseph Klein, who shares their Jewishness and perhaps more significantly in plot terms he collects the autographs of the famous. Hence it is at this event that will prove so traumatic for him that Alex first encounters first hand both celebrity and the idea of its philographic trace:

And then the boy says, 'Oh yes … Philography's very lucrative'.
    Alex: 'Phila who?'
    'It's the word for autograph collecting,' says Joseph, and it's clear he isn't saying this to impress. No, he just wants to tell someone. Still, it's

hard to forgive him for it and Rubinfine won't, ever. He suggests that everything Joseph has is worth four pee. He goes on to bet him this same four pee that his collection is actually worth *less* than four pee. Which is when Jospeh seemingly without malice explains that he has an Albert Einstein worth three thousand pounds.

And that shuts up Rubinfine.

Alex: 'Really? Einstein?' (30)

Later in the novel it becomes self-evident that both an obsessiveness and voyeuristic quality underpin the objects that animate Alex's profession of philography. Equally important is the theme of fame and infamy, initially represented performatively as two polar opposites by the wrestlers Big Daddy and Giant Hasytstacks. Also of relevance are the real actual beings and selves that underpin the curious trans-national world of celebrity. The wrestling match demonstrates the narrative and archetypal nature of the cultural products that contribute to the complex set of beliefs and exchanges that constitute celebrity and in which the four boys participate actively as audience:

> [T]he thing is, they are not here to express genuine feelings, or to fake them and dress them up *natural* like on TV – they are here to demonstrate *actions*. And all the kids *know* that. Any fool can tell a story – can't they? – but how many can *demonstrate* one, e.g., *This is what a story is, mate, stripped of all its sentiment.* This afternoon these two hulking men are here to demonstrate Justice. The kind Mr Gerry Bowen [Block M, Seat 117] can't get from the courts in compensation for his son's accident; the kind Jake [Block T, Seat 59] won't get from school whether he chooses to squeal on those bastards or not [...] the kind Li-Jin [Block K, Seat 75] can't get from God. (38)

In this section as well as introducing religiosity, faith and its absence as major themes Smith evokes variously: the residual narratives that mainly remain hidden but which accompany us; the curious impersonality of the arena; the commonality and visceral importance of archetypes in our lives; and the narrative patterns that underpin them. Clearly for Smith cultural activity and action are as significant as the narratives that accompany them.

Later in life Alex follows a pleasure principle of sorts, which involves the radical avoidance of pain and suffering, including his failure to retrieve the memory of witnessing his father's death, an avoidance that means he cannot come to terms with this loss. Gradually the reader recognizes that Smith's attitude towards certain cultural norms that have permeated her protagonist's life is essentially skeptical and even hostile. A vital clue to her objections comes in the blurb found on the inside front cover of the dust jacket to the original UK hardback publication: '*The Autograph Man* is a deeply funny, existential tour around the hollow things of modernity

– celebrity, cinema and the ugly triumph of symbol over experience' (N. Pag.). Most critics and reviewers including Wood quote the phrase 'the hollow things of modernity'. However I would suggest that the last phrase is more telling, concerning Smith's rejection of both an obsession with symbolism and the attempt to wrench meaning critically and conceptually away from the experiential. I would conjecture that this is further confirmed if a reader takes off the novel's elaborate dust-jacket and opens it out. One of the first things this action reveals are three additional stories by Smith under a general heading 'When You Turn Everything into Symbol, Bad things Happen or The same Instinct Runs through It All' (N. Pag.). In adding these elements in this fashion, Smith stresses both the physicality of the book, its presence and the fact that responding to it involves actions beyond simply reading, that include the handling and manipulation of the object itself in all its 'thinginess'. Throughout Smith uses various devices to emphasize the notion of what Glyn White describes as 'graphic textual phenomena' (1) disrupting readerly expectations with a variety of fonts, scripts, illustrations, other visual graphic devices, and so forth. Additionally in a similar vein if Smith's reader happens to glance down at the cardboard cover that their removal of the dust-jacket has revealed, there they can read a phrase in gold lettering, which is a quotation from the refrain of the headline track from the soundtrack of a movie, the musical *Fame* (1980), written by Irene Cara (who appeared in the film): 'Fame! I'm gonna live forever!' (N. Pag.)

Quite explicitly this takes us beyond Smith's narrative imagination, evoking a particular cultural phase that crystallized a cultural obsession in Western culture with fame and surely for Smith the reference to this particular musical suggests both her early childhood (she was four when it was released) and more general love of musicals that developed over the years. As I summarized in *Zadie Smith* (2010) 'In numerous profiles and interviews Smith is described variously as quiet, awkward and reticent as a child and adolescent, drawn to old Hollywood films and musicals' (27).

In contrast however, this reference to *Fame* might also perhaps refer ironically and retrospectively to her own fate when drawn into the phenomenal maelstrom of success created by her publisher's media people before and after the publication of *White Teeth*, part of a process that I described as follows: 'Smith was being manufactured [...] She was celebrated precisely for her youth, ethnicity, intelligence, and ironically even the suddenness of her emergence from obscurity' (19–20). In marketing her, the publicity machine – and the wider cultural process that machine engaged with – offered her up as a potential icon, created conditions whereby she could be transformed into a celebrity whether or not she liked that new public identity. In its original context Cara's song initially appears to represent the desire, particularly among the young, for fame as an ultimate egoism, achieving success and celebrity through performance. However such desire may be more complex than first appears. If one considers the first two verses of the lyrics by Cara, ironically one finds expressed a desire to transcend the everyday and ordinary that is suggestive:

> Baby look at me
> And tell me what you see
> You ain't seen the best of me yet
> Give me time I'll make you forget the rest
>
> I got more in me
> And you can set it free
> I can catch the moon in my hands
> Don't you know who I am. (N. Pag.)

Fundamentally Smith seems to suggest in *The Autograph Man* that such an aspiration might appear natural enough, but easily becomes perverted variously by the star system itself, but also by an obsession for symbols over substance (and therefore over reality), and the distortion of values by both celebrity culture and a deconstructive intellectualism that is hubristic. Moreover, in opposing the cultural permeation of these and allied concepts or systems of thought what clearly becomes part of Smith's aesthetic problem is that in order to convey the mores of a generation mired in an even wider hyper-self-consciousness, increasingly defined by the essentialist illusions of rampant individualism, and seduced by a belief in the loss of affect, this places severe limits in terms of such characters on their grasp of any concepts that transcend the self. And as Wood indicates Smith in attempting to create empathy for her protagonist (and more generally for his generation) does so for people who exhibit neither few sustainable values nor very much purchase on how the world functions, in short she is asking us to inhabit the worldview of very dysfunctional individuals, a difficult task both aesthetically and morally.

So what exactly are the set of dysfunctions that inform Alex's life, being and identity and are they due to personal failings? Smith indicates that Alex and his friend Adam are guided by a range of overarching contemporary cultural dynamics. Like Wood most critics seem to intuit a broader framework of cultural misdirection or failing beyond the self that Smith describes cumulatively in this novel. Being stymied by rampant reflexivity is part of that process. According to Clark, Alex 'is the embodiment of this narrowing process, this unwitting loss of authenticity, a man who "deals in a shorthand of experience", and who is "one of this generation who watch themselves"'. According to Wood:

> The book's conceptual grid is plausible enough. The problem is Alex, and the novel's assessment of his nullity. He is simply an absence. We learn little about him except that he loves Kitty Alexander and is a rather faithless friend and boyfriend. His chosen profession does not yield pathos, as perhaps Smith hopes, but derision. (N. Pag.)

Terentowicz-Fotyga feels structurally the novel incorporates 'the complex dialectic of the real and imaginary, the authentic and the fake, the fictional and the metafictional [...]' (58) influenced by 'theoreticians such as Jean Baudrillard and Walter Benjamin' (59). Certainly Smith incorporates many critical and cultural concepts drawn from such figures, but does so in terms of their *deleterious cultural effects*. Smith demonstrates how inimical such criticism is for her in *Changing My Mind* when she opines her former enthusiasm for thinkers such as Roland Barthes (44) deciding finally that the trouble with 'French criticism is that criticism's tendentious politics' citing Barthes support for 'capitalism generally and the Vietnam War specifically' (45). In *Changing My Mind* Smith concludes that Nabakov's aesthetic is more appealing than any Barthesian critique that captivated her in her youth, precisely because the latter seems unfavourably disposed to any significant purchase on the real:

> Just as we must give up the urge to know the reality of the text, we must also give up hope of knowing the world in its ultimate reality. There can be no more 'deciphering', we must settle for 'disentangling'. Power is relinquished. (47)

Terentowicz-Fotyga is correct in concluding that in *The Autograph Man* 'metafictionality is the target of parody' (69), but so too is what some academics described somewhat pompously as 'high theory'. Smith's novel critiques the very debates and discourses that had appeared to dominate the academy, precisely by demonstrating the vacuous grasp on life that Alex and others exhibit, young(ish) people full of apparently clever analytical points of reference, but lost in a free-flow of cultural references, and imbued with a cynicism, an inability to identify any authenticity or meaning. The critical vocabulary Terentowicz-Fotyga sees as central actually eludes, bores and alienates Alex. Of his relations with girlfriend, Esther, the narrator ruminates:

> Alex was careless, in small ways, in the ways that count. His inability to remember the title of her Ph.D. ('Modes of Something in the Development of the Iconography of African Jewry in the Something'). The state of his bathroom. The books she recommended and he never read. He had her in his heart, but not always in his mind. (99)

Part of the joke and Smith's underlying critique is that Esther's research is primarily about herself, a common strategy in an age obsessed with a selfhood defined by the essentialist categories of identity politics, with a culture avowing both a fluidity of meaning and reference. Alex's life seems initially animated and defined by a post-adolescent infantilism.

As Terentowicz-Fotyga indicates (63) certainly Smith quotes Walter Benjamin's 'The Work of Art in the Age of Mechanical Reproduction', but she does not do so in the main body of the text, rather in one of what Wood calls her 'silly epigraphs', where surely Smith's tone is dismissive (offering an ironic refusal of received wisdoms which is a recurrent strategy of the narrative that irritates Wood) since the quotation is tagged, 'A definition of "aura" offered by the popular wise guy Walter Benjamin' (43). As Wood points out, Smith refers to the German critic again when describing the cultural iconography that Alex's friend Alex maps out in his living room with paraphernalia including photos and postcards, the latter sporting Adam's limited residual autograph collection. Smith inserts 'The wise guy Walter Benjamin in need of a comb, a better tailor, a way out of France' (126) which Wood describes as '(a deeply unfunny line). This sounds like Smith herself, not her characters'. Certainly it may be somewhat tasteless and yet it does serve to reduce Benjamin to a pop culture icon for aspirant vaguely leftist intellectuals. What Alex values about this cursory collection, and this is presumably an aspect Smith ironizes, is that it is 'Small, selfless, almost entirely arbitrary' (128). As the narrative indicates through mirroring Alex's thought processes Adam has 'lurched from one ill-fitting "identity" to another every summer,' and Alex lists over 20 variations before indicating that finally Adam appears to have achieved happiness:

[H]ow did he get from there to this? How did he get so happy?
    Adam will say God, of course. Except he won't say His name and if you ask him to write it down he will write YHWH. (129)

Alex resists the idea that on the fifteenth anniversary of his father's death he should perform the Kaddish, finding the concept of this ritual alien and repugnant. Like many of his responses this seems animated unconsciously. As Smith indicates much of what Alex really holds true is supressed, with subliminal desires surfacing periodically. The novel's first contemporary section begins with a hangover from taking a drug: 'Legal name: Microdot. Street name: Superstar. For a time it had made itself famous all through his body. And now it was over' (47). The transitory nature of such apparent pleasure is clearly linked to the limits of fame. Alex is confronted by the reality of having crashed the vintage sports car he shares with Adam, various flashbacks, and concrete evidence of unremembered actions such as booking flights to New York to attend as a stallholder 'The Autographicana Fair, an annual extravaganza' (157), thereby missing his girlfriend's operation to replace a pacemaker for her heart.

As a result of his travels beyond his routine, after abandoning the bedrock of familiarity found in Mountjoy (and elsewhere in London), an underpinning that he assumes offers something genuine and authentic, finally what emerges apparently against all the odds, are other experiences *and* qualities that reassure Alex despite his radical uncertainties. Kitty Alexander, the movie star to whom Alex has sent his one-sided and obsessive correspondence fantasizing about her life, emerges as a real old lady whom he tracks down and who travels back to London with him. If this is something he subliminally desired, then what does this longing represent? According to Mars-Jones something spiritual informs Alex, but it is distorted through the prism of his obsession, each autograph signifying a distillation of the search for some transcendental quality:

> it also represents in diluted, distorted form a search for the sacred. The hunger is for a symbol that will have absolute value, beyond the reach of market forces. The holy of holies, as far as Alex-Li is concerned, would be the autograph of a Hollywood actress long retired, famously reclusive. He has been writing to her regularly since he was a boy – nothing crudely soliciting, just little prose poems imagining her mental life.

Smith indicates strongly that Alex might achieve this only when he departs from the routines that have previously defined his life, only then can he recover a sense of the vitality of the world. Previously he has been obsessed with popular culture and film, referencing his life through allusion and quotation of music, movies and celebrities. Alex misses something critical about film, which as a genre according to Benjamin exhibits great potential:

> For the entire spectrum of optical, and now also acoustical, perception the film has brought about a similar deepening of apperception. It is only an obverse of this fact that behavior items shown in a movie can be analyzed much more precisely and from more points of view than those presented on paintings or on the stage. As compared with painting, filmed behavior lends itself more readily to analysis because of its incomparably more precise statements of the situation.

Alex encounters a classic example on his transatlantic flight, which experience in many ways initially encapsulates his fundamental problems in a search for meaning and authenticity of any kind among myriad clues in the symbols and semiotics of the world. Pointedly concerning Lovelear, another autograph trader, the narrative says 'He did not understand an object's status as a "gift"' (218) which refers to *potlatch*, a concept that was incredibly popular with cultural theorists and semioticians following Georges Bataille's analysis in *The Accursed Share*. Significantly Lovelear attempts to crudely deconstruct everything to a point of confusion and irritation, one might suggest to the destruction of any credible meaning. Alex follows suit, finding a promotional slogan on a plastic bag which is intended to encapsulate his confusion. '*Our youth is but a brief night: fill it with rapture*' (219). Once airborne Alex ponders on how little the experience has to do with flight; rather he is faced with something quite different: 'Everything in this plane is an interface, like the windows on his computer. Nothing on this plane has anything to do with flying, just as his desktop doesn't have anything to do with the processing of information. Pretty, pretty pictures. Lovely, distracting stories we tell each other' (220). He can see the replication of this experience, but is then distracted by viewing *Casablanca*. Despite his capacious knowledge of the contradictions and chaos of its production, 'Alex can think of no better example of the accidental nature of great art' (221). He shares a similar recognition to that which Smith describes going through in her youth in 'The North West London Blues' where she discovers after 'an actual argument about art, an early inkling that there might be a difference between a film with good intentions and a good film'.

Much as *Casablanca* might stir something within Alex, his primary epiphany lies in America where he discovers evidence of his own capacity for beauty, in the letters that have been read belatedly, and at that point treasured by their recipient, Kitty Alexander. Knowing this transforms Alex's life and his sense of self-worth. Kitty first describes herself as a *fan* of his (277), and second details the impact of discovering the unopened letters in her agent Max's dirty apartment. Alex's imaginary descriptions of Kitty have anticipated her life in many ways. Clearly, the transition or switching point of the novel centres upon travelling to and arriving in America and his meeting with Kitty. Her transformational effect upon Alex derives precisely from the fact that she is the original ontological presence or source of all of the various copies of her that he had viewed in her film over the years, borrowing such copies multiply from Adam, indicating that the very act of multiple representation might well be inspiring, but still offers an insufficiency. As Smith intimates the living, actual Kitty allows Alex to experience the aura related to nature and authenticity that Benjamin describes:

> We define the aura of the latter as the unique phenomenon of a distance, however close it may be. If, while resting on a summer afternoon, you follow with your eyes a mountain range on the horizon or a branch which casts its shadow over you, you experience the aura of those mountains, of that branch. [...] Unmistakably, reproduction as offered by picture magazines and newsreels differs from the image seen by the unarmed eye. Uniqueness and permanence are as closely linked in the latter as are transitoriness and reproducibility in the former. To pry an object from its shell, to destroy its aura, is the mark of a perception whose 'sense of the universal equality of things' has increased to such a degree that it extracts it even from a unique object by means of reproduction.

Interestingly in this context Smith questions Benjamin in *Changing My Mind: Occasional Essays* (2009) precisely in terms of art's relationship with reality:

> When did we become so inured to the real that it gathered around it this strange *aura*? In the age of mechanical reproduction, prophesied Walter Benjamin, a painting such as the *Mona Lisa* will lose its aura: the more cheap postcards we make of her, the more she will disappear. But he was wrong – it turned out the erotic logic of capital worked the other way round. Her authentic aura increased. (296)

In *The Autograph Man* a crucial point for Smith seems to be that Alex should face the negativity not only of his own existence, but that of a whole generation of younger people of which he is part, sharing common values, concepts and judgements – stimulated by those such as Benjamin – that seem either insufficient to sustain them or without any convincing purchase on the complex realities of modern existence. Hence Wood's recognition of Alex's fundamental nullity and its problematic for Smith. Of course this means that roughly half the novel charts a generational malaise, a set of deep personal and cultural crises, offering a cartography of this generation's social and intellectual failings through the prism of Alex.

Finally after his trip to New York, Alex returns to Mountjoy. After his various travels he is faced with a range of home truths, demonstrations of the opinions and suffering of others which do not add to his pleasure principle. His repaired car is delivered by Joseph, who is unhappy with his life and Alex's exchange with his friend serves to remind Alex of his own problem with authentic communication. Joseph attempts to explain their distance:

> 'We've turned into abstractions of each other, it's obvious,' he said, rather high-handedly. 'We fear each other as symbols of one thing or another. We don't tell the truth.
>
> 'Look, it's *exactly* that sort of thing,' said Alex, exasperated, 'that's just what I'm talking about. I don't know what you mean. Part of the problem is the way you express yourself. We used to be friends. There was none of … this. It used to be easy, between us'.
>
> 'I used to be an Autograph man,' said Joseph coolly, adjusting his wing mirror. And that dog has no male genitalia'. (334)

Clearly for Alex the immediacy of their relationship has been squeezed out by such self-conscious vocabulary, and the supposedly intellectual analysis that permeates their consciousness and conversations. Equally, according to Joseph, any such schism is due to Alex's presumptions, his ordering of the world conceptually, and his hedonistic avoidance of pain.

More awkwardness occurs when Esther discovers an apparently new infidelity on Alex's part. Together the pair sees premature news of Kitty's death on television, the agent Max's revenge on the ageing star for both deserting and challenging him. Ironically it offers Alex a vision, how to manipulate the philographic trade opportunistically to make a fortune for Kitty, to free her from Max by delivering the proceeds of an auction of her autographed items. Alex does so by first convincing a newspaper to print her obituary. After these trades, an even harsher reality intrudes when the philographers visit fellow autograph man Brian Duchamp on his deathbed suffering greatly. Alex finds such pain obscene; he leaves after passing over a cheque for 15,000 pounds, the proceeds of a single Kitty autograph, an action which accentuates the fact that Duchamp will face a later final reckoning, which realization confirms that material gain has profound limits. In fact there may be a glimmering of understanding in that Alex recuperates a more historical sense of potlatch – the concept that so bemused Lovelear, the materialist American – that is explained by Marcel Mauss in *The Gift* (1954):

> Further, what they exchange is not exclusively goods and wealth, real and personal property, and things of economic value. They exchange rather courtesies, entertainments, ritual, military assistance, women, children, dances, and feasts; and fairs in which the market is but one element and the circulation of wealth but one part of a wide and enduring contract. (3)

This idea of a wider set of obligations helps situate the elaborate system of exchanges that provide the a core element of Smith's novel, including offerings, rituals and symbols of friendship, and other loyalties. Initially Kitty is appalled at Alex's subterfuge, revealed to her when she discovers an obituary about her that is less than flattering, and shocked by his dishonesty. Alex realizes the contradictions of his world and his profession when Kitty suggests the money be returned, another epiphany occurs for both of them, drawn by Alex from an intuitive sense of larger set of values and of intersubjective and social interconnections that has animated his scam:

> 'It's *your* money,' he said, 'and it's pointless giving it back. Even when they find out you're not ... then it'll just be worth more because you'll be the actress who everybody thought was dead and her autograph went for such and such on the day everybody thought she was dead – and on and on. Thaat's the way it works. It's all madness anyway. Take it, Kitty. Take it and bloody *run*'.
>
> [...]
>
> 'You're a *good* boy,' said Kitty, patting his face. 'I'm very glad we meet. You're a realist, like me. This is good. You kill me, but then you resurrect me. And you are forgiven'. (397)

Her symbolic resurrection is another gift from Alex to Kitty, just as her discovery of the letters has been, but here she shares his epiphany as a transatlantic phenomenon. As recorded by Tim Martin, Smith admires Lewis Hyde's *The Gift: How the Creative Spirit Transforms the World* (1979), in which he says: 'Because of the bonding power of gifts and the detached nature of commodity exchange, gifts have become associated with community and with being obliged to others, while commodities are associated with alienation and freedom' (69).

So, taken in this overall context what has Alex achieved by the end of the text? Certainly he transcends his recursive patterns of life by accepting both his own vulnerabilities and those of his contemporaries. He also accedes to certain external cultural commitments,. By liberating his own imaginative possibilities, Alex has revealed a key truth underlying celebrity culture by bringing back across the Atlantic to Mountjoy the apparent reclusive actress, Kitty Alexander, confirming the rootedness in an underlying reality even of a system as arcane, mercurial and perverse as celebrity and fame. Finally in the personal sphere Alex confronts the concept of fatherhood, the problem of one's origins, the challenges of the kabbalah and the realities inherent in the early paternal death he has witnessed with which the narrative opened. As Wood says of Alex:

> The man who trades in false signs is finally led into synagogue to do business with the great transcendental signified Himself. Smith is quite explicit about this. Alex has spent his life commercially honouring the worthless dead, dead celebrities. The novel will end with his beginning to honour his own dead, his father. (N.Pag.)

As Rubinfine has indicated endings are a gift from God, something not to be exchanged (409), and although Alex fears the Kaddish with which the novel ends will only be a gesture, it exudes a sense of the ceremonial and of community. This is a resolution of a kind, Alex's reconciliation with the faith of his mother, and the fears of his father about that set of cultural beliefs, and his own horror at the unfamiliar territory of death. As Hyde says, 'A gift when it moves across the boundary, either stops being a gift or else abolishes the boundary' (63). However, despite the apparently moral resolution of *The Autograph Man*, as Wood fears, to a degree it may purvey overall a less than optimistic sense of being. However, any malaise in the cultural trajectory of Britain that Smith charts in her second novel would appear to have in her view been minor when compared to certain other more current contexts, including in particular the state of governance and public affairs, or at least her perception of these issues of polity. In 2012 in 'The North West London Blues' Smith confronted the deep economic crisis facing the world: 'First and foremost I need to become less naïve. The money is gone, and the conditions [...] my generation inherited [...] are unlikely to be replicated in my lifetime, if ever again'. Smith described her ideological position thus:

> Things change. I don't need the state now as I once did; and the state is not what it once was. It is complicit in this new, shared global reality in which states deregulate to privatize gain and re-regulate to nationalize loss. A process begun with verve by a Labour government is presently being perfected by Cameron's Tory-Lib Dem coalition. [...] It's only recently that I had any idea that how a person felt about libraries – not schools or hospitals, libraries – could even represent an ideological split. I thought a

library was one of the few sites where the urge to conserve and the desire to improve – twin poles of our political mind – were easily and naturally united. Besides, what kind of liberal has no party left to vote for, and feels not so much gratitude to the state as antipathy and, at times, fear?'

In contrast to Smith's view of the nation in 2012, despite her cutting and sceptical cultural critique delivered in *The Autograph Man*, the Britain described by Smith in 2002 in the second novel might seem to appear retrospectively as simply misguided in its cultural attitudes and behaviour, but still capable of sustaining a certain hope. This surely contrasts the darker view of a more malevolent and dysfunctional society she traces above in terms of the changing state which is diminished its citizens' lives through its erosion of both public services and any residual communal culture. As she says in *NW* (2012) this has become a world where 'we feel we are more modern and that the change is faster' (225), one full of 'the great mass of cultural detritus' (237), defined by an increasing sense of chaos, alienation and ephemera.

Bibliography

Amis, Martin. *Money: A Suicide Note*. London: Jonathan Cape, 1984.

Bataille, Georges. 'The Gift of Rivalry: "Potlatch"'. *The Accursed Share: An Essay on General Economy. Vol. I. Consumption*. New York: Zone Books, 1988, 63–77.

Benjamin, Walter. 'The Work of Art in the Age of Mechanical Reproduction'. 1936. http://www.marxists.org/reference/subject/philosophy/works/ge/benjamin. htm. N. Pag. Web.

Cara, Irene. 'Fame'. [Song lyrics]. 1980. http://www.lyricstime.com/irene-cara-fame-lyrics.html. N. Pag. Web.

Clark, Alex. 'Signs and Wanders'. *The Guardian*. 14 September 2002. http://www. guardian.co.uk/books/2002/sep/14/shopping.fiction1. N. Pag. Web.

Curtiz, Michael. (Dir.) *Casablanca*. Hollywood: Warner Bros. 1942.

Hyde, Lewis. *The Gift: How the Creative Spirit Transforms the World*. Edinburgh: Canongate, 2006 [1979].

Kakutani, Michiko. 'An Elusive, Whimsical Autograph'. *The New York Times*. 25 September 2002. http://www.nytimes.com/2002/09/25/books/books-of-the-times-an-elusive-whimsical-autograph.html. N. Pag. Web.

Mars-Jones, Adam. 'Name of the Prose'. *The Observer*. 8 September 2002. http:// www.guardian.co.uk/books/2002/sep/08/fiction.zadiesmith. N. Pag. Web.

Martin, Tim. 'Lone Scribblers, Treasure Your Gift'. *The Independent*. 12 November 2006. http://www.independent.co.uk/arts-entertainment/books/ reviews/the-gift-by-lewis-hyde-424028.html. N. Pag. Web.

Mauss, Marcel. *The Gift: Forms and Functions of Exchange in Archaic Societies*. Mansfield Centre, CT: Martino 2011 [1954].

Parker, Alan. (Dir.). *Fame* [musical film]. Hollywood: United Artists, 1980.

Smith, Zadie. *White Teeth*. London: Penguin 2001 [2000].

—*The Autograph Man*. London: Hamish Hamilton, 2002.

—*Changing My Mind: Occasional Essays*. London: Hamish Hamilton, 2009.

—*NW*. London: Hamish Hamilton, 2012.

—'The North West London Blues'. *The New York Review of Books*. June 2, 2012. http://www.nybooks.com/blogs/nyrblog/2012/jun/02/north-west-london-blues/. N. Pag. Web.

—'This Week in Fiction: Zadie Smith'. *The New Yorker*. July 23, 2012. http://www.newyorker.com/online/blogs/books/2012/07/this-week-in-fiction-zadie-smith.html#ixzz28nhy0G4B. N. Pag. Web.

Terentowicz-Fotyga, Urszula. 'The Impossible Self and the Poetics of the Urban Hyperreal in Zadie Smith's *The Autograph Man*'. *Zadie Smith: Critical Essays*. Tracey L. Walters (ed.). New York: Peter Lang, 2008, 57–72.

Tew, Philip. *Zadie Smith*. Basingstoke and New York: Palgrave Macmillan, 2010.

—'Zadie Smith's *On Beauty*: Art and Transatlantic Antagonisms in the Anglo-American Academy'. *Symbiosis: A Journal of Anglo-American Literary Relations*. 15(2), October 2011: 219–36.

White, Glyn. *Reading the Graphic Surface: The Presence of the Book in Prose Fiction*. Manchester: Manchester University Press, 2005.

Wood, James. 'Fundamentally Goyish'. *London Review of Books*. 24(19), 3 October 2002: 17–18. http://www.lrb.co.uk/v24/n19/james-wood/fundamentally-goyish. N. Pag. Web.

5

'I could have been somebody': The Articulation of Identity in Zadie Smith's *The Autograph Man*

Tracey K. Parker

Zadie Smith's second novel, *The Autograph Man*, continues her exploration of the meaning and value of popular culture in the contemporary subject's life, a journey she began with her first novel, *White Teeth*. Smith's engagement with popular culture reveals much about the highly mediated identities of contemporary individuals and how they are shaped and defined in the postmodern era. One enduring element in her work is the interrogation of whether the individual's preoccupation with popular culture is illuminating or is a barrier to understanding one's subject position. The book suggests that taken too far, such obsessions can create emotional distance in interpersonal relationships, with the individual feeling estranged. Paradoxically, however, popular culture is also employed to articulate one's subject position, sometimes in transgressive terms.

One of the ways Smith conveys a concern with the effect of popular culture on contemporary subjects is her engagement with Jean Baudrillard's theory of the 'hyperreal,' which holds that in the current consumer and media-driven era, the image has increasingly replaced the real. Rather than producing concrete images, industry in the age of capitalism creates hyperreal simulacra, images no longer referring to actual objects. As Baudrillard suggests such simulacra take the place of goods because capitalism creates desires rather than needs; individuals no longer work to satisfy their natural needs but instead want images more than the goods those images represent (26–7). If the contemporary subject is invested in pursuing simulacra with lives coordinated within the hyperreal, then by default, such an existence becomes superficial, devoid of substance. Baudrillard thus posits a deterministic theory of the effects of popular culture (as created by capitalism) on the individual, offering no real acknowledgement of even a possibility of resistance; in his view, the postmodern subject is deprived of agency in the face of the capitalist machine.

Smith's characters do see themselves through the lens of popular culture referents and therefore have a sense that they are estranged from any meaningful identities, with their existence constituted through images rather than a sense of an authentic and rooted self. At the same time, however, Smith suggests that the contemporary subject does have autonomy in comprehending the role popular culture plays in one's life. Even though estranged from themselves and others by their sense of hyperreality, Smith's characters also use popular cultural referents as a tool of identity formation by assigning them their own meanings while simultaneously resisting essentialized notions of others' interpretations. In 'On Postmodernism' Stuart Hall challenges Baudrillard's deterministic theory, taking issue with an essentially pessimistic notion that the postmodern era is characterized by meaninglessness:

> I don't agree with Baudrillard that representation is at an end because the cultural codes have become pluralized. I think we are in a period of the infinite multiplicity of codings, which is different. We have all become, historically, fantastically codable encoding agents. We are in the middle of this multiplicity of readings and discourses and that has produced new forms of self-consciousness and reflexivity. So, while the modes of cultural production and consumption have changed, qualitatively, fantastically, as the result of that expansion, it does not mean that representation itself has collapsed. (137)

Instead of viewing the deluge of simulacra, or more specifically, popular culture referents, as an indicator of meaninglessness, Hall instead affirms in 'Encoding, Decoding' that audiences are active in creating meaning through a dialogical process of communication:

> The so-called denotative *level* of the televisual sign is fixed by certain, very complex (but limited or 'closed') codes. But its connotative *level*, though also bounded, is more open, subject to more active *transformations*, which exploit its polysemic values. Any such already constituted sign is potentially transformable into more than one connotative configuration. (912)

How popular culture is 'read', therefore, depends on the viewer, which is possibly independent of the intended meaning of the individual 'displaying' or employing a popular culture referent. No single, stable relationship between a sign and signifier can be determined, and the provisional meaning that is attached is an 'articulation'. Hall's theory of encoding/decoding is a tool of articulation, which in 'On Postmodernism' he describes as a 'way of understanding how ideological elements come, under certain conditions, to cohere together within a discourse, and a way of asking how they do or do not become articulated, at specific conjunctures, to certain political subjects' (141–2). Hall recognizes that the process of articulation is complicated by the cultural hybridity of the globalized world, as well as by the sheer number of subject positions within a culture, as well as within an individual. Furthermore, Hall is ultimately interested according to Grossberg in 'how particular practices are positioned, into what structures of meaning and power, into what correspondences, they are articulated' (156). In *The Autograph Man*, Smith explores Baudrillard's theory of the hyperreal, but she ultimately affirms Hall's assertion that contemporary subjects are caught in a web of a plethora of readings and discourses of popular culture, which has given rise to the 'self-consciousness and reflexivity' as quoted above, and which ultimately do not trump interpersonal relationships. As Philip Tew indicates, Smith's novel from the very cover of its UK first edition is concerned with 'the contemporary preference for the symbolic over the real, image over substance' (72).

Smith's background in literary theory is evident in her reference to Baudrillard's famous discussion of the simulacrum in *The Autograph Man*, remarking that '(theme parks and their like are a concentration of the *symbols* of pleasure, not pleasure itself)' (303) which directly refers to Baudrillard's use of Disneyland as exemplifying the hyperreal (12–14). Furthermore, Smith creates a sense that her characters live in a hyperreal state, partly through saturating her text with popular culture references. They define the existence of her protagonist, Londoner Alex-Li Tandem, a Chinese-Jewish twenty-something who is an autograph dealer by trade. A fan of Hollywood movies, he perceives the world through the lens of popular entertainment; certainly, the intense degree to which he and his contacts mediate their identities in this way reflects the 'new forms of self-consciousness and reflexivity' that Hall in 'On Postmodernism' regards as a way of portraying the 'hyperreal' (137).

Smith establishes such a self-consciousness at the beginning of the novel, since in contrast to their parents Alex-Li and his friends, as early as age 12, are immersed in popular culture. Alex-Li 'deals in a shorthand of experience. The TV version. He is one of this generation who watch themselves' (3). Clearly, mass media's effects begin early in an individual's life, already being part of the essential fabric of the contemporary subject's identity. Alex-Li's Chinese father, Li-Jin is puzzled such an immersion in capitalist culture:

But what were they talking *about*? References to programs he's never watched, songs he's never heard, films that came and went without him noticing. It is as if there is some busy, high-pitched frequency on the everyday life of his son which Li-Jin is tuned into only once a year, at Christmas, when he is told to go and buy the bright plastic merchandise which accompanies these mysterious entertainments. (6)

Li-Jin observes that 'The children speak in slogans now. Li-Jin grew up with clichés. The slogans make the clichés look innocent' (15). Smith's description here reflects Hall's assertion that contemporary individuals have adopted a new form of reflexivity, responding to the vast number of images disseminated via capitalist marketing to which they are exposed to via mass media and popular culture. Not only is Alex-Li's generation dependent on popular culture to communicate, but he and his peers have become prime targets of capitalist marketing schemes.

As an adult, Alex-Li continues to heavily mediate his life through popular culture; by consciously creating a shield, he avoids being fully emotionally invested in others, a result of the psychological trauma engendered by watching his father die when Alex-Li was 12 years old. Alex-Li is aware of the degree to which he perceives reality through the prism of popular culture; a typical example of his internal dialogue reflects an awareness of his existential self-consciousness (what Baudrillard might label a hyperreal existence):

> At the roundabout, waiting for a safe moment to cross the street, Alex-Li tries to imagine his defense if his life were on trial, that is, if he had to prove its worth. It is a kind of imaginary text he carries around with him, along with his obituary, because somewhere in Alex's head he is the greatest, most famous person you never heard of. And as such must defend himself from both slander and obscurity. Who else is going to do it? After all, he has no fans. (151)

Alex-Li defines himself in terms of celebrity, even though he is by no means famous. His comment that he has no fans is revealing; the book demonstrates that Alex-Li does have friends, but he keeps himself distanced from his friends and family because he is unable to accept his father's death. By not allowing himself to truly feel connections with others, he safeguards himself against feeling such a traumatic loss in the future.

Alex-Li's alienation affects his interpersonal relationships, particularly with his girlfriend, Esther, as his emotional distance is intensified in this more intimate relationship. Alex-Li yearns to connect with her, yet at the same time he pushes her away. Suggestively, he wants their relationship to resemble the adoration from afar that fans have for celebrities: 'Yes, he imagined his love on a screen in front of a preview audience ... Yes, he wanted his love at a distance, physically close but in some other way hard to reach ... He wanted to always be at the beginning of the movie ... He was in awe of her beauty and he never wanted to lose that awe. Yes, Doctor, yes. I want to be her fan' (84–5). Alex-Li is afraid of being too close to Esther, in part because he is in denial of mortality. A telling part of the narrative reveals Alex-Li's fear of death, something he links to his movie fandom: 'But he was tortured by the idea that she would grow old! He understood that in all likelihood this sort of thinking would lead him to die lonely, without anyone. He told himself the story that this was the great tragedy of his heart. The great tragedy of his heart was that it always needed to be told a story' (85). Aware of her boyfriend's popular culture-obsessed mind, Esther communicates with him in terms he might understand. Explaining that she will be undergoing surgery to have a new pacemaker inserted, she says, 'Look: this is not *Terms of Endearment*, okay? It's not a big deal. Routine. They cut me open, they take it out' (134). She reassures him that she is not going to die, unlike the terminally ill Emma Horton featured in this film. Alex-Li's relationship with Esther reveals much about his inability to connect emotionally with others, demonstrating that his obsession with popular culture, particularly old movies, creates barriers diminishing intimacy and understanding. Alex-Li remains more comfortable with identifying with simulacra or images of what it might mean to be in a relationship than with the actuality. He is, therefore, living in a state of heightened self-consciousness, filtering his emotional life through Hollywood, having been acculturated in a Western world dominated by the mass marketing associated with celebrity culture.

Furthermore, Alex-Li's profession/obsession as an autograph dealer problematizes interpersonal relationships. Not only does Alex-Li participate in the commodification of Hollywood directly, he is also drawn to celebrity culture because he can establish imaginary connections to people with whom he experiences intimacy despite never having met. By adoring celebrities from afar Alex-Li risks neither loss nor rejection. Alex-Li, bereaved so young, conceives memories of his father as if they were part of a movie: 'The cinema is full of fathers and their wisdom, but Alex remembered only this one example: as a boy, watching a Chinese earthquake on the television, he had turned to his father and congratulated him on his luck for being here, instead of there', and his father tells him that 'luck is an insult to the world. The unlucky dead begrudge you it' (299). Alex-Li filters his memories of his father through a Hollywood lens in order to create emotional distance from his grief, therefore articulating a core part of his identity through the superficiality of popular culture.

Rather than nurture his relationships and deal with his grief, instead Alex-Li creates an imaginary relationship, a particular Hollywood obsession, with actress Kitty Alexander which stands-in for real relationships. For years Alex-Li has mailed fan letters to Kitty, morphing from praise to brief stories in which he tells her about herself; for example, he writes:

Dear Kitty,

She walks into the store and winces at the age of the boy serving her. Even his knuckles have no lines. He should be in school, she thinks.

Love,
Alex-Li Tandem (127).

In this way, Alex-Li can completely control this imaginary relationship; he creates Kitty's life and thoughts to suit himself. Since Kitty does not reply, for many years he expands this one-sided non-relationship, in which he invests emotionally. When finally she does reply, he feels compelled to search for her in New York City.

Smith also problematizes Alex-Li's subject position through Kitty; Alex-Li has watched repeatedly her movie, *Peking Girl*, to the point that he has memorized all of the dialogue and gestures. Kitty, a Russian-Italian actress, plays a young Chinese girl, with 'her eyes Sellotaped into an approximation of his own epicanthic fold, wearing her coolie hat and cheongsam' (54) and who becomes a Broadway and Hollywood starlet. In truly postmodern fashion, Alex-Li is untroubled by a non-Chinese actress performing the role of an Asian character. He is untroubled by a lack of 'authenticity' in the portrayal of an Asian character. An important issue in postmodern theory is that of cultural authenticity. Frederic Jameson attributes the turning away from authenticity to a 'lack of historicity'; the postmodern individual has no concept of the past as differentiated from the present, which results in a loss of meaning because the simplification of historical processes and contexts means that history is flattened, misunderstood and used in a superficial manner. Linda Hutcheon, on the other hand, posits that postmodernism has ushered in liberation from traditional paradigms and has enhanced personal freedoms (3). Alex-Li represents those who find freedom from strict labels liberating; one suspects that being a person of mixed racial heritage, Alex-Li is suspicious of cultural authenticity.

Furthermore, Alex-Li engages in false nostalgia in his enthusiasm for Kitty and old films, perhaps as a way to maintain an emotional connection with his deceased father, albeit a distanced, mediated connection. Frederic Jameson's discussion of false nostalgia, the result of postmodern schizophrenia wherein the individual cannot make links between the past and the present (26), applies to Alex-Li in this context. Smith ties Alex-Li's love of cinema to his wish for things to always remain the same: 'Film is an artificial, circumscribed box to him – four walls and nothing but empty International Gestures inside it. Precisely the reason Alex loves it. It is *dealable* with' (114). Alex-Li prefers the concrete, contained narratives that feature neatly resolved conflicts rather than open, fluid, abstract art that lacks 'answers'.

Alex-Li does attempt to make sense of the world through a system other than popular culture as signifiers; he continually decides whether particular objects, ideas, gestures, words, etc. are either 'Jewish' or 'goyish', and is writing a book on the subject:

NOT THEM, NOT as people – there was no fun to be had out of that. Only wars. No, other things. A movement of an arm. A type of shoe. A yawn. A dress. A whistled tune.

It gave him a simple pleasure. Other people wondered why. He chose not to wonder why. All possible psychological, physiological and neuro-logical hypotheses (including the *Mixed-race people see things double* theory, and the *fatherless children seek out restored symmetry*, and *especially* the *Chinese brains are hard-wired for yin-and-yang dualistic thought*) made him want to staple his eyeballs to a wall. He did it because he did it. (75)

Alex-Li denies that his hybrid subject position is the reason he is creating this system of knowledge; instead, he seems to enjoy the act of categorizing in and for itself. Of course, Alex-Li is at times unaware of his psychological and emotional motives, and the reader is left to wonder if simply he denies his true motives. He becomes increasingly obsessed with goyishness, ascribing that label to anything that is not cool; for example, referring to his colleague Lovelear 'making that most goyish of all International Gestures, the *quote-unquote* motion with his fingers' (90). Alex-Li's book project could be described as an act of articulation, in that he is assigning individual, and therefore unstable, meaning to objects, ideas and behaviours based on his socialization, whether he wants to admit it or not. Ultimately, though, the reader can only tell that what is cool or what he likes is Jewish, and what is uncool or what he dislikes is Goyish; there does not appear to be a political meaning involved, so ultimately this becomes a neutral rather than transgressive act of articulation of his identity.

Alex-Li's friends also frame their identities through the filter of popular culture. Through Alex-Li's friend Rubenfine, Smith suggests that postmodern superficiality is intensified in subsequent generations while also ironizing this perception. When Rubenfine discusses going to Career Day at his children's school, he says that 'in a class of thirty-five, nine wanted to be models, four wanted to be actors, two wanted to be pop stars, ten wanted to be footballers, and the remaining wanted to be "entertainers" just "entertainers". I tried to get specifics out of them – nothing doing' (166). Rubenfine indicates that the younger generation is preoccupied with celebrity on an unprecedented scale, yet his friends display this same sort of fascination, especially in connection with Hollywood. Given that his own generation is so steeped in popular culture Smith ironizes doubly Rubenfine's views of the younger generation. Of course, each generation thinks the younger generation is somehow more corrupt or immoral, but Rubenfine even frames his religion and profession through movie culture:

> he had not become a rabbi solely to please his father. In his own small way he wanted to *carry things forward*. Like the continuity man on a film set [...] Rubenfine was simply, and honestly, a fan of the people he had come from. He loved and admired them. [...] This was the only way he had ever found to show it, that affection. (168–9)

That Rubenfine expresses something as profound as his religious heritage through the lens of Hollywood exemplifies Smith's thesis that his generation is equally guilty of a preoccupation with popular culture as the prime source of mediating their identities. Additionally, so viewing younger generations as more lost that his own serves both a mark of Rubenfine's adult maturation and also his limited self-awareness.

Another friend, Adam, is interested in popular culture in a more transgressive and constructive way than is Alex-Li. Adam is an intelligent young man who studies Judaism and Kabballah after having experimented with a number of identities grounded in style and popular culture that are intertwined with race, religion, and politics. Adam had gone

> through hippiedom, grunge, gangsta lite, various *roots*-isms (Ebonics, Repatriation, Rastafarianism), Anglo-philia, Americanization, afros, straightened, corn-rowed, shaved, baggy jeans, tight jeans, white girls, black girls, Jew girls, goy girls, conservatism, Conservatism, socialism, anarchism, partying, drugging, hermiting, schizing, rehabbing [...]. (109)

After going through these phases, Adam eventually attributes his wholeness to Judaism and Kabbalah and studies both traditions individually, as he teaches himself about art, music, and philosophy:

> On the remaining wall, there many shelves of books, mostly in Hebrew. Above them, a huge cross-shaped poster of the popular musician Isaac Hayes dressed in a dashiki and sunglasses, calling himself Black Moses. Some photos of the popular musician Stevie Wonder. A badly framed print of the painter Klee's *Angelus Novus*. The director Steven Spielberg, the popular singer Michael Jackson and the styrofoam alien E.T. sitting on each other's laps. The martial artist Bruce Lee with nunchucks. The wise guy Walter Benjamin in need of a comb, a better tailor, a way out of France. (106–7)

Adam's heroes are not only popular culture ones, but philosophical and artistic ones as well, which indicates that Adam consciously pursues a life beyond popular culture mediation. Additionally, Adam and Alex-Li discuss autographs that Alex-Li could obtain for Adam, who is only interested in autographs by famous Jews. He tells Alex-Li: 'You should get me Sammy Davis,' says Adam, thoughtfully. '*There* was a Black Jew. He opened up Vegas for the blacks. He was a trailblazer' (114). Adam admires the accomplishments of his people, an act of honouring his roots and understanding his place in the world. Adam contextualizes his religious studies through popular culture and intellectual icons but in doing so, he does not trivialize the importance that religion holds for him. Instead, he employs popular culture as a way to contextualize his religious beliefs for himself instead of relying on the authoritative dogma of religious authorities. Adam makes meaning out of popular culture icons specific to his understanding of and belief in Judaism and Kaballah. His act of articulation transforms popular cultural referents into meaningful signifiers and is an example of an individual bringing together ideological elements to create new meaning per Hall's theory. Smith here offers a transgressive way of using popular culture as a tool to create a meaningful identity through religious belief in a contemporary context.

Smith also demonstrates the paradoxes of contemporary identity formation and perception through Honey Richardson, an African-American autograph dealer with whom Alex-Li becomes acquainted at a New York autograph dealer convention. She negotiates with race and history as they are relevant to her subject position. Honey is appalled by stereotypes and racism that permeate the Hollywood industry (and, ostensibly, in the world at large), and while on a surface level she is herself complicit in the preservation of stereotypes, Honey's personal history and behaviour reveal a character whose complexity also interrogates those stereotypes. Furthermore, Honey's aversion to what the Hollywood machine does to minorities is complicated by the small amount of fame thrust upon her due to her involvement in a celebrity scandal.

Honey specializes in memorabilia of African-American actors, and she educates Alex-Li about problems with representation and the compromise of dignity necessary for minority actors to pursue careers in American entertainment, representations that intersect with and illuminate Honey's subject position. Honey educates Alex-Li on the lack of respect that Hollywood offered actors of colour. For example, she offers up the story of Miss Beavers, a black actress who, in order to get one of the few roles available to a woman of colour earlier in the twentieth century, had to gain weight, 'had to fake a Southern accent, and when she played Aunt Delilah someone had to teach that poor bitch to make flapjacks' (203). The name Miss Beavers connotes two identity positions: a single, available and attractive woman who is equated with her female genitalia. Yet the demands of Hollywood and the dominant culture caused this woman to metamorphose from a sexual, and perhaps overly sexualized, woman to a Mammy character epitomized in the American brand icon Aunt Jemima. Honey also mentions Theda Bara, the 'The Silent Vamp', whose 'name was like Arab Death but all switched around' and despite having been born in

Ohio played objectified, exotic Middle Eastern characters: 'she was born in the shadow of the Sphinx, weaned on serpent's blood. According to the publicity. She was supposed to be sex on legs. Hard to believe' (203). Smith conjures up the spectrum of stereotypical American black women and Middle Eastern women, in effect acknowledging that women of colour throughout the world have been objectified as primarily sexual beings.

Honey's autograph business emblematizes her subject position and the stereotypes that she negotiates in her own life as well. Tracey L. Walters contextualizes Honey's character within common stereotypes of black women: Honey, like Miss Beavers, is both the Jezebel, or overly sexualized predator femme fatale, and the Mammy, the kind, take-charge caretaker when she helps Alex-Li find Kitty Alexander. Furthermore, Walters writes, Smith has complicated the stereotypes somewhat by combining them with Honey's independent spirit and agency outside of these roles (135). Thus, Smith has crafted Honey to embody another liminal space – she is both a Jezebel and a Mammy, as well as an independent (post)modern woman.

Added to the complexity of her character is that Honey is based on the real-life prostitute Divine Brown who became briefly famous when she was arrested along with British actor Hugh Grant for giving him oral sex in exchange for money. Likewise, Honey is infamous for a similar incident, although she is a former prostitute and is now in the autograph business. Her past as a prostitute functions as a reminder that often, particularly for women and minorities, financial independence and economic stability are difficult to obtain and involve traumatic struggle. Ironically, as Honey is herself a celebrity of sorts, she realizes the draw of being (in)famous. She has the notoriety that Alex-Li imagines himself to have, and she recognizes the gains and the downside to being a minor celebrity. Smith writes, 'Alex recalled the two mug-shots: the ruffled Scottish actor, squinting in the flashbulb, the hooker, unbowed, familiar with this kind of camera. Front page for a week? Two weeks? And then it had struggled on for a time [...] and then, finally, the tidy resolution: her return to obscurity' (210). Thus, Honey empathizes with celebrities, especially as still 'In certain areas of Brooklyn, I'm Elizabeth Taylor' (213). Although she hates to admit it, as she indicates to Alex-Li, she is disappointed when people on the street do not recognize her:

> 'But the weird thing is, if nobody looks, I notice. I just notice – and I feel . . . I don't even know how to explain it. Like, out of focus. Fuzzy'
>
> [...]
>
> 'Fuzzy. Like I can't sense myself. It's sort of disgusting, isn't it?' (218)

Honey certainly displays both a Baudrillardan sense of the hyperreal sense of identity and enough political awareness to prompt her both to criticize the gaze of the dominant American culture directed towards women and minorities, and to hunger for recognition and therefore a sense that she matters. Like Alex-Li, while she recognizes her penchant for living the hyperreal, she can see through the dominant culture's mythmaking activities and sees other truths with regard to famous African-Americans. Honey's awareness of her simultaneous desire for and hatred of her infamy reflects the unease with which the contemporary subject views his/her mediated identity.

The proliferation of mass media has made people more aware that there are billions of people on this earth, in turn highlighting our finite and potentially unimportant existence. The temptation has been for contemporary individuals to seek validation from others by being famous, or infamous, as a part of media culture. Honey's story in the novel about the African-American actor Lincoln Theodore Monroe Parry, who was renamed Stepin Fetchit and cast in roles that required him to be 'Rolling his eyes, usually saying *Yessuh* in an elevator or a cotton field or su'in like that?' (203) speak volumes about the contemporary individual's need to be noticed amongst the plethora of images that we take in everyday and the willingness of the dominant culture to promote stereotypes. In an era of mass culture, Smith suggests, celebrity life is one way to be acknowledged and valued, even though the cruel trick is that the attention is short-lived and empty. Honey opines that minority actors were forced to essentialize themselves because it 'Wasn't about what they could get, it was about what people'll do to be famous. It's about humiliation' (203). Her words reflect the dark side to Alex-Li's hyperreality – that living through the fantasy of celebrity can result in degradation or living a life is disconnected and inauthentic.

For Smith, then, as is the case with ethnicity, there are so many subject positions that women may consciously or unconsciously adopt, or that are ascribed to them by others in the encoding/decoding process, none can be championed in a dogmatic fashion. It is not 'correct' to aspire to one particular essentialist subjectivity and, therefore, these various position-alities are simply moments that help convey aspects of one's identity but do not determine it wholly. In *The Autograph Man*, Smith continues her thesis made explicit in *White Teeth* – that while aspects of one's identity are charged with historical meaning, at the same time complex, multivalent identities are the defining characteristic of the contemporary West. This assessment of the difficulties of fixing categories with regard to identity reflects Hall's theory of articulation: 'The end of the essential black subject also entails a recognition that the central issues of race always appear historically in articulation, in a formation, with other categories and divisions and are constantly crossed and recrossed by the categories of class, gender, and ethnicity' (201). In other words, the elements that Honey performs may be historically grounded but are subject to change, continuing to undergo scrutiny and transformation in the present. Smith acknowledges that though one may inhabit many contradictory positions in different moments, this makes one no less real or authentic as a human being. Honey's quest to recover the people behind the Hollywood images helps her make sense of the history of African-Americans and their struggles for dignity and economic gain in the face of racism and oppression at the hands of the white dominant culture.

Honey provides a transgressive counterpart to Boot, the woman with whom Alex-Li cheats on Esther. Boot models her womanly wiles on cinematic examples: 'she prattled on, shaping her body into a deliberate echo of the famous silhouette, the Marilyn hourglass. Back arched, abdomen retracted, turning out the lips like blushing petals, tilting the head low but looking to the ceiling – what an incredibly powerful gift! The ultimate in International Sexual Gestures: the metamorphosis from woman to vase' (162). Clearly, Boot has internalized Hollywood's ultimate example of the desirable woman: Marilyn Monroe, and she is aware of the male gaze, used to her benefit. Interestingly, Smith suggests that the Monroe reference is a closed one; certainly, vamping of this nature is recognizable as deriving from the on-screen glamorous star. Furthermore, such behaviour plays into the male gaze and traditional feminine and sexual norms. Boot provides the essence of traditional female allure, which Smith undoubtedly incorporates to remind readers that the capitalist Hollywood machine profits greatly from these limited portrayals of women, which is a danger of popular culture becoming such an influential force in shaping the consciousness of the individual.

While Honey's function in the narrative is to prompt Alex-Li towards a realization that beyond the hyperreal actual life is unavoidable and painful, Smith denies readers a traditional ending with a tidy resolution with regard to this 'moral lesson'. Urzsula Terentowicz-Fotyga analyzes the plot of the novel in context of the hyperreal and posits that Alex-Li does not, in the end, disavow his imaginary, mediated world in favour of true emotional connections: 'Alex-Li's transformation is neither complete nor truly believable. At the end of the novel, he seems suspended between the real and the hyperreal in the same way that the text hovers between the slapstick and the sentimental' (70). Although Honey's presence emphasizes the need to negotiate with the past in order to affirm one's identity, Alex-Li does not fully embrace this philosophy. Instead, he makes a gesture towards actualizing it. At the end of the novel, after years of urging by his friends to perform a Kaddish ceremony in honour of his deceased father, Alex-Li does so, yet his reactions are mixed. After having this epiphany, when he is alone he 'said his Kaddish without gesture or formality – just a wet song into his hands' (325). Afterwards, he yearns to connect with his girlfriend, Esther: 'He wanted, desperately, to touch her scalp, to draw her into him. To save them both from all this second-rate dialogue, the stuff that love engenders, the stuff of lovers" and he muses on an argument he has sustained throughout their relationship that 'This is what relationships *are*: stage shows that run and run until all the life is drained from them and only the gestures remain' (331). The book ends with Alex-Li performing the Kaddish ceremony at the synagogue with his friends and family present.

Thus, while Alex-Li engages in, and is aware of, real life, concrete inter-actions and the importance of emotional connection, he still maintains that 'only the gestures remain' (331). While the ending in part seems to suggest that gestures, and therefore mediated reality, take precedence over real life experience, I would argue that gestures, images, and popular culture referents are the tools by which the contemporary individual expresses emotion and identity, and they do not necessarily preclude the ability to connect with others. After all, Alex-Li has done so, and allowed himself to grieve and to face his fear of death. While the language of popular culture and fandom may be his *method* of connection, his way of seeing the world, he does ultimately negotiate his identity and sustain interpersonal relation-ships, even as the articulation of his identity reveals a heightened reflexivity as a postmodern subject. Jonathan P. A. Sell argues that in *The Autograph Man*, identity has become completely malleable:

> [F]or Smith the issue of identity in a multicultural society has become a non-issue; or, if it is an issue at all, it is so only on the plane of the individual where, divested of cultural significance, emancipated from history, identity is an index of personal individuality, not of racial, ethnic or cultural affiliation, and comprises an endless series of reinventions. (34)

While Smith downplays deterministic identities based on particular ethnic or religious backgrounds, she highlights the importance of new ways of speaking about and embodying hybrid subject positions, and her treatment of ethnicity and culture reflects Hall's theory that because the postmodern subject occupies a number of subject positions simultaneously, and since signifiers are unstable, representation is expressed through conditional and temporally limited articulations.

Bibliography

Baudrillard, Jean. 'The Precession of Simulacra'. *Simulacra and Simulation*. Trans. Sheila Faria Glaser. Ann Arbor: Uiversity of Michigan Press, 1994, 1–42.

Grossberg, Lawrence. 'History, Politics and Postmodernism: Stuart Hall and Cultural Studies'. *Stuart Hall: Critical Dialogues in Cultural Studies*. David Morley and Kuan-Hsing Chen (eds). New York: Routledge, 1996, 151–73.

Hall, Stuart. 'Encoding, Decoding'. *Cultural Studies: An Anthology*. Michael Ryan (ed.). Malden, MA: Blackwell, 2008, 907–16.

—'New Ethnicities'. From 'New Ethnicities' *Black Film, British Cinema* ICA Documents 7, London: Institute of Contemporary Arts, 1989. *The Post-Colonial Studies Reader* 2nd edn. Bill Ashcroft, Gareth Griffins and Helen Tiffin (eds). New York: Routledge, 2006.

—'On Postmodernism and Articulation: An Interview with Stuart Hall'. Lawrence
    Grossberg (ed.). *Stuart Hall: Critical Dialogues in Cultural Studies*. Morley,
    David and Kuan-Hsing Chen (eds). New York: Routledge, 1996, 131–50.
Hutcheon, Linda. *The Politics of Postmodernism* 2nd edn. London: Routledge,
    2002.
Jameson, Fredric. *Postmodernism, or The Cultural Logic of Late Capitalism*.
    Durham, NC: Duke University Press, 1991.
Sell, Jonathan P. A. 'Chance and Gesture in Zadie Smith's *White Teeth* and
    The Autograph Man: A Model for Multicultural Identity'. *The Journal of
    Commonwealth Literature*. 41(3) (2006): 27–42. *Academic Search Premier*.
    Web. 5 October 2009.
Smith, Zadie. *White Teeth*. New York: Random House, 2000.
—*The Autograph Man*. New York: Random House, 2002.
Terentowicz-Fotyga, Urszula. 'The Impossible Self and the Poetics of the Urban
    Hyperreal in Zadie Smith's *The Autograph Man*'. *Zadie Smith: Critical Essays*.
    Tracey L. Walters (ed.). New York: Lang, 2008, 57–72.
Tew, Philip. *Zadie Smith*. London and New York: Palgrave Macmillan, 2010.
Walters, Tracey L. 'Still Mammies and Hos: Stereotypical Images of Black Women
    in Zadie Smith's Novels'. *Zadie Smith: Critical Essays*. Tracey L. Walters (ed.).
    New York: Lang, 2008, 123–39.

6

'Temporal Layers': Personal and Political History in Zadie Smith's *On Beauty*

Susan Alice Fischer

On the surface, Zadie Smith's third novel, *On Beauty* (2005), appears to be a significant departure from her first and best-known novel, *White Teeth* (2000). While *White Teeth* celebrates multicultural London, *On Beauty* takes place in a staid, mostly white academic town in the US and centres ostensibly on the mixed-race Belsey family and the rivalries in an academic institution central to their lives. Yet, just as *White Teeth* explores the impact of British imperial history, World War II and migration on contemporary life, *On Beauty* looks, perhaps more subtly, to a past rooted in slavery and the more recent battle over affirmative action (similar to 'positive discrimination' in Britain) as defining moments in the formation of contemporary American identity.

While not an historical novel, *On Beauty* can be seen as part of contemporary literature's 'historical turn', often used, as Keen explains, 'to address a wide range of present-day concerns' (167, 176) and, as Lane and Tew write, to highlight 'the place of history in our everyday lives' (11). In drawing upon the historical roots of the contemporary world to show the ways in which the past is inscribed in the present, *On Beauty* represents not only past events of national import, but more significantly what Smith refers to as the 'temporal layers' that constitute both personal and political relations. The entrenched positions that the characters take on in their intimate and public lives have a destructive effect, which halts progress in both arenas.

Set in the fictitious Massachusetts college town of Wellington in the early years of the new millennium, *On Beauty* centres on two major conflicts. In the household of Kiki and Howard Belsey, the question is whether a history of 30 years of love is enough to hold together the marriage after Howard's infidelity. The primary debate on the Wellington College campus has to do with whether the continued effects of historical events makes affirmative action and open access to higher education beneficial to individual and society, as its proponents claim. At first glance these two questions may seem to have little to do with one another, yet they are connected through the novel's conception of history as a 'temporal layer[ing]', in which the past infuses and is inseparable from the present, and specifically of the history of race relations in America as having a place in 'our everyday lives'.

Personal histories and their political contexts

In *On Beauty*, the presence of the past in 'everyday lives' centres on race relations in the US and the ways they permeate both personal histories and wider societal issues. As in American society at large, the legacy of slavery is an underlying, though often silenced or subterranean, presence for many of the novel's characters and their interpersonal relations. At the heart of the story is the interracial Belsey family. Howard is a white Englishman of working-class London origins, while Kiki is an African-American woman whose family hails from Florida. Their house, described early in the novel, evokes in its details the history of slavery and the Civil War and symbolizes the ongoing rift within the nation as a whole. Built in 1856, during the country's most divisive historical moment and one that still shapes its race relations – as can be seen from recent calls for secession from some quarters following the recent re-election of President Obama – the house contains a skylight with a window in a motley design. As light from above refracts through the glass it bathes the top of the stairs in a many-hued pattern (16). It is the Belsey family tradition to avoid stepping into this multicoloured light, which symbolizes the nation's avoidance of recognizing its history and diversity (17), as discussed by Fischer in '"A Glance from God": Zadie Smith's *On Beauty* and Zora Neale Hurston'. In the novel the family gallery of photographs along the central staircase contains portraits of Kiki's maternal family line: a house-slave, a maid and a nurse (17). The latter inherited the house from a doctor with whom she had worked, thus enabling the family to move into the middle class. While Kiki is aware of this history and its importance, Howard's family history is represented by only one portrait of his father 'which has lifted itself out of its low origins, like Howard himself' (18). Yet Howard 'hates' the picture, as he does his father (18).

That the Belsey's is a 'house divided' is not only an allusion to a broader national conflict, but to strained relations at home, despite real affection that binds the parents and their three children, Jerome, Zora and Levi. While each of the children can be seen as developing a different ideological position in the course of the novel – religious, academic liberal, and a politicized diasporic identity respectively as Fischer details in 'The Shelter of Each Other' – the frayed relations in the Belsey household centre on the parents, as Kiki has discovered a condom in Howard's suit pocket. While he claims to have had a one-night stand at a conference, for which she is beginning to consider forgiving him, the marriage is further shaken by Kiki's subsequent realization that Howard has compounded his infidelity with a lie obfuscating the length of the affair and the fact that it was with their friend, and his colleague, Claire Malcolm. Kiki learns this at the party she and Howard throw for their thirtieth wedding anniversary, which, though not directly mentioned, falls on 11 September, an allusion to another historical event brought about by ideological entrenchment which cleaves the world in two and thus symbolizes the deep rift in their marriage and how much further it is imploding.

Personal relations in the novel are inextricably tied to history, and the legacy of slavery reverberates in intimate interactions. That Kiki casts her hurt at Howard's betrayal in specifically racialized terms is not surprising given several earlier scenes highlighting white perceptions of black people in Wellington. For instance, earlier Kiki runs into Claire in town and finds herself performing blackness, as she shakes 'her head from side to side in a manner she understood white people enjoyed' (52). Similarly, Kiki's son, Levi, is aware that white, and at times black, people can see a young black man only as a criminal. Before the party at which Kiki makes her awful discovery, Zora sarcastically assures someone who is passing by the house and staring at her brother Levi that he in fact lives there and is not about to break in. This context of precarious belonging in mostly white Wellington and in a country with a long history of white supremacy deepens the hurt Kiki experiences when she realizes that Howard has betrayed her with Claire: "A little *white* woman," yelled Kiki across the room, unable now to control herself. "A tiny little white woman I could fit in my *pocket*" (206). As a black woman in a white world and in a marriage with a white man she thought she could trust, significantly Kiki tells Howard of the ethnic composition of the world she now inhabits at both his university and the hospital in which she works as an administrator, bound to these environments very largely because of her commitment to their relationship:

'I'm alone in this ... this *sea* of white. I barely *know* any black folk any more [...] unless they be cleaning under my feet in the fucking café in your *fucking* college. Or pushing a fucking hospital bed through a corridor. I *staked my whole life* on you'. (206)

She is responding to Howard's claim she is being 'ludicrous' (206), with Howard failing to see the blow to Kiki not only as his wife, but specifically as a black woman in a white-dominated society.

Yet it is also a long personal history that makes it hard for Kiki to walk away, despite her hurt and anger:

> The only things that threatened to disturb her resolve were the sheer temporal *layers* of Howard as they presented themselves before her: Howard at twenty-two, at thirty, at forty-five and fifty-one; the difficulty of keeping all these Howards out her consciousness; the importance of not being side-tracked, of responding only to this most recent Howard [...] the heart-breaker, the emotional fraud. (203)

While Kiki recognizes these 'temporal layers' of their personal history, Howard fails to see much more than the fact that Kiki has gained weight as she has aged. Howard is unclear about what has gone wrong in his marriage or what has led him to have a relationship with Claire, even as he experiences the inescapability of personal history during a well-intentioned, but disastrous visit that he makes to his estranged father, Harry, in Cricklewood. The weight of their history is palpable as Howard first arrives at the house and sees the 1970s décor still in place alongside the mementos of Howard's long-dead mother. Both father and son are stuck in a history that neither can see clearly nor escape:

> For they fell into the same patterns at once, as if Howard had never gone to university (against Harry's advice), never left this piss-poor country, never married outside his colour or his nation. He'd never gone anywhere or done anything. He was still a butcher's son and it was still just the two of them, still making do, squabbling in a railway cottage in Dalston. Two Englishmen stranded together with nothing in common except a dead woman they had both loved. (295)

Immediately they begin the arguments that, even had they been taken 'through an oral history – with slides – of the past fifty-seven years, day by day', they would have been unable to understand how they arrived at this point after a moment of initial hope; yet, 'once inside, everything was the same as it had always been' (296). It is impossible for Howard to extricate himself from the patterns of childhood and his feelings of shame at his working-class origins, just as it is impossible for his father not to voice racist thoughts, even though he has a genuine fondness for his mixed-race grandchildren. As the narrator explains, Harry's inane small talk riddled with unthinking prejudices which Howard cannot endure is merely 'another way of saying: *It's good to see you. It's been too long. We're family.* But Howard couldn't do this when he was sixteen and he couldn't do it now. He just did not believe, as his father did, that time is how you spend your love' (302).

That history is destined to repeat itself under the weight of these unexamined 'temporal layers' seems a foregone conclusion. Indeed,

Howard's failed encounter with his father is a catalyst to the drunkenness that leads him to enact a new infidelity that also reverses the Oedipal drama, even as it reinforces its blindness. Any resolve he might have had not to succumb to the much younger and very beautiful Victoria Kipps, who is his student, the former object of his son Jerome's affections and the daughter of his professional rival, Sir Montague Kipps, is swept away, and, like Oedipus, Howard runs headlong into a fate rooted in historical blindness.

Political histories and their personal repercussions

Just as Howard is unable to see or to extricate himself from long-established patterns in his personal interactions, contemporary American culture fails to recognize and to transcend deeply engrained positions about race in its public discourse. Not only are the Belseys' personal histories shaped by racial and class hierarchies, but the history of affirmative action and related 'culture wars' has repercussions on the personal lives of several characters. This theme is introduced with the arrival of Kipps, Howard's academic antagonist and ideological opponent, at Wellington College. A Trinidadian migrant to Britain (and now to the US), whose wife Carlene was a passenger on the *Empire Windrush*, Monty has been knighted and mixes with people in politics and the media. The conflict between Howard and Monty, though professional and political, is shaped by a multilayered personal history as well as by a different ideological interpretation of history. Indeed, the liberal Howard's enmity towards Monty is firmly rooted in his belief that what matters to his adversary is promoting an excessively conservative agenda (29). However, Howard has begun to 'hate' him now that Monty has published a book on Rembrandt, while Howard's study of the artist remains in draft form on the floor of his study (29). Worse still, Monty has gleefully and publically poured scorn on Howard for misidentifying a Rembrandt portrait in a clumsily targeted attack on him (28).

Howard is thus jealous of how much further Monty has advanced in his career and despises his political positions, and the two characters are positioned as polar opposites in an ideological war between liberals and conservatives. While Howard is billed as a 'radical art theorist', Monty is a 'cultural conservative' (115) who wants to 'tak[e] the "liberal" out of the Liberal Arts' (148). Their divergent views go back decades. While Howard was engaged in 'direct action' in the 1970s and 1980s (181), during the Brixton riots of 1981, Monty was on the BBC talking about the need for the 'coloured man' to take 'responsibility' for 'his own home' (20), something that perhaps lends credence to Kiki's suggestion later on that his position psychologically is one of 'right-wing black self-hatred' (368); yet, Monty refutes this by calling the notion a 'comforting fairytale', that liberals tell themselves to avoid the reality that 'conservatives are motivated by moral convictions *as profoundly held* as those' of liberals (369).

Although Howard and Monty have had similar trajectories as they have made their way to Oxford and into the academy – one from the white working class, the other through post-war migration – their ideological positions on social mobility through education in the contemporary US are not only at opposite ends of the spectrum, but surprisingly devoid, given their own histories, of any real sense of the repercussions of similar struggles in other people's lives. Howard supports affirmative action, while Monty argues that it degrades those who benefit from it. *On Beauty* not only shows these men's polarized, and very theoretical, stances on affirmative action but also illustrates the very real effects of denying full access to education with the character of Carl Thomas, a young and talented working-class, black poet who is brought onto the Wellington campus as a 'discretionary' student, a practice which grants him access to a poetry course through informal channels and one which Monty abhors. Chantelle Williams, a minor character, is another gifted poet who depends upon such 'discretional' options to hone her talent. The precarious status of 'discretionary' student underlines the ways in which neither ever feels entirely part of Wellington College and ultimately shows how dispensable their status makes them.

Carl first encounters the Belsey family at a concert in Boston after which Zora accidentally takes Carl's Discman instead of her own; thus in a novel modelled after E. M. Forster's *Howards End*, Carl is cast from the start in the role of Leonard Bast to play opposite the Belseys' role as the Schlegels, and he meets a similarly disastrous end because of the 'help' he encounters from his social 'betters', who show little understanding of who he is and where he comes from. Although at first Zora is blind to Carl's good looks because of '[p]ride and prejudice' (74), she ultimately falls for him, as much because he becomes her project as anything else. During his next encounter with the Belseys, when he shows up at the anniversary party to which he has been invited, Carl is turned away at the door because Howard does not recognize him. In fact, throughout the novel, Carl is quite simply not seen for who he is. Similarly to Oedipus' blindness that brings a plague upon the land, this blindness is linked to a legacy of slavery and racism that has both societal and personal repercussions.

Even as Carl is gradually seduced by life at Wellington College, his previous educational experiences make him leery of such institutions. When he first meets the Belseys, he refers to himself as 'not an *educated* brother' (76), and although he is a poet, he recognizes the way his Spoken Word poetry is marginalized by educational institutions as it is not considered legitimate – not '*poetry* poetry' (140). While Zora, who has been brought up in an academic household, is comfortable on campus and focused on her future, for Carl, things are not so straightforward, and he feels that 'The future's another country [...] And I *still* ain't got a passport' (140). Indeed, he will come to learn just how fraught his entry into this world can be.

The 'temporal layers' that are keeping him back are a poor and unequal school system which under-educates black youngsters and in particular treats young black male students with a suspicion that often turns them away from education. Indeed, Carl has previously been hurt in an educational system in which 'his teachers started worrying that he was going to mug or rape them' (260). In high school he had sexual relations with one of his teachers, which turned into 'a bad scene' and marked 'the beginning of when things began going very wrong with him and classrooms' (260). He is thus justifiably diffident as he encounters the world of Wellington College.

Yet Carl's 'passport' seems to have been issued when he is 'discovered' by Zora, her classmates and their creative writing professor Claire Malcolm at a poetry slam at the Bus Stop, and all are enthralled by Carl's performance. As a result, Claire asks if he wants to join the class as a 'discretionary' student. She is one of the faculty that takes such students, believing that opportunities are often closed to gifted students with little access to education, who opt for the military instead, because they lack the funds, while the uninspired Zora Belsey can force her way into Claire's class (160). That Carl needs a 'passport' to enter this world underscores that he is seen as a marginal member of society. As he begins to feel good in Claire's class and supported by her and the other students, he starts to recognize that 'Claire had that special teacher thing he hadn't felt since he was a really small boy [...]: *she wanted him to do well.* [...] And he wanted to do well *for* her' (260). Yet this feeling is tenuousness, and his 'passport' offers only a 'discretionary' leave to stay that can be revoked at any time.

Indeed, Carl and the other 'discretionary' students, such as Chantelle Williams, become the focus of Howard and Monty's battle over affirmative action. While Howard and Monty have managed to move up the class structure because of a British university system that would have paid for their education, young American Carl has not had this opportunity. Moreover, when things heat up with Monty's anti-affirmative action rhetoric, Claire withdraws and puts Zora forward to fight the battle for them (262–3). It is thus through the ensuing drama over 'discretionary' students that *On Beauty* engages with a national discourse about affirmative action in American higher education and shows its effects on individual lives.

While this is the crux of the conflict that shapes the academic discourse on the Wellington campus where much of the action in the novel takes place, *On Beauty* also alludes to other aspects of the so-called 'culture wars [that] were characterized as wars over competing values' about homosexuality, religious expression and the claim made by some conservatives that they are being silenced by an aggressively 'politically correct' left-wing or 'liberal' professoriate, which have shaped the academy since the 1990s, a context Shockley and McNeeley discuss in 'A Seismic Shift in U.S. Federal Arts Policy: A Tale of Organizational Challenge and Controversy in the

1990s' (13). An atheist, Howard bemoans the 'flight from the rational, which was everywhere in evidence in the new century' (38). The religious Monty believes that 'Equality was a myth, and Multiculturalism a fatuous dream', and that 'minority groups too often demanded equal rights they haven't earned' (44). Indeed, as Howard's daughter Zora sarcastically expresses Monty's position, 'Apparently *everybody* gets special treatment – blacks, gays, liberals, women – everybody except poor white males' (148). Yet while *On Beauty* alludes to these diverse aspects of the 'culture wars', it focuses on affirmative action and the virulent backlash against such legislation in the academic sector where race or ethnicity may be used as one of several criteria to select candidates for university admission.

Affirmative action emerges in the US as an attempt to redress the balance in a country with a long history of slavery and segregation. Speaking in 1965 at Howard University, an Historically Black College and University (HBCU), as quoted in Chace, President Lyndon B. Johnson articulated the need to address these wrongs: 'You do not take a person who, for years, has been hobbled by chains and liberate him, bring him up to the starting line of a race and then say, "you are free to compete with all the others," and still justly believe that you have been completely fair'. According to Kim, the first case regarding affirmative action in higher education was *Regents of the University of California v. Bakke, 1978* which ruled that 'racial diversity serves a compelling state interest' (12); thus race could be a consideration in the admissions decision.

These claims have not gone unchallenged. Detractors of affirmative action have posited a false dichotomy between access and excellence that also plays out in *On Beauty*. They demand what they refer to as a 'color-blind policy' because they believe, like Monty Kipps, that affirmative action only 'passes over better qualified students, [...] allow[s] racial discrimination [...] stigmatizes the so-called beneficiaries [...] fosters a victim mindset, removes the incentive for academic excellence, and encourages separatism; it compromises the academic mission of the university and lowers the overall academic quality of the student body', as the conservative Roger Clegg has stated, as quoted in Chace. The relentless legal assault on affirmative action has included a 1996 referendum against affirmative action that was approved in California, as well as a ban on affirmative action at universities in the states of Mississippi, Texas and Louisiana, which resulted the following year in drops in minority enrolment in particular programmes (Barinaga). In June 2003, as Boyd outlines, the US Supreme Court upheld in a close vote the University of Michigan's right to use race as part of the criteria for admissions (2); however, this victory was challenged when voters passed the 'Michigan Civil Rights Initiative', effective in 2006, to amend the state constitution to forbid affirmative action based on race, gender and other points of 'difference' as Chace outlines. At the time of writing, as Dunleavy and Gutman note, the Supreme Court is considering another case, *Fisher v. University of Texas*, brought in 2011 by a white female student claiming that she was not admitted to the university because of discrimination. The case, which threatens to erode current legislation further, will probably be adjudicated in summer 2013 (105).

The battle over affirmative action on Wellington Campus suggests how divisive an issue this is in the US, where a cultural blindness to the legacy of slavery and segregation remains pervasive in many sectors of the population. According to Chace public polls on the subject show that most Americans would side with Monty Kipps against affirmative action programmes; not surprisingly, positions often fall along racial lines, which Smith deliberately reverses in her novel with Howard and Monty. Yet as Kim points out, 'The ambiguity with which people on opposite ends of the ideological spectrum often speak of concepts, such as diversity, equal opportunity, and meritocracy, to refer to those core values clouds, rather than illumines, the basic questions underlying the affirmative action dilemma' (12). Much the same could be said about the ways that Howard and Monty debate the issue on the Wellington campus, as they seem to be more interested in scoring points against one another and holding onto entrenched positions, than with how these issues are rooted in 'temporal layers' of history, affecting actual students in their 'everyday lives'. That neither of them has anything to do with Carl Thomas, the 'discretionary' student, underscores this point, as does the fact that Monty has been having an affair with Chantelle Williams, the young black female student that begs him in vain to let her take courses as a 'discretionary' student. It is only once Zora threatens Monty with exposure of the affair that he is forced to back down on his position and allow Chantelle to take courses – so much for the 'moral convictions' he claims for himself in his conversation with Kiki.

While Howard supports affirmative action, both he and Monty fail to see is how vital access to education is for 'minority' students. For instance, even though the numbers of black women students enrolling and earning degrees in higher education have continued to grow, as Chace explains 'the proportion [of students] who were [black] men was the same in 2002 – 4.3 per cent – as it was in 1976'. The roll back against affirmative action – and the rise of the prison industrial complex – has had devastating effects on the black male student population, something that *On Beauty* perhaps alludes to with regard to Carl who, when an important painting disappears from Monty's office, is the first person Monty thinks of accusing of theft, despite having no evidence whatsoever. Carl may well become a statistic along the lines of the one that Chace cites: 'About one in three black men will go to prison in his lifetime, compared to one in 17 white males', a context also explored by Harper and Griffin in 'Opportunity Beyond Affirmative Action: How Low-Income and Working-Class Black Male Achievers Access Highly Selective, High-Cost Colleges and Universities'. Of course, the novel also suggests that (black) women may encounter another series of problems in higher education, such as inappropriate sexual attention from their male professors.

The history of affirmative action in American higher education thus sheds light on the ideological impasse on Wellington campus regarding their so-called 'discretionary' students, a choice of phrasing that suggests their superfluity for the institution. Yet neither Howard nor Monty really engages in a serious discussion with the other about the subject. When Monty rails against Howard's 'Affirmative Action committee in the *Wellington Herald*', we learn few specifics about what he says about the issues, but rather that he 'challenge[s] its very right to existence' while at the same time claiming the group is 'suppressing right-wing discussion and debate on campus' (156). Similarly, Howard's reaction to this exchange is more about the buzz it creates in his class and in his inbox than about substantive ideas. Like Howard and his father earlier, Monty and Howard are 'just arguing the same stupid dialectic over and over', as Claire Malcolm puts it (263). Smith seems to be suggesting that, in their hubris, both Howard and Monty are so attached to their positions that they are unable to see them clearly or to perceive any argument the other might make, much less the effect that these issues have upon actual people.

Later in the novel, in the section entitled 'On Beauty and Being Wrong', an academic meeting takes place in Keller Library where their colleagues have turned out in force 'to hear the Monty and Howard road show' (323). The references to Oedipal blindness are reinforced here with an allusion to a blind seer, as much is made of the fact that this building is named after Helen Keller, whose portrait hangs in the library, and who, it is suggested, was able to see much more lucidly than the factions blinded by their inflexible positions. The meeting has been called to discuss the issue of affirmative action and specifically whether the recently appointed Monty may give a series of lectures on potentially politically sensitive topics, from affirmative action to homosexuality, or whether these lectures may be vetted by Howard and his pro-affirmative action committee. Howard plans to concede that freedom of speech is important, but he feels it is vital in this instance to protect students from 'the *politics of hate*' (323). While Monty continues to present his reactionary positions, Howard falls into the trap of attempting to silence dissent. Their positions have become so ossified as to stifle a real exchange of ideas in precisely the place that should provide such a forum.

While both Howard and Monty are probably both right about some things – that homophobia is a bad thing, as is forbidding religious practice – they are also both wrong in attempting to silence each other and in refusing to engage in a meaningful exchange of ideas. Like other conservatives, Monty frames the debate on Wellington's affirmative action stance in terms of the rhetoric of access versus excellence. He lambasts a policy

whereby students who are NOT enrolled in this college are yet taught in classes here, by professors who, at their own 'discretion' (as it is so disingenuously put), allow these 'students' into their classes, choosing them over *actual* students better qualified than they – NOT because these young people meet the academic standards of Wellington, no, but because they are considered *needy cases* – as if it helps minorities to be pushed through an elite environment to which they are not yet suited. (329)

This is the most forthright pronouncement against affirmative action in the novel and one which recalls, in suggesting that minorities are 'not yet suited' to an 'elite environment' the more conservative vision of Booker T. Washington (born the same year that the Belseys' house was built), who though seeking to advance black people chose the path of accommodation, as articulated primarily in the Atlanta Compromise, as opposed with the idea, advanced by W. E. B. DuBois, that demanded civil rights and the right to education for the 'talented tenth', to which someone like Carl could be said to belong. However, unlike Washington and DuBois, who were genuinely interested in advancing the cause of education for black people, the discourses of Monty and Howard have degenerated into a 'road show'. In constructing the category of 'discretionary' student, which is *not* how affirmative action actually functions, Smith underscores the marginal status to which society, and those who maintain the power to afford or deny such students access to the academy, has relegated them.

But then, for all his achievements, perhaps even Monty has been marginalized in the academy. Because Monty is so adamantly against affirmative action, it is ironic that, although he is an art historian who has written on Rembrandt, he is housed in the Black Studies Department. As Batra notes, this suggests not only the ways that white majority academic institutions often do not take seriously the mission of such departments, but also that 'The vagueness of Sir Monty's job profile at Wellington or the nature of his duties at Black Studies is in contrast to the neo-conservative anti-affirmative ideas he propounds' (1080). It perhaps also implies a co-opting of a conservative black professor to further the anti-affirmative action agenda of the college, something Kiki alludes to later when she criticizes the conservative attitudes of highly successful black professionals, such as Condoleezza Rice and Colin Powell, who, Kiki believes, have 'this *rabid* need to separate themselves away from the rest of us' (368). As Batra suggests in reference to Monty's position in the department, 'Such tokenism casts doubt – as the author presumably intends – on the very nature and purpose of Black Studies at Wellington' (1080). Much the same could be said of the fact that the Black Studies Department also 'invents' the job of Hip-Hop Archivist for Carl Thomas to give him a 'legitimate' connection to Wellington. While Carl takes this job and his research into the 'crossroads' as a trope in rap music very seriously, there is little evidence that the college really cares what he – or indeed the department – is doing or that his work might enable him to change the fate often assigned to young black men (375).

Because the characters in *On Beauty* fail to see the 'temporal layers' of history in 'everyday lives', Carl is, perhaps irrevocably, hurt in his encounter with the Belseys and Wellington College. Zora will come to regret her role in Carl's disappearance from the college as a 'discretionary' student, as she jealously violates him by breaking up his tryst with Victoria at a party. That Zora now acts as if she owns Carl makes him believe that only her desire for him motivated her fight to allow him to stay on campus as a 'discretionary' student. Consequently, he doubts his talent once more, feeling that she has been toying with him. He thinks that, even as she has supported his presence in class, she has been mocking him all along, making him believe he could write poetry. However now that he fails to do her bidding, she lashes out at him (413–14). He believes that, like Chantelle, whom Monty has been 'screwing' (418), he is being objectified and that the Belseys and other middle class academics are brutal and patronizing, more self-serving than interested in helping people like him, despite the lies they tell themselves and others (417). Carl comes to feel that he is just 'some experiment' for people like Zora who have no sense of the effects that living between exclusion and qualified inclusion have on 'discretionary' students, and he exits the world of Wellington for good (418). In this way, Smith hints at the double-edged nature of affirmative action as it is currently constructed by the discourses in the academy and in American culture at large.

Perhaps because she is not an academic, Kiki engages with the personal consequences of an anti-affirmative action agenda much more directly, whereas Howard and Monty remain in the realm of theory. In her conversation with Monty's wife Carlene, Kiki attempts move beyond the 'binary' thinking of their academic husbands (175). Early on, Kiki summarizes Monty's – and by extension her own – views on the subject, noting that the right-wing politics of a black scholar such as Monty harms black students' bid for equal access to education, by recasting it as preferential treatment. She sees his presence at the college at this particular time as especially problematic as the US Senate is attempting to curtail affirmative action through new legislation (122). Later, Kiki manages to engage Monty in real *dialogue* about affirmative action. She frames the debate in both more historical and more personal, rather than ideological, terms by referring to the recent history of segregation and the need to redress the imbalances of power, access and resources through affirmative action. Kiki reminds Monty that in her mother's Florida neighbourhood, 'you could still see a *segregated* bus in 1973 [...] This stuff is *close*. It's recent' (368). That the historical context still affects people's lives is the most compelling, and least patronizing, argument for affirmative action put forward in the novel. As Kiki says, 'our opportunities have been severely retarded, *backed up* or however you want to put it, by a legacy of stolen rights – and to put *that* right, some concessions and support are what's needed? It's a matter of redressing the balance – because we all know it's been unbalanced a damn long time' (368). The 'temporal layers' of history matter in 'everyday lives'.

By attempting to make the political personal, Kiki tries to undo the unproductive tendencies of the 'thought police' that she has come to feel Howard represents (393). In an argument with her husband, Kiki refers to the way he reiterated, in response to 9/11, Baudrillard's notions of the hyperreal and simulacrum and his argument that the Gulf War did not take place, as his eponymous book title claims. Kiki takes objection to this extreme position: 'simulated wars or whatever the fuck that was [...]. And I was thinking: *What is wrong with this man?* I was *ashamed* of you. I didn't say anything, but I was. Howard [...] this is *real*. This life. We're really here – this is really happening. Suffering is *real*. When you hurt people, it's *real*. When you fuck one of our best friends, that's a *real* thing and it *hurts* me' (394). In this impassioned speech, Kiki emphasizes the inextricable connections between the personal and the political. In sarcastically rebutting her argument by questioning her putative comparison between 'mass murder [and his] infidelity,' Howard misses the point that both Kiki is making and the author makes by having their anniversary – and the day Kiki learns the full story of his infidelity – fall on 11 September. The personal ramifications of political debates – and the 'temporal layers' in 'everyday lives' – that Kiki urges Howard to see, are precisely what Howard and Monty miss in their fight over affirmative action. On the other hand, Howard and Kiki's son, Levi, is one of the few to see the personal consequences of another form of marginalization – that of the 'unseen' migrant workers from Haiti and other parts of the developing world who make Wellington run and whose plight has long historical roots in slavery, colonialism and globalization (264).

Ultimately, *On Beauty* refuses to take either Howard's or Monty's side in the 'same stupid dialectic'. In her essay collection, *Changing My Mind*, Smith writes, 'I'm forced to recognize that ideological inconsistency is, for me, practically an article of faith' (xiii–xiv). Smith thus insists upon the necessity of moving beyond entrenched positions about difficult and historically rooted conflicts. Before the faculty meeting at which Howard and Monty argue their very abstract positions on affirmative action gets fully underway, another character makes a singular appearance: '[o]ne lucky sod now escape[s] through the squeaky double-doors – a feckless novelist on a visiting fellowship' (324). The character's exit suggests that even the author's stand-in – Smith similarly held a visiting position at Harvard, to which Wellington bears a striking resemblance – is fed up with the unproductive and divisive exchange of barbs between Howard and Monty. By refusing to engage in the terms of the debate, the novelist – both fictional and real – shows that Kiki's insistence on connecting with the reality of people's hurt and recognizing that history affects people's lives is the way forward.

Bibliography

Barinaga, Marcia. 'Graduate Admissions Down for Minorities'. *Science* 281.5384 (1998): 1778. *Academic Search Complete*. Web. 3 November 2012.

Batra, Kanika. 'Kipps, Belsey, and Jegede: Cosmopolitanism, Transnationalism, and Black Studies in Zadie Smith's *On Beauty*'. *Callaloo*, 33(4) (Fall 2010): 1079–92. *Project Muse*. Web. 3 November 2012.

Boyd, Melba Joyce. 'The Color Line Redefined in the Twenty-First Century in Wake of the Anti-Affirmative Action Suits Against the University of Michigan'. *Black Scholar* 33.3/4 (2003): 2–4. *Academic Search Complete*. Web. 3 November 2012.

Chace, William M. 'Affirmative Inaction: Opposition to Affirmative Action Has Drastically Reduced Minority Enrollment at Public Universities; Private Institutions Have the Power and the Responsibility to Reverse the Trend'. *American Scholar* 80.1 (2011): N. Pag. *Academic Search Complete*. Web. 3 November 2012.

Dunleavy, E. and A. Gutman. 'Supreme Court to Rule on *Fisher v. University of Texas*: Is *Grutter* In Trouble?' *TIP: The Industrial-Organizational Psychologist* 50.1 (2012): 105–13, *Academic Search Complete*, EBSCOhost. Web. 3 November 2012.

Fischer, Susan Alice. 'The Shelter of Each Other'. Rev. of *On Beauty*, by Zadie Smith. *The Women's Review of Books* 25.2 (2006): 30–1.

—'"A Glance from God": Zadie Smith's *On Beauty* and Zora Neale Hurston'. *Changing English: Studies in Culture and Education* 14.3 (2007): 285–-97.

Harper, Shaun R. and Kimberly A. Griffin. 'Opportunity Beyond Affirmative Action: How Low-Income and Working-Class Black Male Achievers Access Highly Selective, High-Cost Colleges and Universities'. *Harvard Journal of African American Public Policy* 17 (2011): 43–60. *Academic Search Complete*. Web. 3 November 2012.

Keen, Suzanne. 'The Historical Turn in British Fiction'. *A Concise Companion to Contemporary British Fiction*. James F. English Maldon, MA, Oxford and Charlton, Victoria: Blackwell Publishing, 2006, 167–87.

Kim, Joon K. 'From *Bakke* to *Grutter*: Rearticulating Diversity and Affirmative Action in Higher Education'. *Multicultural Perspectives* 7.2 (2005): 12–19. *Academic Search Complete*. Web. 3 November 2012.

Lane, Richard J. and Philip Tew. 'Introduction'. *Contemporary British Fiction*. Richard J. Lane, Rod Mengham and Philip Tew (eds). Cambridge: Polity Press, 2003, 11–12.

Shockley, Gordon and Connie L. McNeely. 'A Seismic Shift in U.S. Federal Arts Policy: A Tale of Organizational Challenge and Controversy in the 1990s'. *Journal of Arts Management, Law & Society*. 39.1 (2009): 7–23. *Academic Search Complete*. Web. 3 November 2012.

Smith, Zadie. *White Teeth*. London: Hamish Hamilton, 2000.

—*On Beauty*. London: Hamish Hamilton, 2005.

—*Changing My Mind: Occasional Essays*. Toronto: Hamish Hamilton, 2009.

7

The Right to a Secret: Zadie Smith's *NW*

Lynn Wells

Zadie Smith's essay 'That Crafty Feeling', which is included in *Changing my Mind: Occasional Essays* (2009), was composed, it seems clear, during the same period that she commenced writing *NW* (2012), her most recent novel in which the prefatory letters of the postcode of the main area where it is set provide the book's title. In her essay Smith proclaims a change in direction for her writing of fiction:

> Much of the excitement of a new novel lies in the repudiation of the one written before. Other people's words are the bridge you use to cross from where you were to wherever you're going.
>
> Recently I came across a new quote. It's my screen saver now, my little scrap of confidence as I try to write a novel. It is a thought of Derrida's and very simple:
>
> If a right to a secret is not maintained then we are in a totalitarian space.
>
> Which is to say: enough of human dissection, of entering the brains of characters, cracking them open, rooting every secret out! For now, this is the new attitude. Years from now, when this book is done and another begins, another change will come. (102)

Smith's attraction to Jacques Derrida's aphorism as a model for her fiction marks a clear departure from her approach to the novel prior to *NW*, such as in *On Beauty* (2005) where her characters' inner workings are exposed through the frequent delving of her Forsterian narrator into their thoughts and their occasional, often disastrous urge to self-revelation and confession. One need think only of Kiki Belsey's painfully honest description to her husband Howard of the effects of menopause on her once beautiful body, counterpointed by narratorial reflections on female aesthetics, or, Howard's partial confession of adultery, which act's magnitude of betrayal is revealed by his body language at their wedding anniversary part. In contrast in *NW*, however, despite a range of narrational modes, the emphasis is on the withholding of information while foregrounding experimental modes of writing as if almost to distract the reader; each of the three central characters – Leah Hanwell, Felix Cooper and Leah's best friend Natalie (Keisha) Blake – keeps a secret that defines their lives. All three grew up in the same council estate (in North American terms, a housing project) in the fictional area of Caldwell in northwest London, an area of the city notorious for poverty, crime and interracial tension, where lower-class citizens of many backgrounds live in apartment towers ironically named after the giants of English philosophy – 'Smith, Hobbes, Bentham, Locke, Russell' (265). Natalie, who grows up to be a highly successful married lawyer with children, clandestinely hooks up with strangers over the internet for group sex, reverting to her 'black' name and her birthplace for her secret email address, 'KeishaNW@gmail.com' (259). Leah, a married woman in her thirties who seems to be trying to conceive, surreptitiously foils any success in getting pregnant by taking the birth control pill without her partner's knowledge; Felix, also in his thirties and in a stable relationship with his new girlfriend, travels across London to buy her a surprise gift but stops to have a final illicit encounter with his Russian lover Annie, after which he is involved in a random incident on the underground (subway) after which he is followed, attacked and dies. While Leah and Natalie do not know Felix, they become connected to him through one of his murderers, their high school friend Nathan Bogle (whose last name means 'bogey' or 'spectre') who is living a life of addiction and violence on the streets. Although these characters' secrets are personal in nature, they are kept in a fictional context clearly inflected with the politics of contemporary England of the last decade, with the novel's title itself mapping the contours of the setting and the action. The narrative lines of all three main characters are brought together at the novel's end, with a symbolic return by Natalie with Nathan to the impoverished area she had tried to leave behind, not a reasoned decision, but more reactive, made after leaving her home following a disastrous revelation to her partner about her secretive, closet sexual activities.

In order to grasp the interplay between the personal and the political in *NW*, one perhaps needs to dig deeper into Derrida's saying, which forms part of his dialogue with Maurizio Ferraris in *A Taste for the Secret*. In this passage, Derrida articulates his belief that secrecy is essential to individual liberty but is faced by the spatial demands of social control which is essentially panoptic, in that all individuals become perhaps uncomfortably complicit in each other's oppression:

> I have a taste for the secret, it clearly has to do with not-belonging; I have an impulse of fear or terror in the face of a political space, for example,

a public space that makes no room for the secret. For me, the demand that everything be paraded in the public square and that there be no internal forum is a glaring sign of the totalitarianization of democracy. I can rephrase this in terms of political ethics: if a right to the secret is not maintained, we are in a totalitarian space.

Belonging – the fact of avowing one's belonging, of putting in common – be it family, nation, tongue – spells the loss of the secret. (59)

In Derrida's sense of the word here, 'belonging' entails a capitulation of the self to collective definition, a state of being 'put in common' with others of the same clan or race or nationality or gender, ironically among the major coordinates of much identity politics with its essentialist tendencies. This collective (stereo)typing, of course, is a staple of comic writers such as Smith, who uses characters to represent various racial, socioeconomic, political and gendered identities – the agonizingly 'politically correct' white liberal Joyce Chalfen in *White Teeth* (2000), for instance, or the right-wing black and highly flawed Christian moralist Sir Monty Kipps in *On Beauty*. Certainly, most of Smith's characters in those novels exceed their stereotypes through particularity of action and personal idiosyncrasy, and the intimacy of the narration plays a key role in facilitating the reader's understanding of a specific character's complex individuality; Irie Jones's struggle for acceptance as a woman of half-Jamaican descent in British culture in *White Teeth* becomes clearer to the reader with the narrator's penetrating description of her ordeal at the salon where she tries to have her hair straightened to look more 'white'. This sympathetic identification with characters of racialized backgrounds is central to the project of postcolonial literature, which creates imaginary spaces in which voices from outside the mainstream can speak and be heard. As James K. A. Smith notes in *Live Theory*, Derrida views all literature as 'a kind of glossolalia that destabilizes hegemonic communities by rupturing the univocal ideal of language' (52). But, according to Smith, while Derrida applauds literature's role as a public and 'inherently *democratic* institution' in which 'excluded and marginalized' (53) views often repressed in other contexts can be expressed, he also insists that that openness must be balanced with respect for privacy of the individual; for Derrida, 'literature is a kind of public clandestine – the right to say anything, and thus the right to keep a secret, to *not* say anything' (53). The right of the individual to refuse full exposure conforms to Derrida's ethics, which value the alterity and absolute uniqueness of the Other above all. In *A Taste for the Secret*, he claims that memoirs, biographies and autobiographies 'are the general form of everything that interests [him]', since they assert the 'irreducibility of *who* to *what*' (41) by telling the stories of individuals whose uniqueness is defined, in part, by the secrets they do not wish to share.

Seen in this light, the characters in *NW*, with their secretive double lives, play dual roles as representations of certain aspects of the multicultural reality of contemporary urban Britain and as manifestations of the ethical danger of reducing others to essentialized identities based on race or other factors while denying their uniqueness. Felix encounters and even engages skeptically in a social narrative based on such impulses derived from a localized sense of identity when he encounters someone from Caldwell (to which area importantly Felix had only moved when eight years old), a 'kid' who recognizes him immediately, but whom Felix does not identify until he notices a clue in their ongoing exchange:

> This trigger gave up at least the surname: Khan. Of Khan's minimart, Willesden. All that family looked the same, many brothers, running the place for their father. This must be the youngest. Caldwell boys back in the day, two floors below the Coopers. He didn't remember them being especially friendly. Felix had arrived too late in Caldwell to make good friends. To do that you had to be born and bred. 'Good times,' said the Khan kid. To be polite, Felix agreed. (89)

The seemingly casual encounter and brief exchange is still replete with underlying meaning and narrative purpose, demonstrating an on-going feature of Smith's writing that Philip Tew notes in *Zadie Smith* (2009) as follows: 'Smith's technique of overlaying and multiplying view-points, often refracted by others, is highly effective, adding depth to her perspectives' (102). The distinction between the public and private registers runs through the passage above, demonstrating the often suppressed conflict between the two, a seemingly social demand that one acts or speaks as the group does which is undercut by inner, mostly private views and desires, one antithetical to the other.

While all three main characters are products of the same marginalized racial and socioeconomic environment, they each exhibit distinctive responses to the circumstances in which they were brought up (with only the two women being 'born and bred'). The only white character of the three, Leah displays the least interest in rising above her upbringing, settling for a middling education and a low-paying job in a local social agency. Unlike her African-born husband Michel, a hairdresser who tries to better their lot through on-line trading, Leah prefers a life of indolence, smoking dope with her neighbours and wishing to remain 'eighteen always' (22) in her mind. In a sense, Leah occupies the stereotypical position of ambitionless under-achievement often assigned by mainstream British culture to immigrant and non-white Londoners. On the other hand, Natalie, who changes her name from Keisha to distance herself from her impoverished black heritage, is relentlessly ambitious, willing to reject her family and her religion to pursue a legal career; as a young woman, she 'thought life was a problem that could be solved by means of professionalization' (177). After leaving her Christian boyfriend Rodney for the more financially successful Frank De Angelis, an investment banker, Natalie becomes 'crazy busy with self-invention' (183), fabricating a white middle-class lifestyle that Leah finds hypocritical, thinking of Natalie as a 'coconut' (55) who is black only on the outside. Natalie lives 'just far enough' from the council estate (housing project) 'to avoid it', while Leah 'can see it from her backyard' (55).

Between these two extremes lies Felix, an incomer to Caldwell in childhood, the son of a Rastafarian father and an absent schizophrenic mother, who began life as a stereotypical lower-class black male, directionless and in trouble with the law. After completing a General National Vocational Qualification in catering, he bounced around to a number of low-paying jobs, including various ill-conceived ventures with his father Lloyd, before doing gopher jobs for the film industry and becoming a drug-dealer and addict. Having had two children when he was young, Felix rarely sees them, unable to cope with their mother Jasmine, 'an oppositional woman' (112). The reinvented Felix, an aficionado of self-help books and motivational slogans, has cleaned himself up, determined to turn his life around, and is working relatively steadily as a mechanic. In keeping with his name, he claims ironically (given his fate) to have 'always been lucky' (110), and finds his good fortune most vividly expressed in his aptly named girlfriend Grace, an up-and-coming waitress with big plans for their future, including more children.

All three characters, then, clearly represent the challenges of contemporary life in London's poorer neighbourhoods, and all three disrupt racial stereotypes, to some degree. Yet the power of Smith's novel goes well beyond the surface contrasts described above. Each character is given her or his own discrete section of the novel, separated by titles – 'visitation', 'guest', 'host', respectively – terms that resonate both with the Christian symbolism of Divine Birth and Communion, as well as with Derrida's dual sense of 'hospitality' as that which can either exclude or accommodate the Other. Within each section, the mode of narration is matched to the character's state of mind: Leah's deeply introspective soul is conveyed partially through stream-of-consciousness reminiscent of Virginia Woolf's *Mrs Dalloway*, a key intertext for *NW*; Felix, whose sudden death is reported, like Septimus Smith's in Woolf's novel, at a party, moves purposefully around London on errands designed to propel himself into his bright future, and is described through Smith's patented ironic focalization, which allows the reader privileged access to his and others' thoughts while keeping the action and dialogue foremost; and the story of Natalie, whose life is most characterized by fragmentariness and self-reinvention, is related through 185 numbered segments, each with its own brief and often provocative title. The sense of division within and among individual characters is enhanced by a general thematic of doubling: from the split identity of Keisha/Natalie; to the mention of hostile twins (Felix has twin sisters, Tia and Ruby, who hate each other; Annie has a twin brother James who wishes her dead); to the activity of the annual Notting Hill Carnival in the background of the novel, which adds Caribbean cultural flavour but also creates a context in which identities are changed or masked or set on stage, and characters break out of their accepted social roles in true carnivalesque fashion.

With their secretive behaviour, all three characters disrupt traditional notions of social morality and monogamous domestic life. For Felix, who is determined to put his past behind him and move forward with his relationship with Grace, the final sexual encounter with the flamboyant Annie is like a turning-point scene that he is acting out from one of the brightly optimistic futuristic movie scripts he composes in his head; from the moment he arrives at her doorstep and pushes past the prostitutes he used to frequent there, he has 'the sense that someone was watching and taking it all down ("Felix was a solid bloke, with his heart in the right place")' (120). Although Felix's intentions seem to be to tell Annie that their affair is over and then leave, he is affected by her dramatic performance of bravado in the face of her own waning sexuality and fertility; the likelihood that Annie, who lives a life of self-absorbed dissolution, will never marry or have children is thrown into sharp relief by tableau of the mixed-race family eating lunch on the adjacent roof terrace, an image that she mocks before breaking down. Felix's decision to make love with Annie one last time certainly stems from lust (since he feels guilty enough to lie to Grace on the phone about his whereabouts), but also seems to relate to his general sense of compassion. This same emotion shortly thereafter gets him knifed when he comes to the rescue of a pregnant woman on the Tube and incurs the wrath of Nathan and Tyler, who confront him on the street and try to steal the precious zirconia ear-studs given to him by Grace, the one possession with too much sentimental value for him to let go. Like Felix, Grace too had a former lover, Marlon, whose final departure from her life was achieved in stages, with him returning to the flat to collect forgotten items and to seek another chance. Despite his tryst, it is probable that Felix, had he not been killed, would have continued faithfully in his relationship with Grace, who seems to have no knowledge of Annie, and that she would have never been aware of his secret.

For the female characters, however, the keeping of secrets is less innocent, especially given the pain experienced by their husbands when their acts are revealed; it is also more intricately related to their sense of sexual and personal identity. While Leah and Natalie, as we have seen, are on opposite tracks with regard to career, they both find themselves trapped in the social script prepared for women before they are born. In *Relating Narratives: Storytelling and Selfhood*, Adriana Cavarero argues that 'the gender identity cannot avoid producing [...] a contradictory effect, in so far as it invites the uniqueness of each woman to identify herself with all other women [...]. Put simply, *who* I am and *who* you are seem to surrender to the urgency of the question of *what* Woman is' (60). In Cavarero's terms, similar to Derrida's, the need to value the *who*, the uniqueness of each individual, is critical to an ethical framework in which the Other is not reduced to simplistic and often antipathetic or exploitable political positions. The preservation of each complex existence depends on the recognition of what Cavarero calls 'the narratable self' (59), defined by Paul A. Kottman in the Translator's Introduction as 'the uniqueness and unity of a self, which is disclosed through that self's actions and words, and which is then narrated as a unique and unified life-story' (x). On one level, this narration is an internalized activity; Cavarero notes that 'every human being, without even wanting to know it, is aware of being *a narratable self* – immersed in the spontaneous auto-narration of memory' (33). This internalized narration, however, is incomplete, since the individual can only know her own life story through memory, which is necessarily partial (one cannot remember one's own birth or infancy, for instance) and prone to lapses and errors. In order to have a complete narrative, the individual 'long[s] for' (63) an Other who will supplement and piece together the fragments of her life, giving it coherence and meaning. The narratable self thus does not belong to the individual alone; rather, 'The self – to the extent to which a *who* is not reducible to a *what* – has a totally external and relational reality' (63). In the case of women, the telling of their stories by others in ways that will recognize their uniqueness is complicated by the societal pressure to conform to the conventional narrative of womanhood, which includes heterosexual marriage and childhood. Any desire that deviates from that narrative is often suppressed and kept secret by the woman herself.

For Leah, whose story begins the novel, the longing for a coherent story capturing her individual complexity is not fulfilled by marriage, which is constructed as a social narrative that is told and retold in various ways, but always with predetermined roles for both men and women. Leah's mother frequently recounts the story of her marriage to Colin, which came later in life after she had established her career, since she believed she was beautiful enough to hold out for a husband who was gentle and not a drinker. Leah's decision to marry Michel was based partly on the fact that he was 'kinder than any man [she] had ever known, aside from her father' (21); it also satisfied their families' desire for conventionality, despite the differences in their backgrounds. Notwithstanding Michel's sexual attractiveness and genuinely caring demeanour towards her, she does not have a deep sense of intimacy with him. Gradually, the romantic privacy of their early married life gives way to social expectation. Whereas Michel is optimistically focused on his masculine role as breadwinner, with the goals of providing financial security for a family, Leah is horrified by the idea that she is expected to produce children according to a pre-established schedule. Close to turning 35, she is under mounting pressure from her mother and husband to do the 'next thing' (39) and get pregnant; her age becomes the focus of others' conversation, and she feels as if she 'is ageing in dog years' (18), seven times as fast as Michel. In one domestic scene, when Leah and Michel are cooking together, she loses her individual identity in the narration and becomes a generic gendered being: 'It is the woman's fault that they never discussed children' (22).

The constant scrutiny and comparisons with Natalie and other women with children force Leah into increasing secretiveness, so that she gets multiple abortions and takes birth control without her husband's knowledge. As Sissela Bok notes in *Secrets: On the Ethics of Concealment and Revelation*, the withholding of information can invest a person with a level of power: 'To be able to hold back some information about oneself or to channel it and thus influence how one is seen by others gives power. [...] To have no capacity for secrecy is to be out of control over how others see one; it leaves one open to coercion' (19). Despite the power of her secret, Leah suffers from a sense of surveillance and guilt that she is not performing according to the expectations of women; at the abortion clinic, she feels 'ashamed before an imagined nobody who isn't real and yet monitors our thoughts' (51). Still weak from the procedure, Leah reels in a church graveyard after reading the monuments of long-dead women who died after multiple child-births and whose names and stories have been effaced by time. The statue of a Madonna with a swaddled Christ child seems like an 'accusation' (63) to Leah, causing her to collapse and lose consciousness.

Under this internalized social pressure, Leah finds herself retreating into the inner world of her hidden desires. Smith's narrational style in the first section of the novel, 'visitation', underscores Leah's separateness not only from Michel but also from the others in her life: her mother Pauline, her co-workers, and even Natalie, with whom her bond of intimacy has eroded over the years as they have grown in different directions. Interspersed with segments of third-person narration are passages of Woolfesque stream-of-consciousness, which create the connection for the reader between Leah and Clarissa Dalloway, another female character with a complex inner life and an inability to reveal certain aspects of herself to her husband, who defines her with narrow gender roles. The only man with whom Leah seems able to communicate in an intimate way is her father Colin, whose ghost appears to her in a marijuana-induced vision similar to Septimus's hallucinations of his dead comrades. The effect of these sometimes disorienting scenes is the enlistment of the reader in the creation of Leah's life narrative, the piecing together of discontinuous thoughts, memories and observations.

Smith's emulation of modernist aesthetics is reinforced by the use of calligrammatic images (popularized by Guillaume Apollinaire in the early twentieth century), including a graphic mouth (27) and an apple tree. The latter image has built into it references to women who defied convention and incurred the displeasure of others: 'Appletreeapple / Trunk, bark. / Alice, dreaming. / Eve, eating. / Under which nice girls make mistakes' (24). The relationship between Eve, the prototype of female dissent, and the novel's female characters is strengthened by the epigraph – 'When Adam delved and Eve span, / Who was then the gentleman?' – which is attributed to fourteenth-century English cleric John Ball and which refers both to traditional gender roles (digging and spinning) and to social equality (there being no hierarchy in the Garden).

Leah is associated with the dissident Eve from the opening scene of *NW*, in which she is listlessly wasting an afternoon in the garden of her basement flat, lying on a hammock beneath a wizened apple tree in the unusually hot weather (another intertextual gesture to *Mrs Dalloway*, in which the heat in London plays an important role). On the radio she hears a line – 'I am the sole author of the dictionary that defines me' (3) – that piques her interest and captures her desire to create her own sense of self. She muses on Michel's assessment of the contemporary economic reality, that 'not everyone can be invited to the party' (3), and disagrees with its calculated exclusionism. Her dissension from her husband's political bias leads her to note mentally that 'in marriage not everything is shared' (3).

The artificiality of social narratives such as marriage is put into relief by the first plot incident in the novel, in which Leah is roused from her hammock by a visitor with a seemingly credible story of distress. Shar, a young woman from Leah's neighbourhood, bursts into her home, disheveled and distraught, claiming that her mother has had a heart attack and has been taken to the hospital. Leah believes Shar to be telling the truth and agrees to her request for a loan so she can catch a cab. Playing the role of savioor of the poor appeals to Leah's conception of herself as empathetic and benevolent; she feels 'a little pleasure' (6) in Shar's repeated exclamations about her goodness. Yet, even as the incident draws to a close, Leah becomes conscious of how the reality will be changed by the act of narrativization: 'But already the grandeur of the experience threatens to flatten into the conventional, into anecdote: only thirty pounds, only an ill mother, neither a murder, nor a rape. Nothing survives its telling' (13). When Shar is quickly proven to be a con artist since she does not appear to repay the debt, Leah attempts to rationalize her own actions by accosting her with offers of charity, only to be made to look foolish and naïve. Leah's inability to see through Shar's scam – one, we learn, that is perpetuated on a widespread basis in the area – contributes to the novel's thematization of the difficulty of knowing the Other's life-story, of seeing beyond the 'what' to the 'who'. This failure of vision leads eventually to an altercation between her husband and Shar's pimp, which results later in the death of Leah's beloved dog Olive, the only child substitute she has. Trying to prevent the confrontation on the street from escalating, Leah resorts to lying that she is pregnant, thereby capitulating to the conventional image of female vulnerability. Smith draws the connection between Leah and Shar as two sides of the conventional social narratives for women in a scene in which Shar's photos eerily end up in Leah's envelope by coincidence at the pharmacy; in one of the pictures, the reader is cued to (mis)recognize Leah, herself a thin ginger-haired woman, as the dissipated drug addict she sometimes secretly longs to be: 'The sixth [photo] is a skaggy redhead, skin and bone and track marks, with a fag hanging out of her mouth, and if you squinted – ' (84).

This image provides the transition to the second section of the novel, 'guest', Felix's narrative, in which the themes of misrecognition and the importance of narrating the story of the Other continue to be explored. The section begins with Felix and Grace in their bedroom flat on the morning of what will be the last day of his life; Grace asks him to retrieve from behind the radiator one of the princess figurines – Ariel, 'the ginger one' (87) – that had fallen there during the night. Grace's story, including her ambition to raise herself and Felix to a status befitting her fascination with fantasy royalty, is revealed only in glimpses; her initial meeting with Felix is described as an accident of geography and timing, since she met him at a bus-stop in Caldwell on a day when she had been scheduled to be elsewhere in London. She believes this to have been 'fate' (103) rather than a random encounter; indeed, the city throughout the novel is affected by the same sort of predestination common to other urban narratives, such as *Mrs Dalloway* and Ian McEwan's *Saturday*, in which fateful meetings between characters occur due to geographic coincidences.

Felix's journey around the city begins with a visit to his father, who lives in Caldwell in the housing project known as Garvey House, known as a hotbed of the Black Power movement in the 1970s. In a photographic history of the site given to Lloyd by Grace, there are images that portray the black residents of the time as predictably hip and radical, in a dated way: 'Kids barefoot, parents looking like kids themselves. Afros, headscarves, cane rows, weird stiff wigs, a tall, skinny, spiritual-looking Rasta resting on a big stick. He [Felix] could not be sure if he had a memory of this, or whether the photograph was creating the memory for him' (93). Lloyd's knowledge of the people in the photos goes far beyond the essentialized descriptions presented in the book. One of those people is his Felix's mother, Jackie, who can only be seen partially, as a blurry purple dress, in a photo occluded by the crease of the page. Suffering from mental illness, Jackie left when Felix was seven to have a relationship with a white man, with whom she had a second son, Devon, whom she then abandoned with Lloyd to raise as his own. She continues to show up in the lives of her adult children, including the twin sisters, raving about conspiracy theories and telling outrageous lies. Felix's understanding of her life is filtered through her schizophrenia and collected in pieces: 'He knew perfectly well she could have exchanged this life story for any other narrative and he would have accepted it just as readily' (144).

Felix's encounter with Tom Mercer, the man from whom he buys a car to fix up as a gift for Grace, offers the reader access to the story of another character, but this time from an internalized perspective. To do his business with Tom, Felix journeys by underground to the London district W1 (closer to the world of *Mrs Dalloway*), specifically to the intersection of Oxford and Regent Streets; this is the furthest south that any of the characters goes in the novel, and it takes Felix into a context that is somewhat foreign. Tom is white, but not native to London, having moved into the city from the country after attending Sussex university. His profession – 'It's hard to explain – I work for a company that creates ideas for brand consolidation?' (106) – confounds Felix, who can only see him as an 'advertiser' (113); their inability to go beyond each other's surface characteristics in evident in Tom's assumption that Felix will be able to sell him some marijuana. Despite the impressive-sounding job, Tom has less direction than the reformed Felix and considers himself as 'TOM MERCER. EPIC FAIL' (115); he is hectored by his girlfriend Soph, though we are only privy to his side of their constant phone conversations. Most of what we learn about Tom comes through his internalized narrative in which he dwells on his fecklessness and his parents' general disappointment in him.

While the 'guest' section thematizes the difficulty of recognizing the Other's true life narrative, the 'host' section enacts the role of the narrating Other while demonstrating its limitations, providing intimate insights into Natalie's thoughts and behaviour while insisting on the fundamental unknowability of any person. In a self-conscious gesture, the narrator enjoins us as readers in one of the segments to consider the 'abstract idea', endemic to all households and, by extension, to all human relationships, that the following sentence must always emerge: 'I don't know you any more' (171). Throughout this section, Smith's narrator engages the reader in the re-creation of Natalie's story from a series of fragmented experiences extending chronologically from her early childhood to the moment when her secret sexual activities become known to her husband.

From the outset, Natalie's existence is inextricably connected to that of Leah, whom Natalie saved from drowning at an outdoor pool when the girls were both four; this rescue was recounted to Natalie when she was ten by her mother Marcia, and since as if immemorially for them 'There had been an event. To speak of it required the pluperfect' (151). Therefore it had gained the status as a foundational element in the narrative of the girls' lives. By filling in this piece of Natalie's story, Marcia plays the role of the Other who fulfills the desire of the narratable self for coherence and meaning; she also underscores the difficult expectations placed on women by society, since the near-tragedy in the pool occurred when she was alone and over-burdened with children. Throughout her childhood and into young adulthood, Natalie looks to Leah as a point of comparison for her own life; she envies Leah's white English lifestyle, with tea properly prepared and general domestic tranquility, which contrasts with her own family's poverty and dysfunctionality. While Leah goes through various phases of grunge fandom, political radicalism and environmental activism, Natalie becomes more focused on her own material well-being, virtually ignoring contemporary crises such as the Bosnian conflict in order to exert her 'celebrated will and focus' (162) in the service of achieving a law degree and earning money. Her growing intellectual and professional energy is matched by a vibrant sexual identity, kept hidden, like the dildo given to her clandestinely by Leah, owing to her family's repressive religiosity. Only Leah is aware of Natalie's powerful sexuality, since the two young women share confidences; yet when Leah tells Natalie, 'You're the only person I can be all of myself with,' (182) Natalie confronts the 'fearful knowledge that if reversed the statement would be rendered practically meaningless, Ms Blake having no self to be, not with Leah, or anyone' (183).

Natalie's sense of undeveloped identity seems to be relieved, for a time, by her relationship with Frank, who, like Leah's husband Michel, is sexually attractive and cosmopolitan. After meeting Frank, Natalie rejects her religious upbringing and embraces an up-scale lifestyle as a young professional. She becomes a role model for underprivileged black girls, and gives motivational talks to inspire them. Unlike Leah, Natalie is willing to follow the social script prescribed for women, having 'no intention of being made ridiculous by failing to do whatever was expected of her', she is willing to have children, though 'it was only a question of timing' (236). Once her two children, Naomi and Spike, are born, she enjoys them but mostly in a peripheral way, having the income to afford a nanny to do the actual child-rearing. Most of her life is consumed with long hours at work and weekend social outings with Frank. When the boredom of her situation becomes acute, Natalie begins visiting the sorts of websites suggested by Leah in one of their instant messaging chats, 'www.adultswatchingadults. com' (212). While Natalie's real-life encounters with the people she meets on-line are generally disappointing, she continues in this illicit activity until Frank finds evidence of it on her computer, compelling him to ask what is arguably the central question of the novel, 'Who *are* you?' (259).

The penultimate section of the novel, 'crossing', enacts the devastating consequences of women's secret lives becoming known by having Natalie undertake a physical and symbolic journey across the city into her own past. Having left her home after her confrontation with Frank with no wallet, keys or phone, she leaves behind her identity as wife and mother: 'She had no name, no biography, no characteristics' (264). Disheveled and aimless, she behaves in a manner that is instinctual rather than rational; climbing a hill towards Highgate, she makes 'a queer keening noise, like a fox' (263). This simile recalls the earlier references to the culling of foxes that have wandered into London, and Leah's self-characterization as having been 'a city fox too long'; she associates this image with her desperate desire to run away from the pressure to have children, her longing to emulate Shar and be an 'outlaw' (66), running like a fugitive animal from the forces that want to control her. Natalie realizes this fantasy by roving until she is blocked by the police at the scene of Felix's murder, then ends up in her old neighbourhood of Caldwell, where she encounters Nathan, who acts as a kind of spirit guide into her past. As they leave the confines of the city and enter the Heath, Natalie becomes aware that her new-found freedom from social expectation does not offer an avenue for a more positive definition of self; Nathan, rattled by his recent involvement in Felix's death, is frenetic and potentially dangerous, especially since Natalie figures out his identity as Shar's pimp. Looking down on London through the bars of the Hornsey Lane Bridge (a site long associated with suicides), Natalie sees fragments of the city, including the tower blocks of Caldwell, and is able to piece together from these images a coherent understanding that the 'sudden and total rupture' (282) that would compel her to commit suicide out of shame for her actions has not arrived.

In the final section of *NW*, also named 'visitation' in a circular link to the novel's opening, Natalie returns home to deal with the crisis in her marriage in the aftermath of the revelation of her infidelity. She and Frank agree to maintain the façade of being a couple in order to carry on with child-rearing, though there is hostility and little communication between them. In an apparent effort to explain her actions, Natalie writes Frank a letter and gives it to him in a sealed envelope, but he refuses to open it, saying only that 'confessions are self-serving' (285). The contents of the unread letter represent the unspoken secret that has given Natalie the power to resist her reduction to the 'what' of conventional womanhood, yet Frank's refusal to read them creates a barrier to his ever understanding the true self of his wife, thus exiling her from a real – rather than an enforced – sense of belonging. Frank's assertion to Leah at the Carnival party that the secret of his happy marriage to Natalie is the fact that they 'tell each other everything' (81) is revealed, on second reading of the text, to be especially ironic, given that he makes the statement the day of Natalie's return from the Heath, since it is the day after Felix's murder. Michel, on the other hand, demonstrates the possibility of genuine connection to Leah by wanting to understand the motivation behind her actions. When he finds her birth control pills, he asks Natalie, who has been supplying them, to explain; Natalie's clear statement that Leah 'just doesn't want to have a baby' (290) prompts Michel to react with compassion, inviting Natalie to help Leah through her crisis. The two women, who have known at least some of each other's secrets for some time, agree to exchange stories, and thereby to create between more coherent narratives of their lives.

The final unspoken story of the text, the circumstances of Felix's murder, is close to being articulated at the novel's end, with Leah and Natalie phoning the police to cast suspicion on Nathan Bogle; the narrator notes that 'it was Keisha who did the talking', and stresses in the novel's final phrase that it was 'Keisha Blake, disguising her voice with her voice' (294). With this temporary reversion to her Caldwell identity, Natalie creates the possibility that the truth of Felix's death will be known, and that, in the process, he will be transformed from another statistically unimportant black man to an individual worthy of his own history, that he will become a 'who' rather than a 'what'. With the telling of the secrets of these three characters to the reader, Smith challenges us to look beyond social narratives – whether racial, socioeconomic or gendered – to seek the hidden, complex lives of those around us, stories that they long to tell and to have told.

Bibliography

Bok, Sissela. *Secrets: On the Ethics of Concealment and Revelation*. New York: Pantheon, 1982.

Cavarero, Adriana. *Relating Narratives: Storytelling and Selfhood*. Trans. Paul A. Kottman. London and New York: Routledge, 1997.

Derrida, Jacques and Maurizio Ferraris. *A Taste for the Secret*. Trans. Giacomo Donis. Giacomo Donis and David Webb (eds). Cambridge: Polity, 2001.

Kottman, Paul A. 'Translator's Introduction.' In *Relating Narratives: Storytelling and Selfhood*. Adriana Cavarero (ed.). Trans. Paul A. Kottman. London and New York: Routledge, 1997, vii–xxxi.

Smith, James K. A. *Jacques Derrida: Live Theory*. London: Continuum, 2005.

Smith, Zadie. *White Teeth*. London: Hamish Hamilton, 2000.

—*On Beauty*. London: Hamish Hamilton, 2005.

—*Changing my Mind: Occasional Essays*. Toronto: Penguin, 2010.

—*NW*. London: Hamish Hamilton, 2012.

Tew, Philip. *Zadie Smith*. London and New York: Palgrave Macmillan, 2009.

8

Revisionary Modernism and Postmillennial Experimentation in Zadie Smith's *NW*

Wendy Knepper

'*Style is a writer's way of telling the truth*'.

ZADIE SMITH

In 'Two Directions for the Novel', an essay included in *Changing My Mind: Occasional Essays* (2009), but initially published as 'Two Paths for the Novel', Zadie Smith identifies 'the Anglo-American liberal middle class' as in crisis and fraught with anxiety (72). Certainly the events of 9/11 and their aftermath, a global financial recession and numerous natural disasters have intensified worries and elicited a traumatic apprehension of contemporary life, which, in turn, have shaped the concerns and styles of postmillennial fiction, much as Rod Mengham and Philip Tew and suggest (xv). The ethical concerns of art and literature in a globalizing world have been the subject of intense discussion through accounts of planetarity by such as Gayatri Chakravorty Spivak, the queer art of failure as in Judith (Jack) Halberstam's work, the claims of precarious life explored by Judith Butler and new approaches to aesthetics outlined by thinkers such as Derek Attridge, Elaine Scarry and Jacques Rancière. In the face of catastrophe, the modernist quest for a new aesthetics responding to war, revolution, terror and global economic crisis seems highly relevant once again. Various efforts to renew modernist aesthetics in the light of contemporary concerns have emerged in the form of revisionary modernisms, including altermodernism, a post-millennial, globalized aesthetic discussed by Nicholas Bourriaud (15) and Alison Gibbons (239) expressive of what Gibbons describes as 'a contemporary experience that is pluralized, decentralized and itinerant'

(240); also remodernism, a rejection of postmodernism and the quest for a new spirituality in art explored by Billie Childish and Charles Thomson; metamodernism, which Robin Van den Akker and Timotheus Vermeulen explain is 'the oscillation between a typically modern commitment and a markedly postmodern detachment' to express a new structure of feeling (2); and digimodernism, which responds to the cultural effects of new technologies and is expressive of the sense of what Alan Kirby describes as the 'onwardness, haphazardness, evanescence' (N. Pag.) of radically altered relationship between authors, texts and readers. While postmodernism has exhausted its energies, a keen interest in both the failures and possibilities of modernist aesthetics and avant-garde movements signals a productive engagement with the ethics of style as a means of reconstituting the imaginary in an era of global anxieties.

In this context, outlined above, I intend to demonstrate that Zadie Smith's *NW* (2012) – a highly experimental, revisionary late modernist novel – maps new relations to locality through a spatial aesthetics that registers the anxious dynamics of a globalizing neighbourhood. Her work investigates the ways in which socioeconomic pressures, especially following the credit crunch of 2007, come to shape the life histories and aspirations of people living in NW, an area of London that straddles the hill 'rising in Hampstead, West Hampstead, Kilburn, Willesden, Brondesbury, Cricklewood' (47). While *NW* shares many of the thematic concerns expressed in *White Teeth* (2000) and *On Beauty* (2005) about the intersections of race, class and gender in multicultural London, the style of the novel seems closer to *The Autograph Man* (2002), also a self-consciously experimental work. Divided into five sections, *NW* eschews chronology in favour of a spatially configured story concerning various 'visitations' or encounters in the space of NW, which frequently erupt into violence as economic disparities surface. The novel draws on techniques found in experimental writing through its inclusion of concrete poems and graphical textual representations, web and online references, stream-of-conscious narration, games with numbers and disrupted chronologies, to name but a few examples. As will be seen, the novel's concern with experimentation is part of Smith's own revisionary modernist project, which calls for what in 'How to Fail Better' she describes as 'an expansion of the heart – in order to comprehend the human otherness that fiction confronts them with' (N. Pag) and celebrates the imperfect, difficult processes of both writing and reading. Through her spatial poetics, which requires new reading practices, Smith embraces experimentation in order to express alternative, ethically-oriented constructions of locality in a globalizing world.

Revisiting late modernist aesthetics: Zadie Smith's changing styles

Smith's keen interest in alternative and revisionary modernisms surfaces in *Changing My Mind* – which includes essays on Zora Neale Hurston, E. M. Forster and Kafka – with references to the influence of Virginia Woolf, James Joyce and Graham Greene on her writing and in her own late modernist fiction. Where *On Beauty* took its cue from Forster's *Howards End*, *NW* seems to favour Joyce's *Ulysses*, especially in the sections related to Leah, a character who bridges Jewish and Irish cultures. Joyce Carol Oates notes that 'Smith's *NW* is a boldly Joycean appropriation', which includes stream-of-consciousness techniques, overheard conversations, prose-poems, fragmentary and disjoined passages and numbered vignettes, such as found in the 'Host' section of her novel, which are modelled on the 'Aeolus' chapter of *Ulysses*. In a recent interview with Foyles bookstores, Smith herself describes Joyce's influence on her approach to literary experimentation:

> I think we should be a bit wary of labelling certain techniques 'experimental' as if it's just a set of tools one picks up to lend whatever you're writing a trace of hipster cool ... Everything I do is an attempt to get close to the real, as I experience it, and the closer you get to the reality of experience the more bizarre it SHOULD look on the page and sound in the mouth because our real experience doesn't come packaged in a neat three act structure. For me, Joyce is the ultimate realist because he is trying to convey how experience really feels. And he found it to be so idiosyncratic he needed to invent a new language for it. All I was trying to do in *NW* was tell fewer lies then last time, and it came out the way it came out. (N. Pag.)

As Smith points out, style is not a catalogue of pre-formulated experiments, but rather a quest for a new kind of mimesis, which expresses felt and lived experience.

Smith's aesthetic is shaped by an awareness of (dis)continuous realities and literary traditions. 'Two Directions for the Novel' is often read as a polemic against lyrical realism, evident in Joseph O'Neill's *Netherland*, and a celebration of a new kind of avant-garde, exemplified by Tom McCarthy's *Remainder*. However, her discussion is more nuanced than these apparent antagonisms. She begins by describing one version of the literary critical tradition, which rejects both realism and postmodernism. Where realism takes for granted 'the transcendent importance of form, the incantatory power of language to reveal truth, the essential fullness and continuity of the self' (73), postmodernism has been dismissed as 'a fascinating failure, intellectual brinkmanship that lacked heart' (73). This leads her to examine future options for literature, significantly through two post-catastrophe novels. Significantly, along the way, both are criticized for their representations of racial and cultural others; a point that Smith seeks to address in her own work. Ultimately, however, Smith does not approach style as a choice between lyrical realism, represented by *Netherland* and her own work (perhaps she has *White Teeth* in mind), or avant-garde experimentation, often associated with *Remainder* (and we might add Smith's *The Autograph Man* to this list). Instead, she opts for the 'crossroads', where authors are claimed by both camps: a tradition represented by 'Melville, Conrad, Kafka, Beckett, Joyce, Nabokov' (93). In so doing, Smith makes a case for reading McCarthy's novel as part of a crossroads tradition.

'Two Directions for the Novel' works towards a poetics that interrogates prevailing conceptions of the self and space. Writing about *Netherland*, Smith does not reject lyrical realism: 'I have written in this tradition myself and cautiously hope for its survival, but if it's to survive, lyrical realists will have to push a little harder on their subject' (80). What she rejects is the redemptive tendencies of a certain brand of lyrical realism, which 'wants to comfort us, to assure us of our beautiful plenitude' (80–1) and 'offer us the authentic story of a self' (81). Instead, Smith asks for a more rigorous interrogation of subjectivity, which recognizes the mutability and contradictions of self: 'But is this really what having a self feels like? Do selves always seek their good, in the end? Are they never perverse? Do they always want meaning? Do they sometimes not want its opposite?' (81). Her quest for a new kind of realism embraces a less coherent account of the subject and the world through 'a rigorous attention to the damaged and the partial, the absent and the unspeakable' (91). Instead of offering solutions or comfort, literature acknowledges that relations to the world and self remain elusive and attends to the improbable, the contradictory.

In this context, *Remainder* is an important text because of its emotional integrity: 'it works by accumulation and repetition, closing in on its subject in ever-decreasing revolutions like a trauma victim circling the blank horror of the traumatic event' (83). Finally, what she admires the novel's spatial aesthetic, which enables it to pose questions about various facets of the world and the self:

> And it's precisely within *Remainder*'s newly revealed spaces that the opportunity for multiple allegories arises. On literary modes (*How artificial is realism?*), on existence (*Are we capable of genuine being?*), on political discourse (*What's left of the politics of identity?*) and on the law (*Where do we draw our own borders? What, and whom, do we exclude, and why?*). (96)

If one takes these two sets of questions, one concerning the contradictory elusive self and the second concerning the possibilities of a spatially-oriented approach to narrative, one has identified the two aspects of the novel upon which *NW* builds. Moreover, Smith's critique of prevailing representations of racial and cultural others also shapes her approach to constructions of self and space.

These tendencies come together in Smith's 'How to Fail Better', a public lecture delivered at The New Yorker Festival in 2006 and 'Some Notes on Attunement: A Voyage around Joni Mitchell', an essay published in 2012, which bring a Kierkegaardian brand of Nordic modernism to bear on contemporary experience and aesthetics. In 'How to Fail Better,' Smith's cites Kierkegaard in order to articulate her approach to space in narrative:

> 'A philosophy of pure thought,' he argues, 'is for an existing individual a chimera, if the truth that is sought is something to exist in. To exist under the guidance of pure thought is like travelling in Denmark with the help of a small map of Europe, on which Denmark shows no larger than a steel pen-point – Aye, it is still more impossible'. (N. Pag.)

She admires his attention to the specificity of the city (a city whose population was closer to that of a neighbourhood in contemporary London), which demands of its inhabitants that they become their own cartographers. Smith remarks:

> When it comes to reading, it's a Kierkegaardian level of commitment that we've forgotten about: intimate, painstaking, with nothing at all to do with Hegelian system-building or theoretical schools, and everything to do with our ethical reality as subjects. You have to make the map of Copenhagen yourself. You have to be open to the idea that Copenhagen might look and feel completely different to what you expected or believed it to be. You have to throw away other people's maps. (N. Pag.)

Her advice is partly intended for readers who interpret narratives through pre-formulated systems of reading in adherence to a particular theoretical approach (such as a prescribed form of postcolonial reading), but she also suggests that the purpose of art is open new imagined routes and pathways through the world.

Smith's 'encounter' with Joni Mitchell and Kierkegaard considers the meaning of failed moments of aesthetic appreciation: her inability to make sense of Mitchell's 'piping' (singing) as music (30). This 'voyage around Joni Mitchell' draws on the coming-of-age story and the road trip story as vehicles that enable her to segue from the question of attunement in Kirkegaard to an aesthetics of oblique complicity with otherness. Smith teases out connections between these aesthetic concerns and the ethics of selfhood, which presents alternatives to contemporary forms of identity politics. Insofar as Abraham, Smith, Mitchell and Kierkegaard are discontinuous with themselves, they are continuous with one another in sharing a sense of the plural, mutable self, '[t]he inconsistency of identity, of personality' (35). Significantly, Smith brings her article to a close with a description of Mitchell's interest in 'black music', notably Duke Ellington and Miles Davis, and expressed desire to write an autobiography that 'begins with the line "I was the only black man at the party"' (35). Mitchell's cross-gender, cross-cultural, cross-racial identifications are also apparent in *Hejira* (1976), an album title that refers to Mohammed's departure from Mecca, and *Don Juan's Reckless Daughter* (1977), where the singer appears in the guise of a black man. In Mitchell's journey of the self, Smith finds an inverse double for her own pathway: 'Turns out that while she has been leading me away from my musical home, she has been going on her own journey deep into the place where I'm from' (35). The journey around Mitchell turns into an encounter with the otherness of self and the self as other.

Smith's methods of attunement, in this article, operate through strategies of immersion, interaction, intersection and imaginative remapping. Smith takes the reader on a trip, but she also prompts her reader to name the unnamed (such as 'Nick Laird' and 'Rain') and fill in the details not provided. Where Kierkegaard repeats the same story with varying outcomes, Smith recounts various narratives that tell the same story about the discontinuous self and moments of aesthetic transformation. Through her textual journey, Smith finds a model for a more rigorous lyrical realism, which is not bound by the conventional identity politics of race/gender, but operates through the disclosure of formerly unrecognized correspondences and points of convergence. Finally, and importantly for *NW*, Kierkegaard's dialectical lyricism, which works through mixed modes, perspectives and forms, offers a model for the various narrative routes and experimental modes to be found in Smith's work.

Revisionary modernist aesthetics in *NW*

Some effort is needed to come to terms with the revisionary late modernist techniques of *NW*, which has been described both favourably by Christian Lorentzen as 'a bit wobbly and lopsided by design [...] a hotpotch in five parts' (N. Pag) and negatively by Michiko Kakutani as 'perfunctory, jerry-built and weirdly contrived' (N. Pag.). Drawing on Marie Laure Ryan's *Narrative as Virtual Reality*, I propose that *NW*'s spatially-oriented aesthetic requires a new approach to narrative immersion, which places emphasis on the interactive experience of worldly/textual navigation and re-routing. 'NW' designates an area of London (the world as text) and an imagined cartography (the text as world), but *NW* (an interactive and immersive book) employs experimental techniques (the text as game) to prompts its readers to remap known relations to place and explore the contested production of localities in a globalizing world.

Smith plays with the tensions between lived, virtual and imagined spaces in the early part of the novel when instructions for walking from Bartlett Avenue in NW6 to Yates Lane in NW8 are provided (33). Users of 'Google Maps' may be tempted to check these instructions, but doing so proves to be a rather frustrating encounter with the 'real'. The instructions do not make sense and any attempt to follow them soon proves impossible as the point of departure and destination do not exist in the named postal codes. One route involves parallel roads: Salusbury Road and Harrow Road. Edgware Road becomes Shoot-up-Hill in Kilburn where it intersects with Willesden Lane. The commentary on the directions seems profoundly ironic: 'These directions are for planning purposes only. You may find that construction projects, traffic, weather, or other events may cause conditions to differ from the map results, and you should plan your route accordingly. You must obey all signs or notices regarding your route' (33). This parody of map instructions seems to establish the reality of the world to which they refer, but they also signal the discrepancies between mapped and lived spaces, virtual and material worlds, imagined and actual places. Following the instructions leads nowhere. Metaphorically, the parallel roads may suggest the parallels between the space of the novel and the world. But perhaps there is a more pragmatic purpose for any reader unfamiliar with the area described by Smith as 'NW' for he or she will have learned something about the area by referring to Google Maps. Finally, however, the reader might reflect that Smith has offered an allegory of reading and writing itself: that we must create our own maps. Indeed, the A to B redux of Chapter 10 may serve a more useful guide to NW, offering as it does a sensory, perceptual encounter with the vital, diverse and perilous space of the urban environment.

NW also provides a symbolic map or entry into its narrative. Divided into sections of varying lengths – entitled 'visitation', 'guest', 'host', 'crossing' and 'visitation' – the narrative follows a circular or recursive form. The dust jacket to my edition of the text explains that that we are to read guests and hosts as 'those with power and those without it' (N. Pag.) while visitations are described as 'the rare times a stranger crosses a threshold without permission or warning, causing a disruption in the whole system' (N. Pag.). Ostensibly, on first reading, this is a loosely written narrative about the coming-of-age experiences of Leah and Keisha (later Natalie), beginning with childhood and leading up to scenes of crisis in their married lives. However, the novel eschews chronology in favour of a spatially coherent account of events: the text navigates a series of seemingly unrelated encounters in NW in order to expose overlooked narratives of dis/connection and violence. In the first part of the narrative, Michel (Leah's husband) views a television report about a stabbing which has taken place on Albert Road. The details about the man, named Felix Cooper, and his life in Garvey House project in Holloway and Kilburn do not concern him (80), but the outbreak of violence in the neighbourhood does because it bears on his own recent encounters in NW. This 'minor' event takes centre stage in the next section, entitled 'guest', which tells the story of the events leading up to Felix's stabbing. In 'Crossing', Natalie and Nathan meet a roadblock and are forced to detour because an unnamed man (Felix) has been killed on Albert Road. 'Visitation' reveals important information concerning the slaying of Felix, gained during her traipse through NW. The novel ends with a call to the police to identify the murderers of Felix. Because the novel buries its dead in spatial references and disrupted chronologies, the crime story is challenging to piece together on a first reading. The reader is therefore prompted to revisit the narrative: to navigate Smith's revisionary late modernist aesthetic in order to make sense of the multiple routes that converge on the scene of the crime. NW is, after all, a parable at heart: an absurd tale about the death of a man named 'Felix' (meaning 'happiness') who comes to a violent end because of his undying love for 'Grace', a woman who has expressed her true love through the gift of zirconia (artificial diamonds). Perhaps, this episode is an allegory about narrative itself: grace – meaning beauty of form, manner, motion or action – finds authentic expression through artifice. Alternatively, an artifice, rather unexpectedly, reveals a truth.

The visitation as a disruption to the system finds its poetic correlative in the use of experimental narrative techniques, which subvert the conventions of the prose narrative. For instance, in Chapter 7, Leah's stream-of-consciousness reflections concerning apple trees and their fruit take the form of a concrete poem in the shape of an apple tree (24). Significantly, the description of the apple tree also offers a model for spatial thinking with references to the symbolic meaning of the 'Network of branches, roots. Tunnelling under' (24). While Leah's husband, Michael, rants about the socioeconomic barriers to advancement, her thoughts about apple trees mix with fragments of his conversation and other musings. The symbolic meaning of the apple in connection with Eve's temptation and original sin, a motif introduced through the epigraph to the novel, which is taken from John Ball's discourse about social equality on the occasion of the Peasant Revolution in 1381: 'When Adam delved and Eve span / Who was then the gentleman?' At the same time, the allusion to the nursery rhyme, 'Rock-a-bye-baby', foreshadows the abortion procedure she later undergoes suggesting that her mind really is elsewhere, considering the impact of the baby growing inside her to whom she is host. In Chapter 8, one finds a visual map of Leah's colleague's mouth: as Adina drones on, her words give way to a visualization of her teeth and tongue in the form of a circular text that maps her dental work. This graphical text suggests that the meaning of the words has been lost as Leah's attention wanders and she is no longer fully present in the moment. These whimsical interventions go beyond the metafictional trope of postmodernism, with its emphasis on the text as an artifice, to convey a form of psychological realism. Somewhat paradoxically, the use of concrete poetic techniques, which effectively immerses the reader in Leah's consciousness, disrupts the body of the text in order to embody another kind of narrative reality: disclosing the workings of the mediated self.

Resistance to realism and the quest for a truer form of mimesis can be found in textual 'visitations' that disrupt the narrative, such as the repeated intrusion of the number 37. In 'visitation', Chapter 37 appears four times (37, 50–1, 64, 83–4), undermining the chronological numbering of chapters (from 1–23, followed by 37 as the final chapter in the section). A kind of textual game emerges as the reader comes to remark on the absence or presence of 37 in the body of the text: 37 is present as a page reference to *The Autobiography of Malcolm X* in 'guest' (94) and absent from the enumeration of chapters in 'host'. Significantly, the first instance of Chapter 37 occurs on page 37, where the narrator reflects on the meaning of the number 37:

> Lying in bed next to a girl she loved, years ago, discussing the number 37. Dylan singing. The girl had a theory that 37 has a magic about it, we're compelled towards it. Websites are dedicated to the phenomenon. The imagined houses found in cinema, fiction, painting and poetry – almost always 37. Asked to choose a number at random: usually 37. Watch for 37, the girl said, in our lotteries, our game shows, our dreams and jokes, and Leah did, and Leah still does. (37)

This quasi-mystical account of 37 takes place while Leah is standing in front of 37 Ridley Avenue (a fictional address) where squatters live, including Shar. In terms of its signification, the number 37 carries with it the hope of unanticipated connections and windfall, but the narrative undercuts these hopes and dreams. Instead, the chapters numbered 37 call attention to aborted social, spiritual and biological relations, namely through Leah's visitation (37) to 37 Ridley Avenue (which fuels a sense of animosity between the middle class and the poor), the story of Leah's abortion procedure (50–1), the account of the Black Madonna's half-forgotten presence in *NW* (64) and an odd scene in the pharmacy, where the photos of Shar and Leah are mixed up, which leads to an emotional outburst (83–4). Thus, the number 37 may represent a call for unanticipated unity and fortuitous connection, but its actual presence in the narrative calls attention to the disrupted communal fabric of the neighbourhood, particularly through economic disparity.

Furthermore, the affiliation of the Black Madonna with the number 37 calls attention to Smith's transnational feminist approach to narrative nesting or embedding. In *Changing the Story: Feminist Fiction and the Tradition*, Gayle Green argues that the embedded narrative features prominently in postmodern feminist writing (14–15) while Roberta Seelinger Trites claims that the 'housing of one narrative body within another narrative [...] implies feminine fertility, so nested narratives can themselves become a child-of-the-mother textual representation of a mother's pregnant body'

(165). Smith's feminist mapping of the Black Madonna's maternal presence in *NW* is especially striking: she is both visitor and host to NW (northwest London), a figure of crossings and visitations. Prior to the Black Madonna's visitation in Chapter 37, Leah and Natalie visit the shrine of Our Lady of Willesden, where they come across a carved sculpture of a Black Madonna, a recent incarnation of the former one 'destroyed in the Reformation and burnt, along with the ladies of Walsingham, Ipswich and Worcester' (63). In *Britain in Old Photographs: Willesden*, Adam Spencer notes Willesden's Roman connections through road building (today's Edgware Road), but observes that its main claim to fame, prior to the Reformation, lay in the shrine to Our Lady (5), which became a site of pilgrimage. The tradition of the Black Madonna alludes to a number of sacred feminine presences: the Virgin Mary, mother of Christ; Mary Magdalene, the converted prostitute associated with Christ; and Isis, the Egyptian and universal mother goddess, frequently depicted holding her son, Horus. As such, Smith's Black Madonna invites a rich and fertile reading of presence and identity politics in Britain, which disrupts a dominant white, English narrative of place. Instead, the Black Madonna incarnates an alternative rendering of history; she bears witness to the long history of global circulations, black presence, syncretic processes of intermixture and national as well as religious conflict that have shaped the globalizing dynamics of NW.

Smith remaps the sacred and the secular by reworking the Biblical account of the Visitation. In the Christian tradition, the 'Visitation' refers to Mary's stay with Elizabeth when both women were pregnant, Mary with Christ and Elizabeth with John the Baptist. According to Biblical interpretation (Luke 1: 42–5), John was touched and blessed by the saviour and filled with grace while still in the womb. Mary, a bearer of the divine, served as a mediatory between worldly beings and sacred presence. Christ himself comes to save the meek, poor and humble of the earth. Smith's narrative seems to be haunted by half-obliterated reminders of the duty to care for the poor and the homeless. Chapter 37 offers a strongly politicized representation of the Black Madonna's visitation when she addresses the reader as follows:

How long have you lived your whole life in these streets and never known me? How long did you think you could avoid me? What made you think you were exempt? Don't you know that I have been here as long as people cried out for help? Hear me: I am not like those mealy-mouthed pale Madonnas, those simpering virgins! I am older than this place? Older even than the faith that takes my name in vain! Spirit of these beech woods and phone boxes, hedgerows and lamp posts, freshwater springs and tube stations, ancient yews and one-stop shops, grazing land and 3D multiplexes. Unruly England of the real life, the animal life! Of the old church, of the new, of a time before churches. [...] Did you hope for something else? [...] Is the sky falling? Could things have been arranged differently arranged, in a different order, in a different place? (64)

Smith's Black Madonna bears witness to a long global presence, present and past, of confrontations with life, human and non-human. Speaking from the fabric of known history, her narrative reveals the concealed presence of difference and otherness to the hegemonic order, which has been there all along. Otherness is already encoded and encrypted within the fabric of the neighbourhood and the world.

From a narrative perspective, the figure of the Black Madonna provides a way of reconciling the various spatial paradigms and literary experiments of the novel. The Black Madonna interrogates the fiction even as she speaks from it. Thus, she represents both an immersive and interactive fiction, a bridge between diegesis and mimesis, but her presence also elicits an alternative interpretive framework. If one reads the novel through its transnational circuits, which bring the story of Isis and her son, Horus, to Britain, then one finds a model for an alternative kind of crime fiction in which it is the Black Madonna's task to locate and piece together the dismembered and scattered body of her son. As a numinous presence in *NW*, this Black Madonna calls the reader's attention to the lives fragmented throughout the narrative. As R. E. Witt explains Isis represents the friend of slaves, sinners, artisans and the downtrodden, but she also hears the prayers of the wealthy, maidens, aristocrats and rulers (7). As such, she is a figure who bridges the growing division between rich and poor, offering an alternative mapping of locality at once critical and hopeful. A syncretic figure, she represents an encounter with the wholly other, which is also part of *NW*'s fictional claims on the British space and history. But, as will be seen, her claims on space and place may resonate throughout *NW*, but remain largely unfulfilled in the eponymous space of the world.

For Smith, the motif of the Black Madonna is associated with an experimental aesthetics of (dis)connection. In *On Beauty,* the figure of Erzulie, the African-Caribbean incarnation who blends sensual and sacred associations, circulates in the form of a painting by Hector Hippolyte, which travels from Haiti through the world. This Black Madonna is commoditized: her beautiful image becomes caught up in a wider struggle for economic, sociopolitical and cultural capital. In *NW,* the maternal and erotic as well as sacred and profane aspects of the Black Madonna are embodied by Keisha/Natalie who becomes her avatar (a term that commonly refers to the adoption of an online presence in contemporary digital culture, but originally refers to the descent of a deity to earth in incarnate form). In the final section of *NW,* Leah says to Natalie, 'Mother and child. Look at you. You look like the fucking Madonna' (292). Elsewhere, Keisha is described as 'a goddess' (258) during a sexual encounter with strangers whom she met over the internet via an adult website. As a member of this online/offline community, she adopts the email address of 'KeishaNW@gmail.com' (259), a name that remaps her earlier, youthful self through the virtual/real worlds of NW. Through Keisha's virtual (online) sex games and offline encounters, Smith highlights the quest for passion and sense of disconnection in everyday life as mediated erotic games in the online space of virtual encounters become a substitute for actual, erotic encounters between bodies and selves in the world. Although the rerouting of identities and bodies through virtual exchanges elicits a sense of desire, actual encounters with others in the lived space of NW are frequently unfulfilling. However, this is not to say that Smith's digimodernism is emptied of affective potential. Where the web reference to the adult website leads nowhere, the URL for Kierkegaard (223) produces many interesting search results about the philosopher. Smith's narrative prompts the reader to consider the links between Kierkegaard's celebration of the 'Fullness of Time' as a transient but decisive apprehension of the moment (223) and Natalie's philosophically-oriented quest for an orgasm that will enable her to experience eternity in the moment (223). Smith's narrative plays on multiple meanings of the word virtual, as Rob Shields indicates a word derived from the Latin *virtus*, meaning virtue (2) and as Shields specifies referring to the 'power or operative influence inherent in a super-natural or divine being' (3). Natalie's infidelities may seem less than virtuous to the husband she betrays, but her actions are virtuous in the sense that she is true to the divine presence of the Black Madonna at work in her life. Thus, the text plays with the theme of the virtual, embodiment and the (dis)connected society through the virtual, broken links that lead nowhere and others that provide access to rich and varied sources of reflection.

Smith maps a passionate connection to the planet as she traces Nathan and Natalie's crossing of NW, rounding the hill that links populated by both the rich and poor. This 'crossing' bears witness to a new spatial narrative of the imagined community of Britain, which reclaims histories of resistance and presents alternatives to the divisive constructions of race, cultural difference and class. Taking shelter from the rain, they stand in the threshold of Jack Straw's Castle, a former pub in Hampstead, whose name alludes to Straw's role in the Peasants Revolt during which he addressed groups of rebels on the heath from a hay wagon, which became known as 'Jack Straw's Castle'. This reference to spatial history is significant, particularly in connection with the epigraph to NW – 'When Adam and Eve span,/Who was then the gentleman?' – which originates with John Ball's call for social equality during the Peasants Revolt:

When Adam delved and Eve span, Who was then the gentleman?
    From the beginning all men by nature were created alike, and our bondage or servitude came in by the unjust oppression of naughty men. For if God would have had any bondmen from the beginning, he would have appointed who should be bond, and who free. And therefore I exhort you to consider that now the time is come, appointed to us by God, in which ye may (if ye will) cast off the yoke of bondage, and recover liberty. (104)

Through these interactive links between the space of the text, and the textual call for a new kind of space on earth, Smith reclaims a long history of calls for social justice. This scene is a prelude to a sexual union that bridges, however briefly, the divide between the impoverished, Nathan, and the sacred, Keisha in her guise as Black Madonna. Whatever this symbolic union represents, however, Smith does not swerve from the more uncomfortable realities of divisions based on class, gender, race and age, which continue to marginalize black men (275). By dramatizing the tensions of the lower-income and middle-classes, irrespective of race (though race still matters), Smith's narrative highlights some of the ways in which the increasing divisions between the rich and poor propel violence and social injustice in contemporary culture. As such, *NW* participates in the wider literary mapping of London as Smith links the well-trod terrain of Hampstead to the space of NW. Jack Straw's Castle – a pub visited by Charles Dickens, Wilkie Collins and William Makepeace Thackeray – represents a space of convivial exchange. But it is also linked to a 'cartography of despair' as Philip Tew points out, arguing that 'Jack Straw's is one of the places where Bill Sikes goes after he has murdered Nancy in Dickens's *Oliver Twist*, and his guilt-ridden, aimless attempt to escape is surely exactly the precursory model for the trek in *NW*' (N. Pag.). Thus, Smith's attention to the long and varied history of imagined and actual human geographies enables an oscillating perspective as the ground of the narrative (the setting) comes to play a vital role in the encoding and decoding of the story's meaning.

A similar case can be made for the more contemporary history of Hornsey Lane Bridge (128), an actual/virtual/imagined site that is mapped as a place of connection and disconnection, vitality and death. In 'host', Annie tells Felix about a reported suicide at this site, commonly known as 'Suicide Bridge' according to her schoolmates in the 1980s, but quickly dismisses this nomenclature as an urban myth (128). However, the numbers of such actual suicides led to the Hornsey Lane Bridge Anti-Suicide Campaign of 2010 seeking to establish a net, fence and barriers to prevent suicide (all verifiable online). Smith's mapping of the bridge attends to this shifting spatial history through lived and online experience, evident when Natalie describes the structure: 'She had remembered only one layer of obstruction, but the six-foot barrier before her was topped by spikes [...]. This must be how they stopped people going nowhere' (281). Smith's narrative is true to these shifting perceptions of the bridge through time and the changes in the built environment thanks to activism. At the same time, the description of the bridge represents a revisionist approach to lyrical realism:

The lamp posts at either end were cast iron, and their bases moulded into fishes with their mouths open wide. They had tails of dragons, winding round the stem, and each lamp was topped by an orange glass orb. They glowed, they were as big as footballs. Natalie had forgotten that the bridge was not purely functional. She tried her best but could not completely ignore its beauty. (281)

Beauty does not so much comfort as distract. The reference to footballs and functionality undercuts the transcendent. Something similar occurs when Natalie looks over the city, seeing St Paul, the Gherkin, cupolas, spires, the 'red gash' of the bus lane and the tower blocks, described as 'separate from one each other, yet communicating' (281). The city's mix of the economic interests, sacred beauty, transport links and housing developments are rendered visible, but Smith deflates the potential lyricism of the cityscape: 'Beautiful view, said the woman. She had a French accent. She didn't sound at all convinced by what she'd said' (281–2). Thus, Smith's lyricism is tempered by realism.

This narrative representation of the Suicide Bridge might be read in response to Kierkegaard's reflections on modern life in *The Present Age* (1946):

Our age is essentially one of understanding and reflection, without passion, momentarily bursting into enthusiasm, and shrewdly relapsing into repose. [...] Nowadays not even a suicide kills himself in desperation. Before taking the step he deliberates so long and so carefully that he literally chokes with thought. It is even questionable whether he ought to be called a suicide, since it is really thought which takes his life. He does not die *with* deliberation but *from* deliberation. (3)

Natalie's reflections on the bridge, the city in front of her the people around her and the site of her own home distract her so that the potential act of suicide becomes 'a prospect, always possible' for someone else (282). Yet, this is one of the few instances when Natalie seems to feel a sense of connection and presence: the contemplation of life and death enables her to feel alive to the world in an altered fashion. Yet, this too is the scene of rupture in which Natalie becomes 'a fucking liability' for Nathan (282), who is freezing and needs to move on. For Natalie, Nathan is once more a marginal figure, pushed out of her consciousness as her thoughts turn towards home. In this passage, Smith effectively pushes lyrical realism into a complex, contradictory representation of the mutable self, which sees little possibility for bridging the divide between the impoverished and the affluent. As such, it is perhaps not surprising that this rigorous lyrical realism ends in a largely realistic mode with Natalie's decision to turn Nathan over to the police. With the claim that what separates the successful and unsuccessful, rich and poor, is a matter of hard work (293), Natalie reverts to the prevailing ideologies of the aspiring middle class. The lyrical evaporates.

To conclude, Smith's revisionary modernist work involves multiple styles and varied forms of spatial reading practices to critique disparity and social inequality, which bring together the tendencies of various revisionary late modernisms through an emphasis on the heterogenous spatio-temporalities of the globalizing world (altermodernism), the yearning for the spiritual in art (remodernism), the oscillation between modernist and postmodernist tendencies to elicit a new sensibility (metamodernism) and the impact of online and network technologies on the imaginary and reading practices (digimodernism). *NW* is an avant-garde novel to the extent that, in terms of Philippe Sers' exposition, it 'evokes the conditions of conflict that arise between this [avant-garde] creativity and the prevailing society' and 'designates artistic activity as the means for opening up new territory' (849). Yet, in her passages of rigorous lyrical realism, Smith seems sceptical of the socially transformative and transcendent tendencies of the avant-garde as well as the consoling power of beauty: instead, literature frames problematic ethical encounters and elicits a sense of unease. Through the imagined cartography of *NW*, Zadie Smith examines shifting relations to the production of locality in a globalizing world. Her fiction attends to the dynamics of identity politics, global finance and virtual life through the network society, but she also considers the contemporary world in the light of its long, global history, shaped by cultural circulations that link Egypt, the Roman empire and Britain through time and space. The juxtaposition of avant-garde techniques with forms of rigorous lyrical realism serves the revisionary modernist task of confronting the vicissitudes of the post-millennial world order.

Bibliography

Anon. *The Hornsey Lane Bridge Anti-Suicide Campaign Website*. http://www.hornseylanebridge.net (accessed 29 December 2012).

Attridge, Derek. *The Singularity of Literature*. Abingdon: Routledge, 2004.

Ball, John. 'All Men by Nature Were Created Alike'. 12 June 1381. *Speeches in World History*. Suzanne McIntire with William E. Burns (eds). New York: Facts on File, 2009, 104.

Bourriaud, Nicholas (ed.). 'Altermodern'. *Altermodern: Tate Trienniel*. London: Tate Publishing, 2009: 11–21.

Butler, Judith. *Precarious Life: The Powers of Mourning and Violence*. London: Verso, rpt. 2006 [2004].

Childish, Billie and Charles Thomson, 'Remodernism: Towards a New Spirituality in Art', 1 March 2000: http://www.stuckism.com/remod.html.

Gibbons, Alison. 'Altermodernist Fiction'. *The Routledge Companion to Experimental Literature*. Joe Bray, Alison Gibbons and Brian McHale (eds). Abingdon: Routledge, 2012, 238–52.

Greene, Gayle. *Changing the Story: Feminist Fiction and the Tradition*. Bloomington: Indiana University Press, 1991.

Halberstam, Judith. *The Queer Art of Failure*. Durham and London: Duke University Press, 2011.

Kakutani, Michiko. 'Narrating Tangled Narratives'. *The New York Times*. 26 August 2012.

Kierkegaard, Soren. *The Present Age*. Trans. Alexander Dru and Walter Lowrie. London: Oxford University Press, 1949.

Kirby, Alan. *Digimodernism: How New Technologies Dismantle the Postmodern and Reconfigure Our Culture*. New York and London: Continuum, 2009.

Lorentzen, Christian. 'Why am I so fucked up?' *London Review of Books*. 34(21) 8 November 2012: http://www.lrb.co.uk/v34/n21/christian-lorentzen/why-am-i-so-fucked-up.

Mengham, Rod and Philip Tew. 'General Introduction'. *British Fiction Today*. Philip Tew and Rod Mengham (eds). London: Continuum, 2006, xiv–xxi.

Oates, Joyce Carol. 'Cards of Identity'. *The New York Review of Books*. 27 September 2012: http://www.nybooks.com/articles/archives/2012/sep/27/cards-identity/?pagination=false

Rancière, Jacques. *Aesthetics and its Discontents*. Trans. Steven Corcoran. Cambridge: Polity Press, 2009.

Ryan, Marie Laure. *Narrative as Virtual Reality: Immersion and Interactivity in Literature and Electronic Media*. Baltimore and London: The Johns Hopkins University Press, 2001.

Scarry, Elaine. *On Beauty and Being Just*. London: Duckworth, 2006.

Seelinger Trites, Roberta. 'Nesting: Embedded Narrative as Maternal Discourse in Children's Novels'. *Children's Literature Association Quarterly* 18.4 (Winter 1993): 165–70.

Sers, Philippe. 'The Radical Avant-Garde and the Contemporary Avant-Garde'. Trans. Jonathan P. Eburne. *New Literary History* 41(4)(Autumn 2010): 847–54.

Shields, Rob. *The Virtual*. London and New York: Routledge, 2003.

Smith, Zadie. *White Teeth*. London: Penguin Books, 2000.

—*The Autograph Man*. London: Hamish Hamilton, 2002.

—'How to Fail Better'. *The New Yorker*. New York, 30 October 2006 (audiobook).

—*On Beauty*. London: Hamish Hamilton, 2006.

—*Changing My Mind: Occasional Essays*. London: Hamish Hamilton, 2009.

—*NW*. London: Hamish Hamilton, 2012.

—'Some Notes on Attunement: A Voyage Around Joni Mitchell'. *The New Yorker*. 17 December 2012: 30–5.

—Untitled interview with Foyles: http://www.foyles.co.uk/zadie-smith (accessed 29 December 2012).

Spencer, Adam. *Britain in Old Photographs: Willesden*. London Borough of Brent. Phoenix Mill, Sutton Publishing, 1996.

Spivak, Gayatri Chakravorty. 'Planetarity'. *Death of Discipline*. New York: Columbia University Press 2003: 71–102.

Tew, Philip. 'Subject: RE: *NW*'. Email to Dr Wendy Knepper. 07.57 8 February 2013: N. Pag.

Van den Akker, Robin and Timotheus Vermeulen. 'Notes on Metamodernism'. *Journal of Aesthetics and Culture* 2 (2010): 1–14.

Witt, R. E. *Isis in the Ancient World*. Baltimore: Johns Hopkins University Press, 1971.

9

'That God Chip in the Brain': Religion in the Fiction of Zadie Smith

Magdalena Mączyńska

Alex believed in that God chip in the brain, something created to process and trigger wonderment. It allows you to see beauty, to uncover beauty in the world. But it's not so well designed. It's a chip that has its problems.

THE AUTOGRAPH MAN (101)

Zadie Smith is celebrated for her ability to capture the vertiginous diversity of twenty-first century life. Since the success of *White Teeth* (2000), she has been fêted as the poster child of the new multicultural millennium. Maya Jaggi in *The Guardian* applauded her fiction for recording the 'polyphony of postcolonial London' (9), while Frank Kermode in the *London Review of Books* praised Smith for 'being in the world, for knowing and loving its diversity' (13). Scholars emphasize her ability to orchestrate the heteroglossia of the cosmopolitan landscape; interviewers play up her youth and her hip hybrid black-Britishness. However, while much critical attention has been given to Smith's examination of racial and national identity, relatively little has been said about her interest in religion – a central concern in all of her novels. Smith's fiction is populated with characters who acquire, reject and redefine traditional beliefs and practices, illustrating the various uses to which religion can be put in a purportedly secular modern world. Alert to the ironies and contingencies of her characters' beliefs, and to the absurdities of the late capitalist spiritual market, Smith offers one of the most compelling fictional portrayals of religion's persistent hold on the contemporary imagination.

In a conversation with Ian McEwan, Smith responded ambivalently to his professed impatience with religion by confessing: 'I suppose I feel the same, but I feel strange about feeling it' (185). Unlike many of her peers, Smith understands that religion continues to shape the experience of modern subjects in ways that cannot be easily ignored by a novelist interested in offering a panoramic snapshot of the present moment. Nevertheless, her writings do not add up to any kind of cohesive statement concerning the state of modern day belief; rather, she aims to capture the heterogeneity and potential complexities of twenty-first-century engagements with religion. The author admits, in the introduction to her collection *Changing My Mind: Occasional Essays* (2009), that consistency is not one of her creative goals: 'I'm forced to recognize that ideological inconsistency is, for me, practically an article of faith' (xiii–xiv). As an essayist, novelist, and satirist, Smith seems less interested in constructing neat philosophical or sociological schemata than in recording, with astuteness and empathy, the gendered, racial *and* religious experiences of her characters in general and protagonists in particular.

The few existing critical considerations of religion in Smith's writings examine it as an aspect of a postcolonial, diasporic, or (post)ethnic identity construction. Praising the novelist's hybrid poetics, Andrew Furman hails *The Autograph Man* (2002) as 'the most thoughtful recent artistic exploration of the problematics of Jewish identity in our broader post-ethnic contemporary culture' (7). Z. Esra Mirze's discussion of Muslim fundamentalism in *White Teeth* focuses on the characters' use of religion for non-religious purposes, such as coping with socioeconomic inequity (Hortense) and traumatic immigrant experience (Samad), or forging new modes of belonging (Millat). Susan Alice Fischer's analysis of Smith's references to Caribbean spirituality in *On Beauty* (2005) posits the voodoo tradition as an alternative way of understanding and affirming an embodied black female identity. As these critics demonstrate, Smith is acutely aware of the ways in which questions of religion are bound with questions of nationality, race and class. She is equally interested in private quests for meaning, and the ways in which such quests may be articulated in quasi-, neo-, or anti-religious terms.

Smith's debut novel is set in a metropolitan milieu where atheism is the default, and faith considered a kind of pathology: Londoners fear 'they might catch religion like an infection' (29), or 'come down' with it like a 'nasty disease' (330). *White Teeth*'s cast of believers, an assembly of social misfits, unassimilated immigrants, and sexually repressed teens, seems to confirm such misgivings. Worse, faith is associated with violence: the novel's Jehovah's Witnesses relish the prospect of watching sinners 'sink under a hot and terrible fire that shall separate their skin from their bones, shall melt the eyes in their sockets, and burn the babies that suckle at their mothers' breasts' (28). The book-burning, gun-wielding Keepers of the Eternal and Victorious Islamic Nation (KEVIN) embrace a more earthly vision of purifying violence. Such elements align *White Teeth* with the emerging subgenre Arthur Bradley and Andrew Tate call the 'New Atheist' novel in their study of post-9/11 fiction. One of the key turns in Smith's novel is the 'conversion' to atheism of Jehovah's Witness Clara Bowden: 'I'm a goat. I like bein' a goat. I wanna be a goat. An' I'd rather be sizzling in de rains of sulfur wid my friends than sittin' in heaven, bored to tears' (36). Similar de-conversions are experienced by lesbian Neena and rationalist Magid, as well as their fictional precursors in Salman Rushdie's work: Adam Aziz in *Midnight's Children* (1980) and Gibreel Farishta in *The Satanic Verses* (1988), both of whom, like Clara, experience their loss of faith as both a bereavement and a liberation.

Like Rushdie, Smith in *White Teeth* sets out to deconstruct the myth of religious purity as manifested in the Islamist ideology of KEVIN and in the reductive 'mono-intelligence' (421) of Jehovah's Witness Ryan Topps. As in matters of race and nationhood, Smith is an anti-essentialist: under close scrutiny, nothing is ever pure or simple, all roots are entangled, all binary structures open to dismantling. The founder of KEVIN, Ibrāhīm ad-Din Shukrallah, is revealed to have been born to Presbyterian parents as Monty Clyde Benjamin; his five-year-long study of Islamic scriptures was made possible by a generous Mormon aunt. Abandoned by her English lover, Clara's Jamaican grandmother (teenaged and pregnant) became a Jehovah's Witness under the tutelage of a Scottish spinster, who herself had embraced the Bible and Tract Society after falling under the spell of Charles Taze Russell's 'mighty beard' (297). These irreverent genealogies underscore the hybrid nature of religious identity. Similarly, Smith's use of the twin/double motif (Magid becomes an atheist in religious Bangladesh; Millat joins an extremist Muslim group in 'godless' London) serves to undo simplistic binaries. Finally, Smith's distrust of the sacred/profane dichotomy (analogous to her suspicion of Englishness/foreignness or whiteness/blackness) is especially apparent in the way she employs religious vocabulary in unexpected, mundane contexts: atheist Marcus Chalfen is 'tempted' to call Magid Iqbal's appearance in his life 'a miracle' (352). Accosted by the disturbed Mad Mary, Samad is convinced 'She had spotted the madman in him (which is to say, the prophet)' (148) and proceeds to improvise a bizarre ecumenical sermon: 'I am trying to say that life is a broad church, is it not? He pointed to the ugly red-brick building full of its quivering believers. 'With wide aisles'. He pointed to the smelly bustle of black, white, brown, and yellow shuffling up and down the High Street' (149). Such juxtapositions blur the boundary between the categories of the profane and the sacred, revealing their mutual interdependence and interpenetration.

If Smith dismantles the myth of purity promoted by religion, she is equally critical of fanatical materialism. Like Mohsin Hamid's *The Reluctant Fundamentalist* (2007), *White Teeth* demonstrates that fundamentalist positions can be found outside the realm of religion. Marcus, a brilliant professor of genetics, aspires to create a perfectly predictable life form: the Future Mouse©. This Faustian/Frankensteinian pursuit is consistently described in religious terms, foregrounding the analogy between religious and anti-religions ardour: 'He went to the edges of God's imagination and made mice Yahweh could not conceive of' (259). Professor Chalfen's sidekick Magid openly describes himself as a convert to scientific thought (echoing the public declarations of Richard Dawkins); responding to his brother's faith, he proclaims, 'I have converted to Life. I see his god in the millionth position of *pi*, in the arguments of the Phaedrus, in a perfect paradox' (354). At his most theological, while witnessing the genetically manipulated creation of Future Mouse©, Magid dreams of a god-like certainty: 'No second-guessing, no what-ifs, no might-have-beens. Just certainty. Just certainty in its purest form. And [...] what more is God than that?' (405). Magid's phrasing reveals the rigid fundamentalism of his atheist worldview.

The novel's fundamentalists (religious and otherwise) are contrasted with hybrid characters like Alsana Iqbal, who embraces traditions and moral precepts of Islam but not its belief system: 'she was really very traditional, very religious, lacking nothings except the faith' (53). Alsana identifies as Muslim but has no patience for Millat's fanaticism and refuses to pray with Samad during the storm that wrecks their neighbourhood. Her idiosyncratic, flexible and highly individualistic approach to religion represents the novel's preference for heterodox solutions and identities. Ultimately, *White Teeth* casts its vote on the side of the impure and the uncertain, symbolically represented by the escape of Future Mouse© into the sewers of London. Elaine Childs argues that the novel rejects 'humanism and fundamentalism – twin paradigms of the known' in favour of 'the unknown' and 'an intense desire for the impossible' (12). However, given its mediatory stance, *White Teeth* could be described more accurately as a rejection of the twin fundamentalisms of religion and scientific materialism in favour of a humanism that celebrates the hybridity and contingency of life. As the unnamed young airport reader of Marcus Chalfen's book put it: 'I'm not religious or nothing, but you know, I believe in the sanctity of life, yeah?' (346).

Smith's second novel, *The Autograph Man*, picks up a number of thematic threads introduced in *White Teeth*: the hybridity of contemporary religious experience; the use of religion as marker of social belonging; the spillage of religious categories into everyday life; and the power of reverse conversion. The protagonist Alex Li Tandem's epiphany closely echoes that of Clara Bowden: 'He wanted to be in the world and take what came with it, endings local and universal, full stops, periods, looks of injured disappointment and the everyday war. He liked the everyday war' (340). Unlike *White Teeth*, however, *The Autograph Man* uses religion not only as a theme but also as a metatextual structuring device. The plot, inspired by Leon Wieseltier's 1998 memoir *Kaddish*, follows Alex, a young, nominally Jewish autograph trader, struggling, 15 years after the event, with the sudden loss of his Chinese father. The narrative is divided into two books: the ten chapters of Book One (*Mountjoy: The Kabbalah of Alex-Li Tandem*) correspond to the ten branches of the Kabbalistic Tree of Life; Book Two (*Roebling Heights: The Zen of Alex-Li Tandem*) follows the trajectory of the Ten Bulls, a Zen parable recorded in the twelfth century by Chinese Zen master Kakuan (introduced to Western audiences in 1957 by Paul Reps and Nyogen Senzaki). The novel is framed by a prologue entitled *Zohar, The Wrestling Match* and an epilogue entitled *Kaddish*. This elaborate intertextual structure positions the narrative in dialogue with the religious texts it appropriates. Smith's borrowings range from Joycean references to symbolic body parts (the left leg in Chapter 4, the womb in Chapter 9), objects (the rainbows in in Chapter 1), and colours (red in Chapter 7), to more systematic structural engagements: in Book Two, the progression of the Zen narrative (The Search for the Bull, Discovering the Footprints, Perceiving the Bull, Catching the Bull, and so forth) provides a framework for the protagonist's trip to America, where he searches for, finds, and befriends the object of his obsession, Hollywood star Kitty Alexander. Echoing master Kakuan's Taoist-inspired drawings, illustrative sketches accompany each chapter.

When incorporating religious imagery and plot patterns, Smith uses the strategy of carnivalesque juxtaposition, first introduced in the novel's opening image of the Kabbalistic Tree of Life. The drawing, which precedes the text of the novel itself, consists of ten interconnected sephiroth, complex symbolic structures representing the transcendent and earthly attributes of the divine. In Smith's rendition, the sephiroth contain names of secular figures: Muhammad Ali in Yesod/Foundation; John Lennon in Hod/Splendor; Virginia Woolf in Hochmah/Wisdom and so on. The highest sephira, the Crown, remains empty, until it is filled with the name of Alex's deceased father. This highly personalized use of Kabbalistic imagery parallels the protagonist's reverence for private 'sacred' objects and rituals: 'Alex heaved his bag onto his shoulder and touched, in order, the things he always touched before leaving his bedroom: a small chipped Buddha on his desk, a signed Muhhammad Ali poster, and an old pound note, Blu-Tacked to the top of the door frame' (53). Similarly, the postcard with Kitty Alexander's autograph, which the protagonist believes had been sent to him (religious pun intended), becomes an object of veneration.

Alex's propensity for sacralizing the mundane is mirrored in the culture that surrounds him. His childhood trip to a wrestling match is described as a suburban 'exodus' (6), with cars full of boys clutching Bible-like event posters: 'big, red, with gold lettering' (7), eager to see the god-like Big Daddy vanquish his evil opponent. Professional exchanges between Alex's colleagues have a ritualistic aspect: 'Every conversation between those two men was actually the same conversation, different words, same meanings. A sort of modern Kaddish, a religious chant' (90). The auction room where the protagonist trades his autographs is a mock-temple: 'It is not a real place but a sort of cathedral or synagogue to which Alex comes every other week and speaks by rote' (87). The autographs themselves are revered as precious material traces of human greatness, their function echoing those of relics, their authenticity debated with a fervor worthy of sacred scriptures. The most fanatical of the novel's philographers, Ben D. Goodall, is described as 'a religious man, religious about fame' (92). Fame, especially its postmodern iteration, celebrity, provides many of the novel's quasi-religious moments. Elvis fans display 'undaunted belief' (92); a Julia Roberts billboard inspires a 'strong urge to kneel' (155); the astronomic value of Kitty Alexander's signatures is magnified by her reluctance to indulge her worshippers: 'Kitty was as awkward and invisible as Jehovah' (56). Drawing on the insights of postmodern theory, Smith demonstrates that, in the era of the triumphant simulacrum, professional sports become sites of collective religious experience and film stars play the role of deities.

Smith's characters are attuned to the ironies of the late capitalist spiritual marketplace: when describing his desire for revenge in religious terms, Alex demonstrates the mix-and-match mentality of a modern consumer: 'this is not an issue to which Zen should be applied. This is an eye for an eye, tooth et cetera issue. This is a time for the application of Judaic law' (104). When Honey explains her experience of pleasure, Alex responds dismissively, even flippantly:

'It ain't a thing. It's a no-thing'.
    'You should go on the shopping channel. They need more Buddhists on that channel'. (225)

Smith's playful tone places her narrative within two overlapping traditions: the recent subgenre of spiritual comedy, whose emergence in American fiction was noted by John McClure (16), and that of Jewish humour, whose relevance to contemporary fiction's post-colonial project was examined by Sigrun Meinig (following Homi K. Bhabha): 'While exploring the features of Jewish culture in terms of performativity, Smith's second novel engages in the "joke-work" Bhabha describes and makes light of its own journey' (74).

Smith's serio-comic approach is best exemplified by her rendering of the Kaddish. When Alex first attempts to rehearse the ceremonial prayer, the effect is anything but reverent:

'MAGNIFIED AND SANCTIFIED,' said Alex loudly, 'be His great name'.
    This last came out in the voice of the popular actor James Earl Jones, a rich basso that often appeared in his throat when he attempted religion. (262)

Even the final Kaddish ceremony – which constitutes the novel's emotional centre of gravity and, in Philip Tew's words, 'partakes of secret and mystical values that subtend both celebrity and death' (90) – is sprinkled with irreverent comic references to the body language of the attendees. While Smith's renditions of religious subject mater are humorous, her humour is underpinned with surprising seriousness. For example, the voice of the 'Zen Lady' on a meditation tape offered to Alex during a transcontinental flight delivers one of the novel's central lessons: 'Knowledge is the reward of action, because it is by doing things that we are transformed. Executing a symbolic gesture, truly living through a role, this is when we come to realize the truth inherent in the role' (185). Another set of teachings concerns the importance of human relationships. Alex's girlfriend defines love as a kind of faith: 'You draw a circle in the sand and you agree to stand in it and believe in it. It's faith, you idiot' (291); the loyalty of friends coming to pick up Alex after a night of drinking is 'godly' (315). Through the strategy of sincere irony, the narrative distances itself from traditional forms of religion, while simultaneously recuperating the transformative potential of religious vocabulary.

One of the most important intertexts in *The Autograph Man* is the Zohar, a work of Kabbalistic mysticism believed to have been compiled in the thirteenth century by Moses de León, but purporting to be the second-century work of Rabbi Simeon bar Yohai. Smith's rabbi Rubinfire dismisses the Zohar as a fabrication: 'At best, it's a thirteenth-century fake, Alex, at best. The letters, the lights, the mystic writings. The Zohar is a pretty good novel, no more no less' (61). If a sacred book can be read as a work of fiction, the fictional narrative can, conversely, take on sacred aspects. Smith enacts this leveling by using the name YHWH, sometimes printed in English capitals, sometimes in Hebrew script enclosed in graphical thought balloons, as a section breaker throughout her prologue. Later in the novel, we learn that Alex had employed the exact same device in his book; this conflates the protagonist's work with the author's, and the secular text of the novel with the sacred text of the Zohar. Sigrun Meinig argues that *The Autograph Man* maintains a balance 'between not asking us to see salvation in the cultural strategies of Jewishness and at the same time presenting them as a feasible and probably successful path for the conundrums of identity building in the contemporary multiple world' (73). However, in light of the novel's subversive metafictionality, Smith's serio-comic levellings can also be read more radically as an attempt at transcending religious categories altogether, while acknowledging the efficacy of their performative gestures.

Zadie Smith's third novel, *On Beauty*, follows two transatlantic families, the biracial Belseys and the Kippses, modelled loosely on the Schlegels and Wilcoxes in Forster's *Howards End*. The fathers, Howard Belsey and Monty Kipps, are both art historians specializing in Rembrandt, and the conflict between their respective positions (Marxist materialism and Christian idealism) provides the novel's central ideological tension. *On*

Beauty is set against the background of the post-9/11 resurgence of religious rhetoric in the public sphere. Howard, a champion of secular modernity, feels discouraged by this development: 'The flight from the rational, which was everywhere in evidence in the new century, none of it had surprised Howard as it had surprised others, but each new example he came across [...] weakened him somehow' (38). This distaste is shared by the author herself, as evidenced by her critical portrayal of fundamentalist excess. On the other hand, Howard's atheist vision of reality, like that of Marcus Chalfen in *White Teeth*, is found sorely wanting. Once again, Smith's vote is for the middle ground.

The self-absorbed, emotionally stunted Howard is made uncomfortable by religious belief, 'as if "beliefs" were a kind of condition, like oral herpes' (38), and goes as far as repeatedly upbraiding his lonely elderly father for enjoying the companionship of a local parish lady:

'Why do you let these bloody people in? They're just bloody proselytizers'.

[...]

'Christian nutters – pushing their crap on you'. (295)

Howard's lack of emotional generosity is shared by several of the novel's younger characters: Zora Belsey loves committing blasphemy when in the company of believers; Victoria Kipps laughs at her father's custom of saying grace before meals, and mocks her brother's obsession with chastity. On the other side of the ideological divide, Monty Kipps, Christian philanthropist and pillar of society, carries on an exploitative affair with a young assistant, while his son Michael, who sees himself as 'a forgiving Christian' (36), is revealed as a sanctimonious, sexist and arrogant hypocrite.

Next to the caricatures of religious hypocrisy and atheist arrogance, Smith introduces a number of characters who break out of constricting binaries: Monty's wife Carlene, at first glance a stereotype of submissive Christian femininity, transcends the letter of her religion to support a gay friend of the family: 'Life must come first over the Book. Otherwise, what is the Book for?' (178). Pious Jerome is endowed with the saving graces of humour and self-irony. Howard and Kiki's younger son Levi, takes the beliefs of others in his stride: 'Everybody got their own way of getting through the day' (237). Kiki tempers her reaction to Carlene's conservatism by taking into account her friend's age and condition: 'Kiki regretted raising her voice. The lady was old, the lady was ill. It didn't matter what the lady believed' (176). Kiki's humaneness, Levi's tolerance, and Carlene's empathy are vindicated over the callousness of Vee, Zora and Howard, proving, once again, that flexibility and the ability to see things from other points of view rank higher than purity in Zadie Smith's ethical universe.

While *On Beauty* returns to familiar themes, it also introduces a new preoccupation: the relationship between beauty and the sacred. In both her fictional and non-fictional writings, Smith is increasingly drawn to what Harold Bloom calls 'the irreducible effect of the aesthetic' (36). This interest is indicated in Smith's choice of title, referencing Elaine Scarry's *On Beauty and Being Just* (1999). Both Scarry and Smith are interested in the relationship between the good and the beautiful, and in exploring what Sophie Radcliff terms 'the occult category of beauty' (10). *On Beauty* juxtaposes a religious and a materialist understanding of art, refusing to settle for either of the two perspectives (each severely compromised by the inadequacies of their proponents). The novel's rigid non-believers are barred from a personal experience of aesthetic delight: Howard, Zora and Vee study the arts but remain incapable of moving beyond intellectual analysis, as seen in Howard's academic ruminations on Rembrandt's *Jacob Wrestling with the Angel*: 'What is the logos of this light, this spiritual light, this supposed illumination? What are we signing up to when we speak of the "beauty" of this "light"?' (252). The believer Monty is similarly handicapped: although he affirms and is thrilled that 'Art was a gift from God' (44), and, as Fiona Tolan points out, subscribes to the Christian idea of beauty as spiritual perfection (131), he is incapable of aesthetic rapture. The flexible, open-minded characters, on the other hand, take pleasure in classical music (Jerome, Kiki), religious artworks (Kiki, Carlene, Levi) and pop (Levi, Carl).

Smith explores her characters' responses to beauty through a series of canonical works. During a performance of Mozart's *Requiem*, Jeremy weeps in ecstasy while Howard resists the piece's religious dimension: 'I just prefer music which isn't trying to fake me into some metaphysical idea by the back door' (72), and mocks his family's emotional response: 'Everyone been touched by the Christian sublime? Can we go now?' (71). Kiki, in contrast, simply calls the *Requiem* 'God's music'(72). Smith also includes several works of visual art, all of which embody the idea of feminine beauty: the statue of the Virgin Mary that Levi observes from his bus stop, whose 'pretty, sorrowful face' and hands filled with pious offerings ('little chocolates, photos, crucifixes, a teddy bear' (353)) evoke a tender, familial aspect of religion; the Haitian voodoo painting of Maîtresse Erzulie, whose multivalent figure represents 'love, beauty, purity, the ideal female and the moon', but also 'jealousy, vengeance and discord', and whose powerful appeal seals Kiki and Carlene's unlikely friendship (175); and, finally, Rembrant's 1654 painting of his model and mistress Hendrickje Stoffels entitled *A Woman Bathing in a Stream*. In the novel's closing scene, this secular portrait acquires the status of sacred icon through which a redemptive reconciliation of Howard and Kiki can be intimated.

Zadie Smith's most recent novel *NW* (2012), which follows the trajectory of two thirty-something married London couples (Natalie and Frank, Leah and Michel), returns both to the author's home turf and to familiar themes.

Like *White Teeth*, *NW* takes on the question of fundamentalist Islam, showing both the triteness of dinner party conversations on the topic: 'Everyone is suddenly an expert on Islam' (98), and the ways in which the West produces fundamentalist positions: 'But in a sense I really did not become a good Muslim until I came to Kilburn. This is really where I became very holy' (397). Like *The Autograph Man*, *NW* examines the intersection of the capitalist commodity market and religion, best illustrated by Smith's Woolfian descriptions of the street scene in London's northwest: 'Deal or no deal? TV screens in the TV shop. TV cable, computer cable, audiovisual cables, I give you good rice, good price. Leaflets, call abroad 4 less, learn English, eyebrow wax, Falun Gong, have you accepted Jesus as your personal call plan?' (42). The novel also returns to the theme of ritual, the importance of which can be seen in Leah's yearning for confession: 'Wish we had confession. Wish I could confess' (52), and in the strength of her marriage to Michel: 'the proper names "wife" and "husband" had a power neither party had expected. If it was voodoo, they were grateful for it' (26). Finally, Smith reemploys the motif of youthful rebellion: as a child, Natalie is 'relegated to the conceptual realm of "those church kids", most of whom are Nigerian or otherwise African' (224); as a teenager, she enters a courtship with the proselytizing Rodney (and guiltily explores her sexuality by skipping church to play with a vibrator). Likewise, as a young adult, she finds an alternative object of faith in culture: 'Natalie Blake was crazy busy with self-invention. She lost God so smoothly and painlessly she had to wonder what she'd even meant by the word. She found politics and literature, music, cinema. "Found" is not the right word. She put her faith in these things' (247). Natalie's search for alternative (cultural) sources of meaning echoes the themes of *On Beauty*.

The importance of the aesthetic is also apparent in Leah's relationship with religion. She is not a church-goer, but loves places of worship: 'The smell of the censer, the voluptuous putti babies, the gold sunburst, cold marble floor, dark wood carved and plaited, women kneeling whispering lighting candles' (52). One such place is the Willesden parish church: 'A little country church, a medieval country church, stranded on this half acre, in the middle of a roundabout. Out of time, out of place' (77). Leah loves the building's 'force field of serenity' (77) and its 'deliciously cool' interior. This romanticized image is juxtaposed throughout the novel with an acknowledgement of religion's darker aspects: more forcefully than any of her previous fictions, Smith's latest work tackles the problems of corrupt church institutions and hierarchies, including the Catholic child abuse scandal, financially fraudulent pastors, and (most gruesomely) a vicar accused of murdering prostitutes. In spite of such damning evidence of ecclesiastical corruption, Leah continues to be drawn to the Willesden church: 'Walking back from a training day in Harlesden she finds herself lost in the back streets. She takes a series of random left turns to keep moving, to lose a surely innocent hooded stranger, and then here is that strange little church again, tolling six o'clock. She goes in. Half an hour later she comes out. She does not tell Michel or anybody. She begins to do this most days' (103). Smith's rendering of this 'conversion' is very subtle: we don't learn anything specific about Leah's beliefs. All the reader knows is that a depressed secular woman suddenly takes to praying in an old church, and finds the practice meaningful enough to make it part of her daily life.

Leah's unexpected turn towards religion is triggered by a quasi-mystical experience she undergoes shorty after getting an abortion. In the abortion clinic, Leah feels 'ashamed before an imagined nobody who isn't real and yet monitors our thoughts' (65). Her feelings of guilt resurge when she first visits the Willesden church: 'At her back a Madonna, fashioned of jet limewood. The Madonna holds a mammoth baby in swaddling clothes. *The Child Christ* it says on the sign, his arms stretched out at either side, *his hands big with blessing* it says on the sign, but to Leah there seems no blessing in it. It looks more like an accusation' (81). The shock of this imagined accusation causes a fainting spell during which Leah is addressed by a voice: 'How have you lived your whole life in these streets and never known me? How long did you think you could avoid me? What made you think you were exempt? Don't you know that I have been here as long as people cried out for help? Hear me: I am not like those mealy-mouthed pale Madonnas, those simpering virgins!' (83). The voice goes on to identify itself as an ancient spiritual power: 'I am older than this place! Older even than the faith that takes my name in vain! Spirit of these beech woods and phone boxes, hedgerows and lampposts, freshwater springs and tube stations, ancient yews and one-stop-shops, grazing land and 3D multi-plexes. Unruly England of the real life, the animal life! Of the old church, of the new, of a time before churches' (83).

Leah's 'vision' takes up a single paragraph that constitutes a specially numbered Chapter 37, oddly placed between Chapters 17 and 18. The abortion is described in another Chapter 37, this time inserted between Chapters 15 and 16. Smith's inclusion of such rogue chapters into an otherwise linear sequence highlights the special status of the number 37, also emphasized by one of Leah's lovers: 'The girl had a theory that the number 37 has a magic about it, we're compelled toward it' (46). Once again, in keeping with the novel's strategy of subtle enigma, nothing more is explained about either the magic of the number or Leah's spiritual transfor-mation. Instead, Smith freely mixes Christianity, numerology and animism to meet the particular needs of her modern protagonist.

Zadie Smith's essay collection *Changing My Mind* opens with an epigraph from David Foster Wallace: 'You get to decide what to worship'. This statement is not, as Smith explains in an interview with Kurt Anderson, meant to suggest that one 'can just pick and choose like some bad New York Buddhist'. On the contrary, the epigraph is an invitation to 'a very serious commitment': 'You do get to decide what you worship, but that also means you have to decide carefully, work hard, and you have to make choices that are genuinely meaningful to you'. In all four of her novels, Smith has created characters who follow this creed of personal responsibility by embarking on unorthodox, quasi-spiritual quests that frequently lead them to atheistic, rather than fideistic conclusions. These quests tend to run along generational lines: turning away from the beliefs of their parents, Smith's young protagonists struggle to forge their own allegiances, making idiosyncratic uses of inherited religious vocabulary and gestures. Such truncated, iconoclastic spiritualities reflect the complexity of religious belonging in a contemporary multicultural world. In this aspect, Smith's narratives accord with John McClure's concept 'postsecular fiction': writing that rejects theological dogmatism and secular materialism to propose 'new, weakened and hybridized, idioms of belief' (4). While sympathetic to her characters' spiritual yearnings, Zadie Smith deflates the seriousness of their pursuits by satirizing the global religious marketplace in which believers are consumers, and everyone is invited to mix and match creeds and practices according to the promptings of desire and fashion.

On the level of fictional form, Smith supplements her penchant for literary allusion with references to canonical religious texts, symbols, rituals and narrative patterns. This extensive borrowing shows the novelist's awareness of the many ways in which religious paradigms continue to shape modern secular experience. On the level of metafictional reflection, Smith interrogates the relationship between secular and sacred textuality, an interest she shares with a number of contemporary British novelists, including Julian Barnes, Jeanette Winterson, Philip Pullman, Salman Rushdie and Will Self. Far from rigorous or systematic, Zadie Smith's fictional renditions of religion are 'baggy, inconclusive, garrulous and broad', to borrow the author's endearing description of her own mind in the introduction to *Martha and Hanwell* (vii); they are also deeply empathetic, tender, thoughtful and funny. Smith's fiction from *White Teeth* to NW offers a welcome alternative to the antagonistic rhetoric of today's culture wars. Her oeuvre confirms Alain de Botton's conviction that 'it must be possible to remain a committed atheist and nevertheless find religions sporadically useful, interesting, and consoling – and be curious as to the possibilities of importing certain of their ideas and practices into the secular realm' (11–12).

Bibliography

Anderson, Kurt. 'Conversations in the Library: Zadie Smith & Kurt Anderson'. 30 April 2006. Video and transcript. http://www.pen.org/viewmedia.php/prmMID/793/prmID/1064

Bloom, Harold. *The American Religion: The Emergence of the Post-Christian Nation*. New York: Simon & Schuster, 1992.

Bradley, Arthur and Andrew Tate. *The New Atheist Novel: Fiction, Philosophy and Polemic After 9/11*. London: Continuum, 2010.

Childs, Elaine. 'Insular Utopias and Religious Neuroses: Hybridity Anxiety in Zadie Smith's *White Teeth*'. *Proteus* 23(1) (2006): 7–12.

De Botton, Alain. *Religion for Atheists: A Non-believer's Guide to the Uses of Religion*. New York: Pantheon Books, 2012.

Fischer, Susan Alice. '"A Glance from God": Zadie Smith's *On Beauty* and Zora Neale Hurston'. *Changing English* 14(3) (2007): 285–97.

Furman, Andrew. 'The Jewishnesss of the Contemporary Gentile Writer: Zadie Smith's *The Autograph Man*'. *MELUS* 30(1) (2005): 3–17.

Hamid, Mohsin. *The Reluctant Fundamentalist*. London: Hamish Hamilton, 2007.

Jaggi, Maya. 'In a Strange Land'. *The Guardian*, 22 January 2000: 9.

Kermode, Frank. 'Here She Is'. *London Review of Books* 27 (6 October 2005): 13–14. http://www.lrb.co.uk/v27/n19/frank-kermode/here-she-is

McClure, John A. *Partial Faiths: Postsecular Fiction in the Age of Pynchon and Morrison*. Athens: University of Georgia Press, 2007.

Meinig, Sigrun '"What's More Important than a Gesture?": Jewishness and Cultural Performativity'. *Anglophone Jewish Literature*. Axel Stähler (ed.). New York: Routledge, 2007, 65–76.

Mirze, Z. Esra. 'Fundamental Differences in Zadie Smith's *White Teeth*'. *Zadie Smith: Critical Essays*. Tracey L. Walters (ed.). New York: Peter Lang, 2008, 187–200.

Reps, Paul (comp.). *Zen Flesh, Zen Bones: A Collection of Zen and Pre-Zen Writings*. Rutland, VT: Charles E. Tuttle Co., 1957.

Scarry, Elaine. *On Beauty and Being Just*. Princeton: Princeton University Press, 1999.

Smith, Zadie. *White Teeth*. New York: Random House, 2000.

—*The Autograph Man*. New York: Vintage, 2002.

—*Martha and Hanwell*. London: Penguin, 2005.

—*On Beauty*. New York: Penguin, 2006.

—'Zadie Smith Talks with Ian McEwan'. *The Believer Book of Writers Talking to Writers*. Vendela Vida (ed.). San Francisco: Believer Books, 2007, 165–98.

—*Changing My Mind: Occasional Essays*. New York: Penguin, 2009.

—*NW*. New York: Penguin, 2012.

Tew, Philip. *Zadie Smith*. Basingstoke: Palgrave Macmillan, 2009.

Tew, Philip and Rod Mengham (eds). *British Fiction Today*. London: Continuum, 2006.

Tolan, Fiona. 'Identifying the Precious in Zadie Smith's *On Beauty*.' *British Fiction Today*. Philip Tew and Rod Mengham (eds). New York: Continuum, 2006, 128–38.

10

The Novel's Third Way: Zadie Smith's 'Hysterical Realism'

Christopher Holmes

The novels we know best have an architecture.
ZADIE SMITH, 'REREADING BARTHES AND NABOKOV'.

All knowledge claims have to begin from the experience of limitation.
TOM MCCARTHY, INTERNATIONAL NECRONAUTICAL SOCIETY.

I begin with the supposition that Zadie Smith's writing on the novel is contiguous with, and co-determinate of, her novel writing. Smith's larger project of advocating for literary form that both responds to, and produces our contemporary moment is manifest in the proliferation of novelistic experiments that have distinguished her as one of Britain's great stylistic chameleons: from comic realism in *White Teeth* (2000), to pastiche in *On Beauty* (2005), to 'constructive deconstruction' in *Autograph Man* (2003) and *NW* (2012*)*, and back again, often in the course of single piece of writing. In her critical writing, she carries two seemingly paradoxical torches: the first, a ferocious devotion to canonical novelists of the Western tradition, particularly as expressed in *Changing My Mind: Occasional Essays* (2009) to those who avoid 'overtly lyrical language, mythic imagery [...] or the love tribulations of women' (3): Eliot, Hurston, Kafka and Nabokov; and the second, the promotion of literature that presses the limits of form 'wherever they may be' (41). I argue that these two sometimes divergent interests coalesce around a belief that the architecture of literature is not constructed merely to house ideas, but as well to give rise to thinking, to give birth to future ideas as of yet unimaginable, and to create what Virginia Woolf admonished were 'the new forms for our new sensations'

(30). In her most admired, and most misread piece of critical work, 'Two Paths for the Novel', Zadie Smith's writing endeavours to dismantle the house of novelistic ideas, and to read the novel, as Rita Felski has suggested in 'Context Stinks', 'not as something to be known, but something to *know with*'.

From the earliest moves in her collection of critical essays and cultural critique, *Changing My Mind: Occasional Essays*, Zadie Smith makes clear her interest in describing how readers and critics know a work of literature. When it comes to Nabokov's *Pnin*, a novel Smith has re-read a dozen times, she admits to 'an old desire, to possess a novel entirely' (43). In confessing this possessive love, she brings to bear Barthes's pivot from structuralism to post-structuralism in 'The Death of the Author' as a signal of the radical tension between authorial control and readerly creation; this would be something of an anathema to Nabokov's iron fisted authorial intent, but that is indeed her point. In this way she praises Nabokov not as the authorial strongman, but as the architect of structural accommodations left for readers to think in, through, and with, often with divergent, if not incompatible ways of perceiving the work. Smith writes of her habitation in *Pnin* 'Even the architect's claim on his creation seems secondary to your wonderful way of living in it' (43).

Here one locates a touchstone in Smith's critical work, a refrain on the interiority of the novel as analogous, or at least hospitable, to the interiority of the mind. That hospitality to the workings of the intellect has been described by various schools of theory and criticism as architectural. Smith's contribution is to interrogate the value of those structures for what literature can and should be able to do.

In her essay on the evolution of George Eliot's *Middlemarch*, Smith offers a provocative vision of how novels think or, rather, how they are preparing space for think*ing*. Eliot's notebooks, produced in the draft-stages of *Middlemarch*, attest to a long period of writer's block followed by what Smith describes as musical movement, 'a contrapuntal structure is set in motion, in which many melodic lines make equal claim on our attention' (30). Eliot's fluidity of construction in the latter stages of writing *Middlemarch* is for Smith a marker of the shift in the novel's form from knowing to feeling, and from static structure to a dynamic process in which many forms make a play for our attention. The structure of this novel-thinking – a form that Smith equates with the gestation of a novel in the process of becoming, and with the unfinished translation of a work (Eliot never completed her own translation of Spinoza's *Ethics*) – appears embryonic, unfinished, 'messy, decentered, unnerving' (39). As is so often the case in Smith's *Changing My Mind: Occasional Essays*, what appears at first to be a sentimental reading of Eliot the auteur, turns quite suddenly to broad theoretical claims for the possibilities of the novel, and here those possibilities are on the move.

Smith's discussion of *Middlemarch* as a gestation metamorphoses into a twenty-first century claim for Eliot's 'radical program for great fiction': a move away static traditional forms, and away from 'programs' of any kind, and towards 'crystalline masses', forms at their 'limits, wherever they may be' (41). The distinguishing of works as either programmatic or crystalline, those that pursue the limits of form, 'wherever they may be', presents a challenge for interpretation, particularly for those who rely on static conceptions of genre. One sees in an examination of Smith's critical-distancing from the ideologies of realism in her literary dustup with James Wood, that the pursuit of limits does not imply a boundlessness of form. Rather, the capabilities of literature shift dramatically from the expectation that form represent ideas, to something more along the lines of what Anthony Uhlmann suggests in *Thinking in Literature* (2011): that 'literature should be understood as attempting to develop an analogue of thought itself' (18).

In this essay, I will be pursuing that 'analogue of thought' in Smith's work as critic and novelist, looking to her collected essays as arguments for an architecture of literary form that depends upon the contrapuntal movement Smith hears in Eliot's work. Eliot's somewhat cryptic model for this movement describes (via *Middlemarch*'s Will Ladislaws) 'a soul in which knowledge passes instantaneously into feeling, and feeling flashes back as a new organ of knowledge' (40). These lines aspire to a great deal but might be more precisely delimited as a theorization of how thinking works as an unceasing oscillation between affect and knowing. Smith gets close with an analysis of Deleuze reading Spinoza as a marker of the way certain texts appear to think through how novels structure the coming into being of 'knowledge', of thought:

> That is why Spinoza calls out to us in the way he does: you do not know beforehand what good or bad you are capable of; you do not know beforehand what a body or mind can do, in a given encounter, a given arrangement, a given combination. (37)

Deleuze's interest in Spinozan ethics rests with those lines of flight for the mind, the irreducible, or what Deleuze borrowing from Leibnitz calls the incompossible of a given encounter with contradictory ideas. The Spinozan ethic depends on not knowing beforehand, rather than in the expectation of a predetermined movement or idea. To be crudely, but helpfully simplistic: Spinoza was a process guy.

Uhlmann, who writes extensively on a Deleuzian/Spionzan model of thinking that emerges from not knowing, but from the process of coming to know, imagines literary form as offering gaps in relationality. Those gaps are catalysts, Ulhmann writes in *Thinking in Literature*, to 'the process of leading to thought, rather than thinking. That is, in art the relation still has to be drawn, has not yet been fully drawn, and we need to think in attempting to bridge the gap' (15). While Eliot's characters of 'practical morality' appear to relate to their world in complete thoughts, shaped by a mode of Victorian realism, in Smith's framing, Eliot's gestating works enable thinking, not by framing what is already known, but by moving between these two modes of operation, knowing and feeling, as Smith describes them in *Changing my Mind* 'with wondrous fluidity' (40). Spinozan ethics turn out to be the setup for an argument about our 'need' for novelists who 'know and feel and who move between these modes with wondrous fluidity' (40). The 'Eliot effect', as Smith names it, produces 'a riot of subjectivity' (30), and a prototype for a dynamic of form that prepares for a 'given encounter' that cannot be foreseen.

Smith shares Eliot's interest in Spinoza's indeterminate mind, but it is his process of ideation that gets us closer to what Smith does with form. Spinoza's figuration of the idea, which as Anthony Uhlmann reminds us is not an object, 'not identified with words or images', and is instead, 'the very process of understanding' (10). Thus, while the idea is always limited, not precisely identifiable as a singularity, it similarly cannot be objectified. In this way the Spinozan idea, or what might best be called the ideational process, cannot be contended with in useable pieces, only as a dynamic process.

If the contemporary novel, as some have suggested, has outgrown what in 'Introduction: Temporalizing the Present' Bewes describes as 'structures [...] for understanding the art and literature of the twentieth century' (160) – in particular the tired oppositions between realism and some version of the avant-garde, politics and aesthetics, history and form – then literary criticism appears ripe for a paradigm shift, something akin to the move from programmatic literature to the pursuit of limits as a dynamic of form. One can find a similar interest in a radical break from ill-suited binaries in many of the recent returns of formalism ('new' and otherwise): described by Best and Marcus as 'surface reading', which proposes a return to the 'complexity of literary surfaces' as a new 'way of thinking' that counteracts a 'nascent fascism' in more symptomatic modes of reading (1); in the wariness of literary criticism that draws knowledge from a text with 'considerable certainty', in Thom Dancer's 'modest criticism' (206); a fatigue with context as the omnipotent theoretical apparatus, in favour of criticism that in Felski's terms 'think[s] of texts as "non-human actors"'(574); and in Judith Ryan's categorization of contemporary literature as those novels that negotiate with theory on the level of form and content, and which even produce theory (2). In each of these examples, there is an explicit move away from theoretical absolutes, combined with a clarion call to engage literature according to its 'ways of thinking'. The limit of presupposed thought, and the potential for thinking-to-come coexist in these new principles for reading form. It is within this energized debate over the need for limits and structures of thinking that I place Zadie Smith's criticism, and her experiment with thinking form.

In order to best demonstrate Zadie Smith's broader manifesto for the novel-to-think with, I reconsider her now infamous literary feud with the critic James Wood over the manner of literary form best suited to the concerns of the contemporary novel. This paradoxically means bracketing, or at least destabilizing, their competing terms of engagement: Wood's 'hysterical realism', and Smith's 'lyrical realism', and focusing instead on Smith's implicit argument for form's possibility not as a representational agent, but as structuring model for future forms of thought. The feud which took place in the pages of *The New Republic, The New Yorker* and *The New York Review of Books* between 2000 and 2008 offers a way of contextualizing Smith's literary project as a series of formal experiments with the novel as an object for thinking with. Such an approach departs from the most prevalent categories of criticism of Smith's work, those that locate in her novels what Terentowicz-Fotyga calls 'the new voice of multi-cultural Britain' (57), and criticism that places her multi/cultural/ethnicity characters, very often the denizens of contemporary London, on what Kakutani labels 'the chessboard of postcolonial dreams and frustrations'.

Because of Smith's prominence as both a critic and novelist, she has an unusual platform from which to address reviews of her work. Although it is not her habit to confront negative or mixed reviews in terms of the specific critique, in the case of James Wood's 'Human, All Too Human', a scathing treatise on the failure of the MFA workshop model of creative writing to produce anything but a detail-bedazzled mockery of the ferocious talent of the late nineteenth and early twentieth-century novelists, Zadie Smith has a full retort. Wood's broader point transcends the stylistic peccadillos he attributes to the 'hysterical realism' of David Forster Wallace, Jonathan Franzen and Smith, to delineate a particular genre of the novel whose success lies with what E. M. Forster might have called its plentitude of rounded characters. Smith's response takes the form of a side-by-side vivisection of two novels, Joseph O'Neill's *Netherland* (2008) and Tom McCarthy's *Remainder* (2007), each of which represents a 'path' for the novel's potential future forms. The traded polemics on the state of realism, in its many contemporary forms, that characterizes the debate between Smith and Wood stand in for a much broader argument about the limits of form, an argument over essential fullness or absence at the heart of the contemporary novel. Smith does explicitly confront Wood's 'hysterical realism' critique of modern fiction directly in 'This is how it feels to me', and although Smith does not reference Wood directly in her much-cited article, 'Two Paths for the Novel', it is clear that she aims to both explicitly return fire for Wood's unflattering characterization in 'Human, All Too Inhuman' of her work as a style-over-substance structure, which mistakes 'bright lights for evidence of habitation' (41), and to lay the groundwork for the fiction and criticism that will pursue limits at any cost.

James Wood has for the last decade been something like the dean of conservative criticism at *The New Yorker*. If, as I have suggested, archi-tecture can be a illuminating metaphor in reading the structures of the novel's form, Wood's lights taken for habitation reminds one of a similar distrust of form in the quarrels over reading aesthetics in cultural studies, and again one can recover the metaphor of architecture. Castiglia and Castronovo, in their introduction to an issue of the journal *American Literature* on aesthetics and cultural studies, note the regularity with which interest in aesthetics is aligned with apoliticality; reading for form provides 'a sanctuary of illusion where coherence and symbolic unity can be imagined' despite looming evidence of a more politically fractured reality (423). Wood is no ascetic, quite the opposite, but he does find self-conscious literary form that seeks out 'vitality at all costs' in the form of shining 'spectacle' (41) an anathema to the 'picture of life' (44) that can facilitate sympathy with characters in the contemporary novel. In other words, form is just fine, as long as it is not too built up, threatening to obscure a view of the rich interiority of the novel. Yet, Castiglia and Castronovo's 'sanctuary of illusion' seems in concert, both in form and content, with the habitation that Wood values in the house of the novel. Vitality, for Wood, is qualitatively different from 'the real', just as liveliness – what for Wood hangs off *White Teeth* 'like jewelry' – is different from living. Vitality in the novel is powered by theme and idea that glows dimly, and sometimes not at all, in the windows of the encyclopedic, fever-pitched epics of Rushdie, Pynchon and Smith. Wood is having none of it.

Crucial to his admonition of the reader of the contemporary novel, is that our choice is stark: on one hand, a novel like *White Teeth* that Wood finds suffering from hysterical fits of style, all 'shiny externality, all *caricature*' rather than 'character' – the earring without the ear, as it were – and on the other, Dickens's Micawber, who Wood in a moment of critical naïveté, reminds us merely 'went up to his room, and cried very much'. But is the house of Micawber, where crying a terrible lot is allowed to go on undisturbed by 'theme and idea', very much different from Smith's brightly lit, if uninhabited form? Both are what Wood calls a 'cover-up', but not in the way he would use it, not a swindle, but a hoax. Since they explicitly perform the false equivalency that is literature, hoaxes are particularly instructive of the limits of representation in the novel. Smith will go on to use the terms 'hoax' and 'wind-up' (rather than 'cover-up') to praise the novel *Remainder* as the ideal path, and to render impotent the very idea at the centre of Wood's critique: that a formal structure is either full or empty, spectacle or habitation. Form as a hoax then obscures not some innate quality of the human or lack there of, but rather the very expectations that one needs form as a revelation of what is not form. Encountering the hoax, and indeed, in Smith's estimation, desiring it, allows you access to the thinking form of the novel. Thinking about the novel in process, as a dynamic, rather than a static preconception of equivalents, frees the reader from the expectation that form has an analogue in 'natural' ideas.

Smith's severe critique of *Netherland* as the archetype of the popular but empty genre of the lyrical realist novel, is less concerned with the failings of realism, and more with the potential for the non-representational qualities of form. So why then do both Smith and Wood rely on hyphenated forms of realism, forms they would prefer did not exist at all, and yet which they give rise to in the process of naming them? It is clear that Smith's lyrical realism is removed from Wood's nostalgia for Dickensian *vraisemblance*. What appears at first to be a rejoinder to Wood's sensibilities, emerges as a sophisticated theorization of how novels unwed themselves from models of representational facility, and adopt structures which support the act of thinking-to-come. In quite the same manner that she suggests *Middlemarch* avoids fixed form in favour of a gestational process that moves 'fluidly' between knowing and feeling, Smith imagines the future of the novel as a dynamic that does not pause in the act of representation. Smith diagnoses what she deems a tragic popularity for the lyric form of realism in the contemporary novel. She writes in *Changing my Mind* of a 'breed of lyrical realism [that] has had the freedom of the highway for some time now, with most other exits blocked' (73). Notable for its aesthetic certitude, its 'perfection' in the sense of closure and completion, this particular 'breed' fails to marry its form to the questions posed by our contemporary state of being: questions of uncertainty, failure and catastrophe. 'It is perfectly done', she writes of *Netherland*, and 'in a sense, that's the problem' (73). The perfection of such novels stands in contrast to what Smith sees as the last half-century's attempts to disabuse Anglophone literary culture of its illusions of facility in describing the world. *Netherland*, and novels of its lyric-ilk, continue blithely along the path of metaphysical ingenuousness, with an uncritical belief in the 'transcendent importance of form, the incantatory power of language to reveal truth, [and] the essential fullness and continuity of the self' (74).

In contrast to Wood's nostalgia for the sympathetic character and the simply drawn scene (recall the lachrymose Micawber), Smith's critiques *Netherland* not for its emptiness, but the very idea of form as capable of fullness, completeness, perfection. It is no accident that Smith comes to *Netherland* as her exemplar of tragic perfection, as just five months prior to the publication of Smith's 'Two Paths for the Novel' in the *New York Review of Books*, Wood had penned a fawning review of O'Neill's novel entitled 'Beyond a Boundary', claiming it as the 'future of the post colonial novel'. The review, which unsurprisingly references Gogol and Bellow as consanguineous realists, praises O'Neill for what Wood imagines was the 'Eureka!' moment of selecting a 'devastating symbolic structure' for his novel: the unexpected symbol of the Cricket pitch as the dominate metaphor of the post-9/11 American landscape. This particular structure, the literally and metaphorically uneven pitch that draws Caribbean and Southeast Asian players out of urban anonymity and onto a global playing field, might itself have been an abstraction for Wood's realist sensibilities were it not, to his mind, 'grounded by the novel itself'.

Whereas Wood reads the grounding of the symbolic structure as its potential to house the conflicts of the contemporary novel, in 'Two Paths for the Novel' Smith finds *Netherland*'s structure 'voracious', eating away at the *matter* of the novel (80). In her distaste for the symbolic structure in *Netherland*, Smith reveals her distrust of literary representation in general. Such distrust cannot be easily categorized as a post-structuralist's admonition against metanarrative, nor should it be understood as an aligning of her own work with the great metafictionists she praises in 'Two Paths': 'Barthelme, Pynchon, Gaddis, David Foster Wallace' (both *White Teeth* and *On Beauty* display little of the self-conscious irony of those 1980's postmoderns). Rather, paying attention to Smith's third path or third way of the novel brings one closer to a reckoning with form's promise as a mode of thinking.

The opening moves of Smith's manifesto for the contemporary novel call to attention the often-unexamined 'credos upon which realism is built', in order to describe a forking path of two possible directions for the contemporary novel. Most successful writers of literary fiction, Smith begins, have already started down the path of lyrical realism, and the results produce at best what she describes in *Changing My Mind* as 'the bedtime story that comforts us most', and at worst, 'catastrophe' (74). Left unchecked, the tendency of novels like *Netherland* is to 'coloniz[e] all space' in an 'anxiety of excess' (80). Wood's delight with the habitation he locates inside the symbolic structures in *Netherland* reads to Smith like a mummification process whereby everything in O'Neill's post-9/11 world is wrapped in the literary, necrotic and lifeless. 'Everything must be made literary. Nothing escapes [...] Even the mini trauma of a middle-class life are given the high lyrical treatment' (80). Lyricism here sounds less like the poetics of high emotion, and more like the failure of the form of the novel to allow for gestations, for the space of new perception to come into being. Or more succinctly, when the aesthetic becomes colonial, there is a failure in the principal structuring event of the novel – its thinking. In her desire for a novel to wear its 'failures', 'anxieties' and 'nervous breakdowns' on its sleeve, one begins to understand that Smith has left the realm of realism and its sensuous form behind, advocating instead for a new mode of writing and criticism that requires a new form of critical awareness to what is not yet finished in the work of the novel.

In making this move, Smith epitomizes the 'disenchantment amongst literary critics with reading practices' that rely on old binaries of 'formalism/commitment, realism/expressionism, modernism/postmodernism' that Bewes finds in contemporary criticism of the novel (160). The 'usefulness of those structures' Bewes argues, 'even for understanding the art and literature of the twentieth century has become questionable [...] In current discussions, the question is more likely to involve the ontology of the work or the "event" of it' (160). Thom Dancer makes this point explicit in his reading of Ian McEwan's *Atonement*, a novel that he perceives as theorizing the danger of 'epistemological immodesty' (209). McEwan's work, he writes, 'is misunderstood when it is read representationally' (209). Encountering the work of contemporary novelists like McEwan is not, Dancer argues, 'mastering it from afar', but rather acknowledging that our 'fundamental views are as contestable as those of others' (205). This relationship to reading and to the contemporary novel as a catalyst to the event works antithetically to modes of criticism that presuppose a 'special form of knowledge' (215) implicit to the form of the novel Dancer follows Uhlmann's 'analogue to thought' when he looks to Deleuze on literature: form 'should affect rather than be comprehended', a description of the event of form that gets one closer to an understanding of Smith's third way for the novel (43).

Indeed Deleuze furthers the concept of non-representational literary form found in Bewes and Dancer, and most centrally in Smith, by shifting the metaphor of the forking paths (that he locates in Borges's beguiling short fiction) to that of a fold. The fold 'captures' rather than closes, and as Deleuze indicates in *The Fold, Leibniz and the Baroque* even God becomes a process rather than a static form of knowledge:

> Even God desists from being a Being who compares worlds and chooses the richest compossible. He becomes Process, a process that at once affirms incompossibilities and passes through them. [...] Beings are pushed apart, [and] kept open. (81)

Explored in *Cinema 2*, Deleuze's theory of incompossibles, the existence of mutually contradictory worlds, uses the concept of God as an analogue to how thinking occurs. Deleuze comes to his theory of incompossibles by reading Leibniz's concept of divergent, but coexistent compossible worlds alongside Borges' 'Garden with forking paths'. The language here reaffirms form as a process rather than a product: 'This is Borges's reply to Leibniz: the straight line as force of time, as labyrinth of time, is also the line which forks and keeps on forking, *passing through* incompossible presents, *returning to not-necessarily true paths*' (127) [emphasis added]. Rather than producing ideas to confirm himself as a monological being, Deleuze's God is a process that affirms incompatible ideas as coexistent and 'passes through them', keeping open their incompossibility. If god is the stand-in in this theory for the architect of ideas, then one can imagine his process as Bataille did writing, as ' a profoundly antiarchitectural gesture, a non constructive gesture', and having the primary objective of what in 'The Literary Event: Between Destiny and Necessity' Bewes describes as 'reopening a hole … the very holes that works of architecture plugged up' (182). This description of the 'event' as the violent rending of constructed knowledge that obscures the coexistence of contradictory, incompatible ideas – what I have been characterizing as its thinking – allows us to contextualize Smith's approbation of *Remainder*'s 'antiarchitectural gesture' in the language of dynamic process, rather than representational capability.

Despite her terminology, what becomes clear is that while Balzacian realism means a great deal to Wood as a counterweight to the Workshop-era of Anglophone fiction, it means almost nothing to Smith's attempt to define the failure of perfective form in *Netherland*. On the contrary, Smith argues for a way of reading that discards old models for labeling aesthetic genres according to their failure or success in representing the questions of their historical moment. In a pointed moment in her essay that continues to be misread, Smith examines the most pregnant absence in American architecture: The World Trade Center Towers. In a sweeping blow to *Netherlands* colonial aesthetic, Smith argues in *Changing My Mind* that O'Neill had a 'chance to let the towers be what they were: towers. But they were covered in literary language' (83). Even with this piqued example of what Smith finds unsatisfactory about the novel's metaphysics, one remains puzzled by the question of what exactly is covered over with language. Smith's point about *Netherland*'s aesthetic echoes the principle question that has guided and plagued literary theory since Plato's *Republic*: if language can represent what is outside of language, how should it best proceed? Given her predisposition to siding with the self-referential anxieties of the postmodernists of the US and UK, it is unlikely that Smith would rally behind a positivist view of representation, even in the case of the national traumas of very recent memory. This would seem to eliminate the towers-qua-towers as that which lies buried under the suffocating excess of O'Neill's aesthetic. If the towers in *Netherland* can be said to represent both an idea and its absence, then Smith's appeal to 'let matter *matter*' (91, original italicized) laments not the material towers, but the absence of their structure as a conceptual model for thinking about loss.

Here again she details the sins of *Netherland*, but as she proceeds one sees the delineation of sins of thought, rather than sins of form: *Netherland* 'knows the fears and weaknesses of its readers. [...] [It] indulges them' (82), and in the case of the towers, 'An interesting thought is trying to reach us here, but the ghost of the literary burns it away, leaving only its remainder' (82). Realism as an ideal, reliant as it is on a material reality comprehensible outside of language, claims to have a thought, an idea about the world. It is that thought that shapes the form of representation and as such, one can locate in Smith's critique of 'lyrical' realism a more fundamental statement on the value of realism as the nodal heart of literature's relationship to thinking. That statement, situated with the trauma of the Towers covered over in 'literary language', critiques not an excessive version of Realism, but the very nature of our assumptions about the thoughts form contains. If realism presumes an *a priori* thought that pre-exists the writing itself, an authenticity and wholeness that begs a form that will be revelatory of that which it obscures, covers-over, this, for Smith, interferes fundamentally with the relationship between literature and thinking, a relationship that should be structured as a dynamic process that accommodates thinking.

In order to have a working example of how the novel structures and accommodates thinking, one must examine how Smith circumscribes a third way for the novel, neither path nor fork, in what she calls the 'refusal' of *Netherland*, Tom McCarthy's *Remainder*. This literary refusal takes the form of architecture at its limits, neither habitation, nor monument. Whereas *Netherland*, in Smith's appraisal, has an idea, one which has been foreclosed upon by the 'voracious image', *Remainder* evacuates ideas from the novel and engages in a dynamic process of building, razing and rebuilding structures for thinking.

Remainder offers the antidote to *Netherland*'s 'authenticity fetish' in the form of 'antiliterature' (85) – that which refuses a genre by the nature of its ever-changing form. Such a term destabilizes Smith's metaphor of the two paths, in that she conceives of *Remainder* as a violent rejection and 'refusal' of *Netherland* (72), and not simply a road less taken. How to delineate these paths becomes even murkier when one of the possibilities for the contemporary novel negates its very category of existence: *Remainder* is a 'hoax', 'a wind-up' and 'a nervous breakdown' (85–6). As such, the novel's third way evinces a protean architecture, a form without form that is in the process of becoming. To return to Uhlmann's formulation, Smith finds in *Remainder* 'an analogue to thought', or in my formulation, thinking.

In Smith's thesis, as expressed in 'Two Paths for the Novel', '*Remainder* exists as the antipodal to *Netherland*'s lyricism: the novel that 'empties out interiority entirely' (85). *Remainder* makes the production of an architecture of thinking part of the fabric of its novelistic design. One cannot separate the narrator's acts of rebuilding, remaking and reenacting, from the novel's protean, unfinishable form. In the building and razing of its own narrative and formal structures, *Remainder* interrogates its own status as a work of literature. It avoids this problem of burning away the *matter* of the novel by dismantling the very building blocks atop which Wood's affective authenticity would seem to stand. This is Smith's final turn of the knife in the side of Wood's crying Micawber. Smith revels in *Remainder*'s performance of what she calls the 'final MacGuffin', the novel's 'nervous breakdown' (86–7), when distinctions between characters and caricatures are no longer important; Smith sees in *Remainder* the possibility of a novel that deconstructs its own authenticity in order to open the text to counter modes of thinking, new imcompossibles that cannot yet register on the level of structure. If *Netherland* offers the reader the exquisite and formally obscuring 'patterning' of lyricism, what Smith in 'Two Paths for the Novel' calls the novel's relentless aestheticization of the world, the antipodal *Remainder* plays at an 'anti-literary hoax', deconstructing our expectations of what a novel does, and, importantly, how its *doing* will look and feel (85).

The house of *Remainder* is built again and again on structures that cannot sustain it, and which point only to the remnants of a materiality to which no access in or through the novel itself. Smith's credo for the novel as a kind of anti-revelation, unknowing, finds in the gestational form of *Remainder* a novel that can convince us of its relevancy to our moment ironically by erasing itself, one formal construct at a time, leaving the process of what in 'Two Paths for the Novel' Smith calls 'constructive deconstruction' (87). This is the great contradiction of *Remainder*; its authenticity comes from the demolishing of tropes of authenticity from the narrative. This is precisely what Smith esteems in the novel – its spectacle of 'a man who builds in order to feel' (87), rather than to know, plays on without a recognizable finish.

I have set up both Wood and Smith as very different kinds of real estate agents for the novel. One shuffles its readers quickly off the lawn and upstairs to meet the lachrymose owners, the other has them wait in the car to watch the dismantling of the house, brick by brick. But to agree with Bewes's view in 'The Novel as an Absence: Lukacs and the Event of Postmodern Fiction' that the novel in the twenty-first century appears increasingly aware of the 'question of its own possibility, in a context in which it has become, or seems to have become, "impossible"' (5), is to insist on new categories of evaluation that move on from modes of unearthing or decoding knowledge supposedly implicit in the novel's form. But to look instead to the novel as a series of unfinishable structures, formal work that has yet to be completed, but which demands of us a willful openness in imagining the thinking-to-come. For Smith, the novel form must be for critics and novelists something 'to know *with*'.

Bibliography

Barthes, Roland. *Image-Music-Text*. New York: Farrar, Straus, Giroux, 1977.

Best, Stephen and Sharon Marcus. 'Surface Reading: An Introduction'. *The Way We Read Now*. *Representations* 108. Berkeley: University of California Press, 2009.

Bewes, Timothy. 'The Novel as an Absence: Lukacs and the Event of Postmodern Fiction'. *NOVEL: A Forum on Fiction*. 38(1) (Fall 2004): 5–20.

—'The Literary Event: Between Destiny and Necessity'. *Imaginaires: L'interpretation au pluriel*. Paris: University of Reims Press, 2009: 177–90.

—'Introduction: Temporalizing the Present'. *NOVEL: A Forum on Fiction*. 45(2) (Summer 2012): 159–64.

Castiglia, Christopher and Russ Castronovo. 'A 'Hive of Subtlety': Aesthetics and the End(s) of Cultural Studies'. *American Literature*. 76(3) (September 2004): 423–35.

Dancer, Thom. 'Toward a Modest Criticism: Ian McEwan's *Saturday*'. *NOVEL: A Forum on Fiction*. 45(2) (Summer 2012): 202–20.

Deleuze, Gilles. *The Fold, Leibniz and the Baroque*. Trans. Tom Conley. Minneapolis: University of Minnesota Press, 1992.

—*Cinema 2*, Trans. Hugh Tomlinson. London: Continuum Books, 2005.

Dickens, Charles. *David Copperfield*. London: Bradbury & Evans, 1850.

Eliot, George. *Middlemarch*. London: William Blackwood and Sons, 1874.

Felski, Rita. 'Context Stinks'. *New Literary History*. 42(4) (Autumn 2011): 573–91

—'Context Stinks'. Lecture. Providence: Brown University. 11 November 2010.

Forster, E. M. *Aspects of the Novel*. London: Edward Arnold, 1927.

Kakutani, Michio. '*White Teeth*: Quirky, Sassy and Wise in a London of Exiles'. *The New York Times*. 25 April 2000. Web.

Kirsch, Adam. 'A Great English Novelist'. *The Wall Street Journal*. New York: Wall Street Journal Company. 31 August 2012. Web.

McCarthy, Tom. *Remainder*. London: Alma Books, 2007.

Nabokov, Vladimir. *Pnin*. London: Heinemann, 1957.

O'Neill, Joseph. *Netherland*. New York: Pantheon, 2008.

Ryan, Judith. *The Novel After Theory*. New York: Columbia University Press, 2011.

Smith, Zadie. *White Teeth*. New York: Random House, 2000.

— 'This is how it feels to me'. *The Guardian*. 13 October 2001. Web.

—*Autograph Man*. New York: Vintage, 2003.

—*On Beauty*. London: Hamish Hamilton, 2005.

—'Two Paths for the Novel'. *The New York Review of Books*. 55(18), 20 November 2008. Web.

—*Changing My Mind: Occasional Essays*. New York: Penguin, 2009.

—'Two Directions for The Novel'. *Changing My Mind: Occasional Essays*. Smith, Zadie. New York: Penguin Press, 2009, 72–91.

— *NW*. New York: Penguin, 2012.

Terentowicz-Fotyga, Urszula. 'The Impossible Self and the Poetics of the Urban Hyperreal in Zadie Smith's *The Autograph Man*'. *Zadie Smith: Critical Essays*. Tracey L. Walters (ed.). New York: Peter Lang, 2008, 57–72.

Uhlmann, Anthony. *Thinking in Literature: Joyce, Woolf, Nabokov*. London: Continuum Press, 2011.

Wood, James. 'Human, All Too Inhuman'. *The New Republic*. 223(4), 24 July 2000: 41–45.

—'Beyond a Boundary'. *The New Yorker*. 26 May 2008. Web.

Woolf, Virginia. 'Hours in a Library'. *Granite and Rainbow: Essays by Virginia Woolf*. New York: Harcourt, Brace and Co., 1958.

11

Eliminating the Random, Ruling the World: Monologic Hybridity in Zadie Smith's *White Teeth* and Salman Rushdie's *Midnight's Children*

Lewis MacLeod

It does not take a very sophisticated literary critic to know you should not judge a book by its cover; even so, I think it is possible to assess something of its reception by the blurbs on the front and back jackets. Such pull quotes will not necessarily be informative as regards specific narrative features, but they do indicate what influential people and publications think about the books in question. They are small indicators attempting to shape the public's perception of the literary zeitgeist. At the very least, they demonstrate precisely what the publishers want the public to think about any given title.

So, I would like to start this discussion of *Midnight's Children* and *White Teeth* with a brief look at the reception of each novel as evidenced by jacket blurbs. My Vintage edition of *Midnight's Children* reminds me it is the winner of 'the Booker of Bookers' and was, according to the *New York Review of Books*, 'one of the most important books to come out of the English-speaking world in [its] generation'. *The Times* suggests readers will be 'continuously surprised' by the novel, while the *London Review of Books* finds it 'brilliant and enduring'. Not to be outdone, my Penguin paperback of *White Teeth* tells me I am holding the winner of both *The Guardian* First Book Award and the James Tait Black Memorial Prize for Fiction, a book which is 'the outstanding debut of the new millennium', according to *The Observer*.

Inside the academic community, the praise for both novels has also been remarkable. Each has been praised as a high-water mark for cultural hybridity, applauded for foregrounding the polyphony of voices that are possible in the contemporary novel, and lionized for highlighting the possibility of truly 'novel' and pluralistic approaches to fiction. Rushdie has been described by Josna E. Rege as a novelist who insists that it is 'crucial to keep open the space for ambivalence, uncertainties, and multiple truths' (176), and by John Clement Ball as a writer with a clear 'preference for contradiction and multiplicity instead of a totalizing, unitary truth' (218). According to Dominic Head, Smith's achievement lies in a gift for 'harnessing the novel's capacity to embrace heterogeneity'; *White Teeth*, he claims, encodes 'an evolving, and genuinely multicultural Britain' (107). These are just examples. There is a great deal of strikingly similar commentary out there.

Such praise seems to me to be well deserved in a number of ways, and I continue to think that *Midnight's Children* and *White Teeth* are very fine novels indeed. Just not in the ways outlined above. What I would like to do here is, first, express some uneasiness about the nature of the hybridity *Midnight's Children* posits and, second, suggest that the abundant similarities between *Midnight's Children* and *White Teeth* reveal a problematically homogenized (rather than hybridized) set of preferences in the contemporary literary-academic climate. If *Midnight's Children* is both 'continuously surprising' and 'enduring' this ought to beg some questions about how long a surprise can be expected to endure. Can an apparently innovative and counter-hierarchical literary approach become assimilated into the dominant power structures it purports to critique? More directly, do the seemingly heteroglossic impulses in Rushdie's novel actually work to produce a new notion of purity that in its turn works to reify rather than reinvent normative modes of narrative production and reception?

In *Culture and Imperialism*, Edward Said famously suggests that post-imperial experience can be imagined in terms of a multiplicity of cultures intersecting through a process of 'unhierarchical influence' (330) whereby 'people exist between the old and the new, between the old empire and the new state, [and] their condition articulates the tensions, irresolutions, and contradictions in the overlapping territories shown on the cultural map of imperialism' (322). Just as famously, *Midnight's Children* sees 'the chutnification of history' (459) as an emancipatory project by which vast and diverse flavours are juxtaposed, altered and reworked to produce and then 'preserve' a certain vision of (lower case 'T') truth. For Rushdie, all claims at authenticity and purity are faulty because they depend upon isolation and compartmentalization rather than heterogeneous recombination. *Midnight's Children* is a narrative which seeks to 'flout the laws of Halal. Letting no blood drip from the body of the tale' (59). In the novel, Saleem measures the 'degree of internal tidiness' in various people and expresses a clear preference for 'the messier type' (214). Saleem's chutney (and by extension India's history) encodes this mess and operates through factors and forces which refuse to 'stay neatly in separate compartments' (187). This apparent disinclination for compartmentalization and exclusion is so pronounced that Saleem happily accepts 'the flavourful contributions of the occasional speck of dirt' (461) in his recipe. If 'dirt' can be regarded as a positive contribution, Rushdie suggests, then even the lowliest elements have productive roles to play in a perpetual process of recombination; purity, by extension, has no place at all.

This much, I think, is self-evident. What is not immediately clear is what 'dirt' is, and, beyond this, it is not clear how 'dirt *as* dirt' comes to be figured so positively, how the rehabilitation of dirt works. In her landmark study, *Purity and Danger*, Mary Douglas maintains that 'where there is dirt, there is system' (35), that 'dirt is a by-product of a systemic ordering and classification of matter' (35). Without an organizing hierarchical structure, the notion of dirt becomes unintelligible; with such a system it becomes necessary and unavoidable. For Douglas, anything out of its 'proper' systemic position or out of proportion becomes filthy because it violates the organizing structure the subject (or the wider culture) uses to calibrate its position in the world. According to Douglas 'our pollution behaviour is the reaction which condemns any object or idea likely to confuse or contradict cherished classifications' (36). Crudely, desire (what we want, what we cherish) undergirds the production of dirt; what we are seeking determines what counts as pollutant.

More seriously, the absence of any stable definition of dirt means that everything and everyone possesses the potential to *become* dirt, so much so that human history can productively be read in terms of the process of making (and unmaking) dirt, a process directly linked to what Zygmunt Bauman, in *Postmodernity and its Discontents*, calls 'the Dream of Purity' (5). Bauman's argument sees the quest for some kind of purity in terms of paranoid and progressive redefinitions of dirt, in terms of a process by which formerly acceptable signifiers of difference become re-figured as pollutants as the purity seekers pursue their impossible goal. Bauman maintains that 'each order has its own disorders; each model of purity has its own dirt' (11). Ethnic cleansing, for example, operates as a quest for purity inside a radicalized (and specifically racialized) notion of what dirt is. According to Bauman this means that 'thoroughly familiar and unproblematic "neigh-bours next door" [can] turn overnight into terrifying strangers once a new order [of purity] is envisaged' (11). Perhaps more importantly, the purity-seeker does not see annihilation in negative terms. Instead, negation is figured as both progress and process, as a step towards decontamination and order. In the context of the paranoid quest for purity, Douglas – at least in Bauman's account – recognizes that 'eliminating [...] is not a negative movement, but a positive effort to organize the environment' (7).

Midnight's Children provides a number of examples demonstrating the legitimacy of Bauman's idea that all things seem to possess 'the awesome tendency to turn into "dirt"' (11) when they fail to observe hierarchical boundaries. The original characterization of Lifafa Das, for example, operates in terms of an excessive inclusiveness; with his peepshow, Das seeks to put 'everything into his box' (75), to exclude nothing, to mix everything together. In the end, though, he is refigured as human dirt by a mob of Muslims as the historically momentous partition of India and Pakistan approaches. Although he is well known in the neighbourhood, and, in the context of the previous system was regarded as a 'decent type' (77), he becomes a smudge that must be cleansed from the neighbourhood as the quest for religious and ethnic purity intensifies. A well-known neighbour who turns into a terrifying stranger overnight, Das is suddenly and summarily reimagined as 'Mister Hindu, who defiles our daughters [...] Mister Idolater who sleeps with his sister' (76–7). Above all, he is seen as someone who has 'got a *nerve* coming into [the] Muhalla [when] everybody knows [he's] a Hindu' (76); he is someone who has not observed Douglas's 'cherished classifications'.

In Rushdie's novel, it is clear that both Saleem's chutney and his narrative method are meant as hybridity's answer to this kind of compartmentalized sterility. They represent assertions of 'Bombayness' in the face of the impulse to purity, concoctions which recast 'dirt' as 'ingredient'. Obviously, Saleem's notion of Bombayness entails a more inclusive and more multi-faceted worldview than Pakistani puritanism, yet I would like to argue that neither Saleem not Rushdie escapes the quest for purity and order, that neither transcends the contagion anxiety (the fear of dirt) they so often critique. By including 'dirt' in his recipe, Saleem effectively unmakes 'dirt as dirt', but this unmaking does not entail any escape from the systemic processes through which the concept of dirt is produced. By configuring dirt in terms of a flavourful contribution to a complex, but organized, process, Saleem's dirt ceases to be an agent of randomness and disorder and becomes instead a signifier in a recognizable system of meaning. In the chutney, dirt is no longer 'a stranger' and, as such, no longer terrifying; in Bauman's terms, it ceases to be 'something that is out of place' (6) and so becomes clean. What Saleem does to dirt, then, is the precise opposite of what the Muhalla does to Lifafa Das. While Das is recategorized, moved from clean to dirty (from neighbour to contagion), Saleem's chutney moves in the other direction, reclassifying dirt as clean, bringing it within the boundaries of a new notion of what counts as acceptable and tolerable.

More importantly, despite his repeatedly articulated allegiance to 'Bombayness', Saleem is an active participant in what he calls 'a national longing for form' (300). Throughout *Midnight's Children*, he is possessed with a desire to make sure both his story and his chutneys are constructed in 'proper order' (385), consumed by a sense that 'everything must be told in sequence' (338). As his narrative struggles to reach its conclusion, he laments the degree to which it fails to satisfy normative narratological procedures. He thinks, 'this is not how a climax should be written. A climax should surge toward its Himalayan peak, but I am left with shreds' (426). To him, the shreds are dirt in precisely the way that real dirt is not. Throughout the novel, he manifests both the chef's and the storyteller's rage for order, a rage which is the precise opposite of any laissez-fair Bombayness. Whatever else cooking might involve, it involves a detailed understanding of relationships and ratios; too much or too little of one thing or another can destroy the total effect. Saleem is obsessed with 'when to use large (and when small) cardamoms' (461) because he understands that 'clean' things can turn into dirt with very little provocation (Cayenne pepper may not be bad in and of itself, but you do not want to mistake teaspoons for tablespoons when you are using it). Consequently, Saleem's acceptance of a variety of raw materials (including dirt) does not in itself entail a conceptual endorsement of a dirt-free world. It does not constitute any acceptance of randomness because the appropriateness and, more importantly, the desirability of various ingredients remains in the control of some overall organizing, hierarchizing presence (the chef) who will decide how much is enough of any given thing. Again, this is as true of Saleem's narrative as it is of his chutney; both his contempt for the 'fare dodgers' intruding on his narrative and his frustration at all interruptions to his creative/commemorative process speak to his desire for authoritative influence. Bluntly, he has a clear sense of what 'narrative dirt' is and he wants it expunged.

I say all this to contextualize what I regard as some of the more significant points of connection between the two novels. Obviously, *White Teeth* shares *Midnight's Children*'s concern with the question of purity and its relationship to history. It also lends itself very easily to several of Rushdie's descriptions of his own literary output. In *Imaginary Homelands* Rushdie sees his work as both 'a love-song to our mongrel selves' (394) and an assertion that 'cross-pollination is everywhere' (20). In the same collection of essays, he champions London as 'a metropolis in which [a] multiplicity of commingled faiths and cultures' (16) productively coexist. All of these descriptions apply to *White Teeth* in an unreasonably straightforward manner, and the echo of Rushdie haunts several critical assessments of Smith. Head, for example, reads *White Teeth* as a 'summative portrayal of a *de facto* hybrid cultural life' (106), and Laura Moss sees it as an energetic affirmation of the fact that 'what constitutes the ordinary English subject is no longer based on a white Church-of-England norm' (14). In Caryl Phillips' terms, *White Teeth* reflects the 'helpless heterogeneity' (11) of contemporary cultural life.

All of these assessments seem fair enough as regards the world *White Teeth* depicts and the politics it encodes, yet the ease with which Rushdie's fiction and non-fiction can be used to describe Smith's novel ought to suggest something less than hybrid and less than heterogeneous in *White Teeth*. If Rushdie is correct when he contends in *Imaginary Homelands* that the successful contemporary novel 'dissents [...] from imposed orthodoxies *of all types*' (396), it is difficult for me to imagine what kind of dissent or heresy, (what kind of narratological dirt) he finds in *White Teeth*. As Sanjay Iyer recognizes, 'Rushdie, as literary giant, has powerfully set the terms for inclusion in [the] countercanon' (2) and, by the time *White Teeth* comes along there is a lot less 'counter' involved than there once might have been.

Rushdie, it seems clear, has created, endorsed and encoded a kind of orthodoxy out of a specific mode of hybridity. In the space remaining, I would like to point to some of the more obvious ways in which *White Teeth* duplicates *Midnight's Children*, and argue that the heterogeneity of Smith's novel might be less 'helpless' than Phillips suggests; its heterogeneity might be more clean, more pure, than is acknowledged, might demonstrate an essentially monologic response to a reified notion of cultural hybridity. Despite *White Teeth*'s apparent endorsement of a world in which 'roots won't matter' (527), both its procedures and its reception are rooted in its most obvious antecedent. Despite its very clear suspicions about the ethical implications of cloning, *White Teeth*'s vision of heterogeneity often looks like hybridity-by-design, a Monsanto hybrid more than a mongrel. Rushdie might see himself as history's bastard, but *White Teeth*, I contend, is an authenticated and endorsed heir to a well-defined literary legacy, a legacy which is apparent on almost every page of Smith's novel.

To begin with some of the more obvious matters, *White Teeth* makes a clear and direct substitution of the oral cavity for *Midnight's Children*'s nasal cavity; it then proceeds to foreground strikingly similar issues regarding the relationship between the individual and history. While Rushdie's novel uses the nose as 'the place where the outside world meets the world inside you' (17), Smith's narrative uses the mouth as an extended metaphor for the search for some kind of 'uncontaminated cavity' (517), a space outside the influence of complicated individual and collective histories. The various dental problems and root canals that inform each character's life serve as a repeated citation of Rushdie's idea that the space *inside* is inextricably linked to the space outside, that, despite Irie's hopes to the contrary, Alsana is correct to think 'there are no neutral spaces anymore' (453). Just as Saleem's nose becomes the site of a variety of traumas that shape his life as a whole, teeth that are broken, impacted and poorly cleaned figure into many of *White Teeths*'s most important scenes.

Both novels also very clearly revolve around liminal, watershed notions of time. While Saleem is born on the stroke of Indian independence, *White Teeth* uses the idea of both New Year and new millennium to imagine a very similar kind of ontological zero-hour. *White Teeth* leans heavily on *Midnight's Children*'s concept of midnight as the moment 'when we step out from the old [and] to the new' (116). Smith describes every New Year's Eve in her novel as both a new start as an 'impending apocalypse in miniature' (497), simultaneously a chance to begin again, and an admission that Saleem was right to think 'we simply cannot think our way out of the past' (118). In *White Teeth*, when Irie tellingly hears her mother's 'midnight voice' (378) for the first time and discovers Clara's false teeth (and consequently realizes the presence of a decidedly contaminated oral cavity), Clara tells her, 'It's not the end of the world', yet for Irie, 'it was, in a way' (379). Both novels, then, use midnight's status as both the middle of the night and the beginning of the new day to highlight the degree to which the pure is always contaminated (the degree to which the new is simultaneously the old) as part of their almost identical efforts to highlight the multifaceted nature of the identities they are depicting.

In terms of style, there are moments in *White Teeth* when the Rushdie citation gets so pronounced the voices and preoccupations of the novels appear to merge. When Smith writes, 'Ah, Alsana's culinary nose for guilt, deceit and fear was without equal' (147) it is not difficult to imagine she's crossed over into the kitchens of *Midnight's Children*, where Saleem is obliged to eat the 'meatballs of intransigence' (139) and the 'curries of disquiet' (331). When Smith writes, 'Inside Ambrosia, waters broke. Outside Ambrosia, the floor cracked' (361), it cannot help but recall Saleem's notion of the 'eternal opposition of inside and outside' (236). Smith also closely mimics Saleem's ideas of storytelling with her narrator's parenthetical comments about the art of storytelling: 'If this story is to be told, we will have to put [the Bowdens] back inside each other like Russian dolls, Irie back in Clara, Clara back in Hortense, Hortense back in Ambrosia' (356). This not only sounds like something Saleem would say (right down to the use of parentheses), but serves as an endorsement of his comment that 'to understand just one life, you have to swallow the world' (109). All this being so, it is hard to accept Head's suggestion that, in *White Teeth*, Smith has found 'way of harnessing the novel's capacity to embrace heterogeneity (107). Instead, I see a very good novel duplicating the successful procedures of its most obvious predecessor.

The above similarities alone ought to reveal a kind of post-Rushdie orthodoxy in *White Teeth*, but I want to go further to investigate both Smith's use of diametrically opposed twins and her depiction of fundamentalism in light of the template *Midnight's Children* provides. In my view, Millat and Magid are so closely modelled on Saleem and Shiva that they come close to undercutting the novel's larger argument about the problems inherent in cloning, paradoxically endorsing reproductive procedures which are homogenized rather than hybrid. In his essay on Rushdie and the problems of fundamentalism, Mark Wormald suggests that Rushdie provides a narrative method 'that springs from history in the way people do, messily, richly, chaotically' (188), an idea that has also been enthusiastically applied to Smith. Yet, in her heavily influenced construction of these identical twins, Smith seems to reassert the procedures of a known order rather than invite new possibilities, to employ a kind of narrative mathematics in which two multiplied by two equals one. In Bauman's terms, she (inadvertently) becomes a kind of purity-seeker, an agent of a system intent on 'remaining forever identical with itself' (12). Or, to take it directly from *Midnight's Children*, Smith's twins seem

like evidence that the 'ruling dynasty [has] learned how to replicate itself'
(429).

Like Saleem and Shiva, Smith's twins encode a wide variety of religious
and class antagonisms, antagonisms that seem to render the dream of a
pluralistic, tolerant society untenable. Beyond these differences in religion
or cultural affiliation, though, I see both conflicts in terms of hegemonic
masculinity, as conflicts that result in the subordination of the 'sissy'.
In *Manhood in the Making*, David Gilmore maintains that hegemonic
masculinities are ultimately a matter of 'visible concrete accomplishments'.
Real Men *do* things while subordinate masculinities ponder and reflect.
In *Midnight's Children*, Saleem's telepathic powers are always decidedly
invisible and consequently feminized, while his antagonist deals exclusively
in the concrete. Throughout the novel, Saleem is defined in terms of a
kind of metaphorical (and therefore self-reflexive) power, while Shiva is
defined in terms of a mammoth physical force. The opposition of nose and
knees is, in effect, the opposition of the conventionally feminine and the
conventionally masculine. In Saleem's own terms, it is a contest between
a feminized 'passive metaphorical' (he has only the internalized power to
receive thoughts and feelings but cannot actively do anything) and a very
macho version of the 'active literal' (Shiva *does* things as a result of his
physical power and virility). While Saleem is involved in a perpetual process
of self-reflection that leads to his disintegration, Shiva reminds him that
'the world is not ideas, rich boy; the world is no place for dreamers or their
dreams; the world [...] is things' (255). This assertion of the primacy of the
concrete extends into the reproductive arena, as Shiva produces thousands
of heirs while Saleem is physically unable to consummate his relationship
with Parvati.

Perhaps rather too similarly, in *White Teeth* Magid and Millat are
configured along the same divide between a robust masculinity (focused on
the visible and concrete) and an effete, contemplative, feminized interiority.
While the young Millat has a 'passion for obscenities and a noisy show
about an A-Team' (180), Magid appears 'with specs perched upon his nose
like some dwarf librarian' (134). While Millat attracts 'vistas of available
and willing pussy stretching in every direction' (369), Magid is defined (by
his own father) in terms of 'his bow-ties and his Adam Smith and his E. M.
bloody Forster and his atheism!' (424). Magid's single sexual encounter is
motivated by Irie's surplus lust for his brother, demonstrating once again
the disconnection between virile heteronormative masculinity and Magid's
feminized self-reflective tendencies. When Millat's fundamentalist friends
get caught up in 'the question of *translation*' (501) of a particular passage
of the Qur'ān, Millat sees the group's recourse to the linguistic and the
metaphorical as unmasculine and undignified. He asks of them, 'Is that
what we joined KEVIN for? To take no action? To sit around on our arses
playing with words?' (502). Like Rushdie's Shiva, Millat believes the world
is things, and his violent action at the end of the novel is the result of a

doubt-free worldview that is not concerned with complex ideas or contra-dictions. Millat knows what dirt is, and he is more than prepared to clean it up.

KEVIN, of course, is not the only fundamentalist organization in *White Teeth*. The left-wing fringe of animal rights activists parody their right-wing counterparts in their efforts to provide a singularly defined order, and even self-consciously atheistic characters like Clara and Irie feel the impulse towards a pure, uncontaminated world. After rejecting her mother's religion, Clara mourns the loss of 'the all-enveloping bear hug of the Saviour, the One who was Alpha and Omega' (45). Irie, after becoming disillusioned with 'the *purity*' (328) of the Chalfens, begins to imagine Jamaica as dirt-free, 'fresh and untainted and without past or dictated future [...] A blank page' (402).

White Teeth also revives *Midnight's Children*'s interest in issues to do with perfectibility and cloning. In Rushdie's novel, the Black Widow's forced sterilization programme makes the links among 'cleanliness', 'purity' and 'sterility' literal rather than simply metaphorical. The way to clean out the magicians' ghetto is literally to sterilize it; the neigh-bourhood is 'a public eyesore [that] can no longer be tolerated' (429) and the open-ended alterity inherent in the magicians' fertility is a threat to an order determined to remain forever identical with itself. Smith has a similar preoccupation about the correlation between reproduction, infes-tation, order and dirt. A small-scale example occurs very early in *White Teeth*, when Mo Hussein-Ishmael seeks to clean up his environment by redefining (and expanding) the definition of dirt as regards the pigeons that congregate outside his shop. He thinks 'With pigeons you have to get to the root of the problem: not the excretions but the pigeon itself. *The shit is not the shit* (this was Mo's mantra), *the pigeon is the shit*' (5). This idea is amplified and extended through the figure of Dr Marc-Pierre Perret, an agent of the Nazi 'sterilization programme, and later the euthanasia policy' (106). In Smith's novel, the familiar concern about the random (hence dirty) factors in 'natural' reproduction (especially the unregulated reproduction of magicians, pigeons and other undesir-ables) is figured most prominently in the Nazi doctor, who, like other purity-seekers, sees all-encompassing order as desirable and achievable, fragmentation as contagion. As he prepares for what he imagines to be his death, he tells Archie, 'It is such a terrible thing, to know only in part. A terrible thing not to have perfection, human perfection, when it is so readily available' (538). At the end of the novel, when it is revealed that Perret later acted as Marcus Chalfen's mentor, Smith directly links the Nazi programme with Marcus's effort to 'eliminate the random' (366) in reproduction, an effort which amounts to an attempt to eradicate biological dirt. Although Marcus imagines himself to be involved in a process of *generating* a desirable life in the future, the young student he meets at the airport reminds him that that such order can only be defined negatively inasmuch as it seeks to 'eliminate "undesirable" qualities in people' (418).

The fear of the partial (the fragmentary, the hybrid) as dirt is also seen in the desire of the Jehovah Witnesses, Hortense Bowden and Ryan Topps, who cling to the totalizing life recipes their religion offers. As a young woman, Hortense was mortified when the apocalypse *failed* to occur on 1 January 1925, because, in her rigid worldview, 'the continuance of daily life, the regular running of buses and trains' (32) amounted to an affront to her system of order, an error that ought not to have occurred. Under the influence of such a strict system of order, it is hardly surprising that she believes '"Black and white never come to no good. De Lord Jesus never meant us to mix it up"' (384–5); and, such mixing it up, of course, entails disorder.

In *Imaginary Homelands*, Rushdie maintains that 'a bit of this and a bit of that is *how newness enters the world*' (394), yet in *White Teeth* newness is exactly what Hortense and Ryan reject in favour of the perpetual sameness of a divine and stable system. Ryan's faith appeals to his 'mono-intelligence', his 'ability to hold onto a single idea with phenomenal tenacity' (509). Just as Marcus Chalfen's project involves an effort at an 'intellectual faith' (422) that produces 'certainty in its purist form' (490), Ryan believes religion gives him an unambiguous hierarchical position: 'the right to be always *right*' (510), with faith functioning as 'the biggest fuck-off light sabre in the universe' (509).

Given the cultural politics of the novel as a whole, it is not surprising that those who do not have, or do not want, 'the fuck-off light sabre' of absolute certainty emerge as *White Teeth*'s muted, fragmentary, hybrid heroes. While others seek pure (capital 'T') Truth, Alsana rejects absolutist principles, claiming that she 'cannot be worrying-worrying all the time about the *truth*. I have to worry about the truth that can be *lived with*' (80); clearly, this is 'mongrel' not pure, truth. When Samad makes the unilateral decision to separate her sons, Alsana combats him by withdrawing completely from the binary world his decision creates. Determined 'never to say *yes* to him [Samad], never to say *no* to him' (213), she endeavours to teach him a hard lesson about 'never *knowing*, never being *sure*' (214). For Alsana, her '*exquisite* revenge' (214) against the discourse of certitude is not defined in terms of a head to head conflict with her husband, but through a systematic destabilization of the overarching assumptions of authority that made his action possible in the first place.

Again, I think Rushdie's influence is excessively prominent in these constructions. Alsana's may be a mongrel vision of truth, but it is a purebred mongrelization that comes from a clear source with overt authentication. That ought to be a problem when we claim to be celebrating alterity, hybridity, 'helpless heterogeneity' and so forth. Crudely, I think the interior discourse of the novel is in tension with the larger discourses which enclose it. In his essay on satire and the Menippean grotesque in

Midnight's Children, John Clement Ball cites Graham Pechey's argument about polyphonic voices in Bakhtin. In that argument Pechey claims that 'the true priority of heteroglossia is never realised as decisive victory' (52), yet the commercial and critical 'victory' of *White Teeth* is about as decisive as it gets, and it is much more triumphal than it is ambiguous. As a character inside a novel Alsana is aligned against linearity and certitude, yet a larger certitude about reified narrative signals and practices encloses her uncertainty. In the context of a post-Rushdie orthodoxy, we know *for certain* that uncertainty is good, and even if Alsana is opposed to linearity, it is very easy to draw a clear, straight line between Rushdie and Smith.

The characterization of Archie works in a similar way. Inside the narrow context of *White Teeth,* Archie is depicted as an unlikely hero, yet in the larger interpretive context, he is a very likely hero indeed, predictable precisely because we know archetypal heroism has now been refigured as narrative dirt. Archie's dithering, the fact that he is 'never able to make a decision, never able to state a position' (55) works as a clear ironic counterpoint to the novel's various overzealous purity seekers, and marks him as someone singularly incapable of the self-certitude from which atrocities arise. As a result, he reinforces the hegemony of the hybrid, reaffirms the necessity of ambiguous self-positioning and critiques the blinkered shortcomings of linear self-definition. In short, he is precisely the type of hero a post-Rushdie orthodoxy demands. Not surprisingly, *Midnight's Children* provides a summative description of valorized heroic befuddlement which applies to Archie every bit as much as it does to Saleem. Faced with the suggestion that his narrative might be wavering, going wrong, Saleem sees rightness where others see waywardness: 'if you're a little uncertain of my reliability, well, a little uncertainty is no bad thing. Cocksure men do terrible deeds' (212). The problem, of course, is that *White Teeth* is not wayward *enough*, that it relies on an established mode of unreliability for a great deal of its effect.

Given all of the above, it may now seem disingenuous to close by saying that I still think *White Teeth* is a very good book. Yet, I *do* offer just such a judgement. What I have been attempting to suggest here is not that *White Teeth* is a derivative failure, but that the terms under which it succeeds have been seriously misrepresented. I have been trying to demonstrate that critical and popular tastes for 'hybrid' narratives are considerably more homogenized than has been acknowledged, fuelling a self-congratulatory sense that we have developed an eclectic literary culture, when such eclecticism has become an established, authenticated and naturalized aesthetic. I still think *White Teeth* is smart, interesting and funny, but I also appreciate that it appeals precisely to tastes I *know* I have; it abides by its own orthodoxies (ones I generally share), and, as such, it did not and could not shock me into an entirely new understanding of life or literature.

With all of this in mind, I would like to return one last time to the jacket of my edition of *White Teeth* to consider both Rushdie's endorsement of the novel as 'an astonishingly assured debut' and *The Guardian*'s comment that the book is 'relentlessly funny ... idiosyncratic and deeply felt'. Rushdie's judgement about the novel's sense of self-assurance and *The Guardian*'s suggestion that the book is both comic and emotionally resonant are difficult to contest, yet I find it hard to imagine that Rushdie could be astonished by a book that is, in terms of its content, style and thematic preoccupation, so very like his own greatest achievement. In *Imaginary Homelands*, Rushdie famously claims that the novelist can never become 'the servant of some beetle-browed ideology' (98) but must always remain 'its critic, its antagonist, its scourge' (99). 'The greater the writer' he says, 'the greater his or her exceptionality' (425). Yet, his whole-hearted endorsement of Smith seems narcissistic rather than oppositional, applauding work that is closely modeled on his own brand of orthodoxy. Just as in *Midnight's Children* Saleem is not 'immune to the lure of leadership' (227) and seeks his own form of purity, Rushdie, it seems, is not beyond self-affirming modes of (re)production that tend towards the homogenous rather than the heterogeneous.

In her essay on Rushdie's influence on the English novel in India (an essay that first appeared before the publication of *White Teeth*), Rege identifies six key elements in Rushdie's aesthetic. The standard-issue Rushdie text is one which: (i) is multigenerational in scope; (ii) rejects the traditions of conventional social realism; (iii) combines English and non-standard English; (iv) employs a sprawling style; (v) investigates a variety of contestatory narrative forms (including myth, oral tradition and history); and (vi) displays an irreverence for sacred cows of nationalism and religion (171). Clearly this could serve as a critical template for Smith's novel, and that should bother people more than it seems to. Instead, critical responses to *White Teeth* gravitate towards predictable, and perhaps disingenuous, conceptions of a newness that is not really new, an idiosyncrasy that is not very idiosyncratic. A systemic conception of the hybrid is established, and a new model of what I will call 'narrative purity' solidifies into an increasingly orthodox notion of what amounts to the 'proper' method of contemporary narrative construction.

In *Imaginary Homelands* Rushdie claims repeatedly that the purpose of the novel is to 'open up the universe a little more' (155), but here I have tried to suggest that just the opposite might be true, that the extraordinary success of *White Teeth* might have less to do with 'our mongrel selves' than it does with some very predictable and ordered modes of production and reception, that *White Teeth*'s hybridity is a pretty 'purebred' affair. When it comes to contemporary book sales and critical acclaim, *following* established rules and duplicating 'productive' reproductive procedures seems to work very well indeed. In both Rushdie and Smith, the desire to eliminate unanticipated fare-dodgers and reinforce established recipes is perversely pronounced. If the manifold similarities between *White Teeth* and *Midnight's Children* and the mutual admiration of their authors are any indication, Rushdie and Smith have several obvious and cherished classifications, and they maintain them with consistency and zeal. They also do not seem to like unanticipated surprises as much as they immediately appear to. In some odd way, then, the relationships between *Midnight's Children* and *White Teeth* might serve as a paradoxical testimony to hyper-organized, self-duplicating Chalfenism rather than 'helpless heterogeneity:' if you want succeed, stick to the plan, keep the variables to a minimum, keep the place clean. Maybe Marcus Chalfen was right; if 'You eliminate the random, you rule the world' (341).

Bibliography

Ball, John Clement. 'Pessoptimism: Satire and the Menippean Grotesque in Rushdie's *Midnight's Children*'. *Salman Rushdie*. Harold Bloom (ed.). Broomall, PA: Chelsea House Publishers, 2003, 209–32.

Bauman, Zygmunt. *Postmodernity and its Discontents*. New York: New York University Press, 1997.

Douglas, Mary. *Purity and Danger: An Analysis of the Concepts of Pollution and Taboo*. London: Ark Paperbacks, 1985 [1966].

Gilmore, David. *Manhood in the Making: Cultural Concepts of Masculinity*. New York: Yale University Press, 1990.

Head, Dominic. 'Zadie Smith's *White Teeth*: Multiculturalism for the Millennium'. *Contemporary British Fiction*, Richard J. Lane, Rod Mengham and Philip Tew (eds). Cambridge: Polity Press, 2003: 106–19.

Iyer, Sanjay. 'East, West, No More Home is Best: *East West*'. *Indian Review of Books*. 4(3), 16 January–15 February (1995): 2–3.

Moss, Laura. 'The Politics of Everyday Hybridity'. *Wasafiri*. 39 (Summer 2003): 11–17.

Pechey, Graham. 'On the Borders of Bakhtin: Dialogisation, Decolonisation'. *Bakhtin and Cultural Theory*. Ken Hirschkop and David Shepherd (eds). Manchester: Manchester University Press, 1989, 39–67.

Phillips, Caryl. 'Mixed and Matched. Review of Zadie Smith's *White Teeth*'. *The Observer*. 9 January 2000: 11.

Rege, Josna E. 'Victim into Protagonist? *Midnight's Children* and the Post-Rushdie National Narratives of the Eighties'. *Salman Rushdie*, Harold Bloom (ed.). Broomall, PA: Chelsea House Publishers, 2003, 145–83.

Rushdie, Salman. *Imaginary Homelands*. London: Granta, 1991.

—*Midnight's Children*. Toronto: Vintage, 1997 [1981].

Said, Edward. *Culture and Imperialism*. New York: Vintage, 1994.

Shohat, Ella. 'Notes on the 'Post-Colonial'. *Social Text*. 10 (1992): 99–113.

Smith, Zadie. *White Teeth*. London: Penguin, 2001 [2000].

Wormald, Mark. 'The Uses of Impurity: Fiction and Fundamentalism in Salman Rushdie and Jeanette Winterson'. *An Introduction to Contemporary Fiction: International Writing in English Since 1970*. Rod Mengham (ed.). Cambridge: Polity Press, 1999, 182–202.

12

Zadie Smith's Short Stories: Englishness in a Globalized World

Lucienne Loh

Introduction

Before Zadie Smith gained worldwide acclaim in 2000 for her first novel, *White Teeth*, she had regularly published in *The May Anthology of Oxford and Cambridge Short Stories* while a Cambridge undergraduate reading English from 1994 to 1997. These early shorter prose works reflect her continued attention to both shifting and persistent signifiers of Englishness in a post-war Britain which has witnessed unprecedented mass migration, the unification of Europe, and an increasing coalescence of American and British popular cultures. Throughout the writing of her four novels to date, Smith continued to publish short stories which scrutinized the nuances of English class attitudes drawn from tensions between what Caryl Phillips has termed 'a new world order' and 'Britain's desire to promote herself as a homogenous country whose purity is underscored not only by race and class, but, perhaps more importantly, by a sense of continuity' (292). A range of high profile transatlantic literary magazines and journals such as *Granta*, *The New Yorker* and Dave Egger's *Timothy McSweeney's Quarterly Concern* replaced the *May Anthologies*. Smith's stories now included a more intimate understanding of American life acquired during a year-long fellowship at Harvard University in 2002–3.

Certainly, Smith's time in America provided her an opportunity to contemplate contemporary English life anew and occasioned what Christian Lorentzen terms a 'retreat into Englishness' (21). In the 'Author's Note' to *Martha and Hanwell*, a slim volume in which two earlier published short stories 'Martha, Martha' (2003) and 'Hanwell in Hell' (2004) were republished, Smith admits not being 'a natural short-story writer' (vii). However, inspired by her time in America, she decided to commit herself to the form, impressed by the creative industry that surrounds the craft of short story writing in the States. Thinking about how to create such stories with particular English inflections, both in form and sensibility, Smith said, in the 'Author's Note', that she 'wanted to write English stories – emotionally satisfying, character driven – but with the kind of formal polish and control that American stories often possess' (viii). Yet, all her stories evince a particular strand of English humour that is full of irony and self-deprecation.

Smith's stories formally reflect the 'Chekhovian' narrative which William Boyd, writing about the modern British short story's evolution in 'A Short History of the Short Story', has identified as the form most favoured by current short story writers in Britain (N. Pag.). Many practitioners of the contemporary short story, including Smith, owe a debt to Chekhov's typical elements. An understanding of life's endless contingencies and absurdities, a refusal to judge characters or strive for a climax or tidy narrative resolution, stories that appear life-like, and inconclusive endings are all found in Smith's stories.

The Chekhovian narrative is a particularly apt form for Smith's interest in depicting an English post-war identity, tested by a contemporary zeitgeist driven by a rapidly shifting world seemingly unified, yet so conspicuously differentiated, by ever increasing material needs and desires. Smith's characters often struggle within an England placed against a complex global culture with its ceaseless transformation of place, identity and community as people adapt to, and accommodate, new social and political elements with various degrees of success and willingness. Indeed, her stories are particularly attentive to characters living in a neo-liberal society where loss and losing always threaten to overwhelm the self and condemn it to alienation and destitution. As Molly Thompson argues in the context of Smith's writing, 'inhabiting a multicultural society is not easy for *anyone*, and that we are all implicated by [...] our history, corporeality and nationality [which] are constantly in flux' (136) [emphasis in the original]. Thus, despite the frequent association of Smith's *White Teeth* with a celebration of post-war British multiculturalism and contemporary global culture, her short stories almost always also represent a darker, more insidious, and even unsettling aspect to contemporary life. In 'Speaking in Tongues' Smith suggests this might arise out of 'opposing dogmas, between cultures and voices', an opposition which Smith, calls the 'extreme contingency of culture' (149). Smith scrupulously depicts these contingencies through the intersubjectivities of multifaceted individuals forged from the exigencies underpinning the confluence of race, class, gender and sexual identity formations in England. Furthermore, she simultaneously seeks to identify the subtle distinctions and tensions within, and between, broader, more evident, categories of differences which construct any one of these sites of identity.

Smith challenges and eludes a homogenous sense of English culture and identity, even as she so attentively relies on an implicit understanding of the quiddity of Englishness itself. This dialectical tension between the particular, on the one hand, and on the other, the national or communal is central to my reading of her short stories. This essay clusters Smith's short stories around three significant themes. First, it explores Smith's representation of the experience of multiculturalism and Englishness through a working-class lens in a contemporary, globalized world. If Britain's ethnic communities constitute the legacy of colonialism and globalization, the white English bourgeoisie form another crucial element of that legacy in contemporary England. In several of Smith's stories, white English women uphold the values and ideologies of this class; their lives are often portrayed as being both stifling and selfish, driven by a dogmatic adherence to material preoccupations and prejudices. If Smith is particularly interested in white middle-class English women, it is instead working-class and lower middle-class English men who preoccupy her. Residual forms of post-war English masculinity fascinate Smith: she sympathetically attempts to articulate the anxieties and insecurities that affect the familial and domestic lives of working-class men and especially their relationships with their daughters. Many of these stories also serve as a gradual and intimate process of Smith's efforts to work through some of the taboos and unspoken personal histories located within her own lower middle-class, mixed-race family and, more poignantly, to confront her tenuous relationship with her white father, Harvey Smith. Especially in the stories published after *White Teeth*, one finds, too, Smith's attempts to contemplate the role fiction can play in illuminating the career path of a mainstream writer of mixed race and immigrant background only too conscious of the predominantly white middle-class reading public and literati who support her work.

Part I: British multiculturalism in a globalized world

In terms of British multiculturalism within a global culture two of Smith's stories are considered in detail in this section: 'Mrs Begum's Son and the Private Tutor' (1997) and 'Martha, Martha' (2003). 'Martha, Martha', originally published in Granta's 2003 *Best of Young British Novelists*, offers a subtle commentary on the complex modes of race relations in a world, which through globalization networks and the waves of international migration that defined the late twentieth and early twenty-first centuries, is more interconnected and more racially diverse while being simultaneously more conscious of absolute differences in material wealth. These contexts are also reflected in the story's acknowledgement of the 9/11 attacks. Smith, writing in an article titled 'Monsters' in *The New Yorker* on their tenth

anniversary argues that apart from those who died during the attack, it was
'[T]he beginning of a different sort of world for the rest of us' (N. Pag.), one
that Smith's story reflects as being ever more cognisant of class differences
between rich and poor that are at once national and transnational. 'Martha,
Martha' concerns the eponymous Miss Martha Penk, whose 'extremely
English' nature – according to Smith in her 'Author's Note' to her tale – also
shapes Martha's 'personal tragedy' (x), one with transnational dimensions.

Exceeding the brash political rhetoric which ensued in the wake of the
9/11 attacks in New York, Smith's story calibrates the layers of personal
trepidation experienced by various characters living in a small Massachusetts
college town who are all located at a remove from the geographical heart
of the 9/11 attacks. Smith also uses this seemingly innocuous local setting
to explore the consciousness of global class differences prompted by 9/11.
On a snowy day in November 2002, Martha, recently arrived in the town
from London, views a number of rental properties with an independent,
self-managed local estate agent, Pam Rogers. It transpires that their
short temporary relationship contains a microcosm of white middle-class
America's struggle to confront and to acknowledge the implications of
the 9/11 terrorist attacks. Martha's black British working-class anxieties
become heightened in this American context. The short story – largely
focalized through Pam, a middle-aged white woman of Midwestern origins
and long-term resident of the town – explores and extends a central motif
of Smith's work: white Western bourgeois liberalism and its purported
claims to a compassionate humanism. For Smith, this liberalism frequently
masks patronizing solicitousness melded with practiced social graces which
seek to compensate for discomfort from uncommunicated racial, ethnic
and cultural differences or to deflect conflict and tension. In the story,
Pam represents the global petit bourgeoisie of which working-class black
Britons, like Martha, are only too conscious; but Smith further insinuates
that Pam's class is also one whose neo-liberal values are threatened by the
9/11 attacks which had targeted, in an ideological sense, Pam's own class
of privileged capital.

The narrative perspective contrasts Martha's consciousness of being
black working class (but not necessarily poor), and her sense that she lacks
high levels of education against Pam's relative ignorance of, and unfamili-
arity with, British signifiers of race and class. While being in this small
American town frees Martha from these signifiers, she continues to be
psychologically burdened and constrained by them. When Martha arrives
at Pam's office, she immediately betrays her working-class background,
which Pam fails to read, by the declaration: 'I came right from London
and I didn't have any place arranged – I just arksed the taxi to take me
to the nearest hotel – I been there a week' (5). Pam senses a disquietude
from Martha, who is attempting to overcome the loss of an unexplained
separation from a lover in London who writes painfully crass and tacky,
if heartfelt, love poetry. Smith includes these details about Martha's lover

and hints at his education and taste to create a fuller image of Martha's class background.

Pam also suffers a sense of loss, but hers is of a middle-class variety. Pam, in contrast to Martha, appears as the quintessential petit bourgeoisie: entrepreneurial, intellectually led and emotionally guided by the traditions and recognized icons of high culture. Divorced from her husband and ousted from the sizeable family home in a posh district where she once raised her two daughters, she now lives a single life in a flat and seeks comfort in tearful Mozart arias and prides herself on her affinity with PBS. Pam maintains a tacit, seemingly innocuous tolerance towards other cultures and races, a tolerance, however, stretched by the recent events of 9/11 and its attendant racial and religious paranoia. These sentiments are betrayed as she swiftly assesses a man who mistakenly believes her office to be a temping agency. She notes 'a large, dark, bearded man' with 'a heavy accent, quickly identified [...] as 'Middle-Easterny. A Middle-Easterny scarf, too, and a hat' (3). She redirects him in measured patronizing tones and 'stared frankly' (3) back at him and his friends, daring any further exchange or exhibition of the cultural, racial, ideological and class differences she instinctively perceives. Martha, who arrives at Pam's office after the Middle Eastern men depart, appears only too aware of the class and racial differences separating her and Pam, while viewing Pam as an inspiration for her own visions of social mobility. Martha couches her move to America as a journey of self-improvement driven by her perception of white middle-class aspirations: she admits to Pam that she wishes to 'listen to more classical music' (7) as she 'looked at Pam and the surrounding office with determined reverence' before admitting to Pam that she is 'looking for that next level – qualifications, getting forward' (8).

In the wake of 9/11, Smith suggests that the bourgeoisie represented by Pam becomes enlarged, its class dimensions gaining both national and international significance. Prompted by Martha's question about Pam's move to a smaller city apartment from a wealthy neighbourhood lined with large houses, Pam proffers the following explanation: due to age 'and especially in the light of the events of last September, I just think you have to make things work for you, work for you *personally*, because life is really too short, and if they don't work, you just have to go ahead and cut them loose' (16) [emphasis in the original]. The fear generated by the 9/11 attacks, politically represented in terms of a symbolic national assault on America and its neo-liberal values, has purportedly inspired Pam's 'personally' transformative decisions, whereby the public insecurity which underpins a nebulous terror threat becomes a pitiful response shielding her private unhappiness. Smith subtly underscores the self preoccupation lying at the heart of Pam's class which serves as a greater motivating force than any genuine political engagement or ideological consciousness.

The story's central irony and the source of Martha's tragedy lie in her fervent and thwarted desire to possess the material and racial self-confidence that Pam displays, a stance which Smith implicitly critiques. Smith renders the desires of black upward mobility in much fuller detail in her 2012 novel, NW and in 'Martha, Martha', Martha's hopes are temporarily arrested at the end of the story when she becomes distraught during a visit to a potential property she envies but cannot afford. The occupants – a self-assured, mixed-race, cosmopolitan, middle-class couple – undermine Martha's sense of her new self and her material desires and she is met with the crisis of wishing to be something she is not. Her bruised confidence, however, is immutably linked to insecurities from being working-class and black within contemporary Britain where ethnicity is often mediated and experienced through the struggles of the nation's divisive class system. In this moment, Martha experiences contemporary Britain's new racism, where cultural discourses that define identity in terms of exclusion, segregation or banishment, conjoin with class anxieties on a global scale. These generate emotional and psychological vulnerabilities which overwhelm Martha in America where she had most hoped to overcome these very limitations and Smith suggests that race and class relations in Britain can take on the global dimensions which 9/11 precipitated. Indeed, the story resonates with Smith's more sustained effort in NW to depict a black existential crisis of the early twenty-first century.

Smith suggests in an earlier short story, 'Mrs Begum's Son and the Private Tutor' that some of the self-confidence Martha seeks in America may be found in ethnic communities in Britain. However, this self-confidence also promotes a strained liberalism often disguised and misconceived as a flourishing urban multiculturalism. Originally published in the 1997 May Anthology of Oxford and Cambridge Short Stories, 'Mrs Begum's Son and the Private Tutor' focuses on the relationship between a white middle-class writer, Alex Pembrose, working as a part-time tutor, and his tutee, Magid Begum, a young boy of ten from a working-class Bengali family.

Like 'Martha, Martha', this earlier story's milieu is small and localized, but this time the backdrop is Smith's more familiar territory of Willesden Green during the 1990s. Smith sets her story against the broader political landscape of Thatcher's legacies, whose ideologies of the free market, hard work and private entrepreneurship seemed racially inclusive, but whose open hostility to immigrant cultures, through what Caryl Phillips terms her 'continued incantation of a discordant, neo-imperial rhetoric of exclusion' (304) also stoked ethnic and racial tensions throughout the country. Various members of Magid's working-class immigrant family reflect this context: his timid father slaves away as a waiter in an Indian restaurant while his vocal and ambitious mother, Mrs Begum – has placed an unfounded faith in Magid, whom she believes possesses a superior, natural intelligence which he needs to fulfil at all and any costs through extra tutoring in order to ultimately enable Magid to 'one day, save his people' (92). Magid himself appears sensitive to the economic and social marginalization of Bengali and other South Asian immigrants living in multi-ethnic Willesden. While this earlier story lacks the subtlety of 'Martha, Martha', it too represents many of the racial and ethnic strains making a mockery out of British multiculturalism and the spirit of liberalism that aims to support it. Salman Rushdie argues in *Imaginary Homelands* that 'multiculturalism' is 'a new catchword', and 'the latest token gesture towards Britain's blacks, and it ought to be exposed, like "integration" and "racial harmony", for the sham it is' (137). Indeed, Philip Tew argues that the story offers a 'precise critique of a failing liberalism' (155). This failing liberalism, embodied by Pam in 'Martha, Martha' is also inherent in Smith's style in 'Mrs Begum's Son the Private Tutor'. Through the exaggerated and excessive use of colour tones, Smith ironises the sweeping celebration of ethnic 'colour' that white English liberalism associates with immigrant communities, but which are also often the source of mutual hostility and frustration. Mrs Begum's youngest child is described as 'a little girl all in pink' (89) who force feeds Alex some

> sweets [which] were pink like the child and tasted pink, far too much so; between this sickly pink, the outrageous red of the carpet and wall (the wall was carpeted), the strident green of the sofa suite, the gaudy orange of the 24 set children's encyclopedia that dominated the bookshelf, and the blinding yellow of Alsana Begum's selwar khamise – a peculiar synisthesia happened – the room gave you indigestion. (90)

Conjuring an immigrant landscape that literally dislocates Alex's senses and makes him physically ill, Smith uses heightened, hyperbolic and hyperreal language alongside an excess of colour to destabalize the signifiers within a liberal 'positive' multiculturalism which she subjects to postmodern parody. Alex's white middle-class girlfriend, Alison, also an aspiring writer, personifies this perspective of a 'colourful' multiculturalism. She thinks of immigrants such as Magid and his family in flippant phrases such as 'Exodus, Diaspora' (95). In a red sari and fake bindi, she attends the official opening of the local Asian Women's Centre and delightedly declares to Alex how 'happy' she was that they lived in Willesden and how '"colourful" it was after all those little grey University towns' (111). Alison symbolizes another aspect of a failing liberalism which lauds pluralism and shuns bigotry, yet is glibly ignorant about the historical and racial oppression suffered by working-class immigrants within a longer legacy of British colonial exploitation, a legacy that Mark, Magid's brother, 'the white liberal nightmare' (105) resists with violence and outspoken, virulent hatred. E. San Juan Jr, argues that '[C]ultural pluralism via [...] the "multicultural Imaginary" [...] may be regarded as the principal ideological strategy of the ruling bourgeoisie in the post-Cold War era' (12). Indeed, the positive celebration of multiculturalism in Smith's *White Teeth* fails to account for her critique of the vicious politics of difference in Britain's purportedly 'Happy Multicultural Land' (465), a critique that is similarly evident in this story which forms a precursor to the novel.

Smith suggests liberalism can be superficially deployed as a response to this sense of historical injustice to create exclusive working-class ethnic identities and communities in Britain. Mrs Begum declares to Alex: 'Magid is Bengali. I don't expect you to know what this means. You can never be us and we, thankfully, will never be you. Luckily, in this borough, however, we have mutual understandings. We are all *liberals* here!' (91) [emphasis in the original]. The short story, then, depicts a floundering liberalism, whereby different ethnic camps with divergent, self-serving agendas exist in strained mutual tolerance within a society of individualists who occasional defer to collective identities. Certainly, this bleaker vision of multiculturalism is not usually credited to Smith, but as Dave Gunning argues, Smith suggests that 'ethnicity loses some of its connection to definable community structures. Instead a conception of ethnicity as an individual's relation to history begins to emerge: a contingent articulation of a necessary relation to an imagined past' (136).

Part II: Smith's white English bourgeois women

In both 'Martha, Martha' and 'Mrs Begum's Son and the Private Tutor', white middle-class women such as Pam and Alison serve as foils for British working-class ethnic characters, but such women also act as ciphers for Smith's critique of populist, celebratory attitudes towards contemporary multiculturalism. In several of Smith's short stories, however, these women serve as the central characters and receive a more thorough examination within their own social spheres. They feature not only in 'Mirrored Box', the first of Smith's stories to be published in 1995 in *The May Anthologies*, but also in 'Picnic, Lightning' (1997), 'The Girl with Bangs' (2001), and 'The Trials of Finch' (2002). Throughout the first three of these stories, Smith explores female sexual freedom and expression which are constrained and determined by the gendered expectations of middle-class Englishness. In 'Mirrored Box' and 'Picnic, Lightning', upper middle-class English women of considerable wealth and social standing breach the narrow racial and class boundaries which circumscribe their class privilege to discover, and indulge in, their own sexual pleasures. The former story features a recently separated woman of faded aristocratic beauty while in the latter story, a London-based woman travels to Paris daily to fulfil her daily diplomatic commitments. Banal material obsessions stoically pursued by this class of conservative white English bourgeois women encapsulate the repressive social codes under which both women are expected to live: they include concerns with the cleanliness of skirting boards and curtains in 'Mirrored Box' (126), or alertness to the necessity of standing 'up knees together like a lady [...]' in a 'neat navy two-piece (115)' in 'Picnic, Lightning'. Smith suggests these women project their own sexual frustrations and unhappiness onto such material preoccupations and forms of social decorum. Both women cross the class divide to pursue relationships with racial others of an inferior class in a world which is seen to easily present such possibilities. However, the fetishization of class and racial difference appears more prevalent in the Parisian affair between the London diplomat and her young, bisexual Arab lover than in the lesbian liaison between the aristocratic woman and her Spanish housemaid. Thus, Smith uses the sexual awakening experienced by the women in both stories as an implicit critique of white bourgeois English sexual mores and social codes.

In both 'Picnic, Lightning' (1997) and 'The Girl with Bangs' (2001), Smith suggests the narcissistic quality of bourgeois consumerism through narrative perspectives of a world existing to serve and satisfy the self, where other people are viewed predominantly as commodities. In both the stories, Smith's voyeuristic narrative style and perspective are employed as homage to Nabokov. In 'Picnic, Lightning' the narrator observes 'things [that] are the product of the personal, obsessive eye of the beholder' (118). 'The Trials of Finch' (2002), set in leafy Hampstead, further highlights this perspective. The story circles around a group of bourgeois white English women who patronize and objectify Finch, an insecure, vulnerable, guileless woman suffering long-term psychological problems and emotional trauma. Smith scrutinizes the behaviour of a highly feminized circle whose members are thoroughly determined by their material conditions and their relationship to neo-liberal capital: big cars and houses fortify their domestic lives, the challenges they face largely revolve around professionally successful husbands whose substantial salaries sustain their leisured lifestyles, but who prove consistently unfaithful. For these women, Finch's dysfunctionality affords a terrifying index of what they could have become: 'the lonely mad, who were visible everywhere in Hampstead' (116). Despite her comparable wealth and class status, Finch, remains unloved, unsexy, uncared for, childless and desperate for attention. These women use Finch to feel relatively less beleaguered by their own bourgeois despondency and dissatisfactions.

The middle classes are a consistent source of social commentary about white Englishness for Smith. 'The middle classes are irresistible [...] to a lot of people', Smith says to Gretchen Holbrook Gerzina, 'and it's only later that you start to realize the problems with that' (275). In such stories, Smith repeatedly reveals the women's consistent psychological shallowness and material self-satisfaction, falsely buoyed by a sense of class superiority which frequently belies small everyday cruelties towards others.

Part III: Post-war English Masculinity and Smith's men

While Smith often satirizes white, middle-class English women, English men are generally portrayed more sympathetically. Such men hail from either working-class or lower middle-class backgrounds, and frequently contend with the seeming opprobrium of family life, yet they often represent a lingering, admirable, if easily forgotten, expression of Englishness. Nick Bentley has argued that despite Smith's interest in positively depicting the shifting landscape of English multiculturalism, she simultaneously longs nostalgically for a 'residual' form of Englishness embodied by unassuming, apathetic but tolerant white men who nonetheless possess 'an inherent goodness' (497–8). Oftentimes, such men seem alienated within a postmodern world of relentless change and constant self-modification. The father figure in 'The Newspaper Man' represents this manifestation of white English masculinity. The story reveals the tensions in terms of intersecting gender and class perspectives in a father/daughter relationship focalized through a middle-class, moderately successful mixed-race artist, Ruth Mackintyre, who attempts to come to terms with her relationship with her white working-class father whom she has painted in larger than life scale in a work entitled 'The Newspaper Man'. First published in the *May Anthology* of 1996, the story reveals a more autobiographical element than other early stories, since like Ruth, Zadie Smith's father was white, while her mother is black. Indeed, Smith's own academic and artistic success separated the writer from her own lower middle-class origins. In Cressida Leyshon's 'This Week in Fiction: Zadie Smith', Smith reveals that the conscious knowledge of different social spheres underpins much of her own creative work: '[e]very time I write a sentence I'm thinking not only of the people I ended up in college with but my siblings, my family, my school friend, the people from my neighborhood' (N. Pag.). 'The Newspaper Man' demonstrates the self-consciousness of Smith's success as a writer and her more humble beginnings. The story hinges on the ironies created by the juxtaposition between the retrospective innocence of the daughter as a child and the more knowing narrative perspective of the adult daughter who has recently moved to Italy after tiring of England. Ruth's white English father features many aspects of English masculinity she finds depressing and oppressive, but shortly after her arrival in Italy, news that her father may be about to draw his last breath reaches her. The story revolves around this life-changing revelation through which many of the recollected details of Ruth's childhood with her father are refracted.

This story articulates with compassion the unspoken anxieties, tensions and resentments that arise when a child successfully crosses over from working to middle-class identity within a family history which has simultaneously witnessed the parent's own inability themselves to transcend those very class boundaries. Ruth's attendant shame at the recollection of her father's efforts to wrest a bourgeois respectability that she, in contrast, achieves with relative ease through academic achievement and creative endeavour structure the story. As a child, Ruth remembers trying to explain to her primary school English teacher the divide that distinguishes her from her father as he awkwardly and ignorantly runs through a series of classic nineteenth-century novels: 'he is working class I mean and I am educated' (13). Ruth's childish instinctive sense of being assessed by her parentage and her innate desire to distance herself from her father's class insecurities in terms she is only able to articulate as an adult with a more precise vocabulary and understanding of English class dynamics reflect an uncanny acknowledgement of irrevocable biological bonds rooted in '[T]he security and the faith in similarity, in the concrete fact of beget-ing' (32). Smith suggests that childhood exposure to any parent's angst and struggles to overcome the restrictions of English class identity become automatically infused within one's lineage, one's 'begetting'. As an adult, professional differences between herself and her father doubly complicate Ruth's inheritance. While for most of his working life, her father was a subservient assistant in a middling advertising job, Ruth had become a professional artist, inhabiting an artistic world celebrating self-assured freedom of expression, middle-class pretensions and material self-entitlement. Her father responds to this world with disdain: he hated '[T]he university educated "types", the free wine, the glib conversation, the middle-class-ness was something he dreaded, really feared because, of course, he desired so much to be part of it' (23). If Smith herself, like Ruth, absorbed some of her own father's class anxieties, Smith, too, reflects this in her use of fiction. Ruth attempts to express her own conflicted emotions about her father's background through 'The Newspaper Man', just as the story of the same title in which the painting appears represents Smith's own efforts to do the same.

The legacies of empire which surface in contemporary British life, however, further compound Ruth's uneasiness about her class background when, as a schoolgirl, she is judged through the rhetoric of racial difference which lay at the heart of British colonial discourse. Smith asserts in an interview with Gretchen Holbrook Gerzina that 'colonialism is all about class' (275). The belittling thoughts Ruth thinks about her father which childishly elevate her in class terms are undercut by racist assumptions that her father's white English blood has bestowed her with natural intelligence, while her black heritage may thwart her class aspirations, since in England her blackness relegates her to the margins of society. Smith's surely quasi-autobiographical narrator recollects 'a feeling in the school, in the belly of the school in the recess beyond language, that I am smart because I am half-white' (14). Her father affirms this by proclaiming: 'She gets her brains from me,' he says 'and her looks from her mother' (14). While this is said with an element of undeniable affection, the story personalizes the inherited legacies of colonial racism which are difficult for the young child to understand as social and ideological constructs since they are imbricated within the very fabric of the family, and within the wider institution of the school. As an adult, the narrator realizes her early experiences of these legacies become mediated through the minutiae of psychological intimacies that develop between her white father and her as his half-black daughter. The suffocating effects of these discourses, as the story underscores, frequently lie beyond common everyday language itself. Ruth's experiences growing up chronicle an England built around social mechanisms of inclusion and exclusion and based on the fault-lines of class and racial prejudice.

Smith expresses more fully the undeniable influence English fathers cast on their children and the attendant class epistemologies which accompany those relationships in the two Hanwell stories: 'Hanwell Senior', published in 2004 and 'Hanwell in Hell', published three years later. *The New Yorker* initially published both stories, with the former republished in *The Book of Other People* (2007) while the latter was reprinted in *Martha and Hanwell* (2005), alongside 'Martha, Martha'. The common central character is Hanwell, loosely modelled on Smith's own father, Harvey Smith, who died in 2006 aged 81, a year before 'Hanwell in Hell' was published. Smith admits that her father's death rendered her wordless, unable to write, and thus her attempt to recreate the difficulties of fatherhood undermined by forms of abject English masculinity in 'Hanwell in Hell' is surely a testament to the affection and love Smith felt for her father as well as an attempt to overcome his death. Both stories depict white English working-class men, but they are especially concerned with the relationship between masculinity, fatherhood and domestic life in post-war Britain. Like 'The Newspaper Man', these later stories concern an Englishness absorbed through family lineage, the consciousness of inherited parental qualities and the struggle, by children, to balance what in 'The Newspaper Man' Smith describes as a 'great tightrope of need vs independence' (32–3). Although published three years apart, the two stories can be considered usefully together, demonstrating Smith's imaginative retrospective endeavour undertaken in 'Hanwell Senior' to fill in the uncommunicated relationship history between Hanwell and his father, whose own 'history, [...] is partial, almost phantasmagoric' (N. Pag.). Both stories also evince Smith's attempts to recreate inter-war Britain and retrieve the post-war Britain in which her father, Harvey, lived. They are peppered with small 'period details' of the English working classes: Harvey Senior inserts tuppence in a machine for a fag in 'Hanwell Senior' and his son is worried about whether he might have a shilling for the meter in 'Hanwell in Hell'. These small items are both period specific as they identify, but also symbolize, the measured economy of the working class and the pinched efforts at savings balanced by the cost of leisure and necessity.

'Hanwell Senior' appears to be Smith's effort to creatively reconstruct the possible personal contexts which influenced Hanwell's early life contexts which then impinge in unknowable ways on the descendants of Hanwell

Senior. Smith's stories thus intimate that forms of Englishness are preserved across generations. If these stories are tenuously situated within Smith's own life, then they may also attempt to make the unknowable ways of her own relationship with Harvey partially intelligible through art. Both stories have a highly self-conscious narrator seeking to understand the character Hanwell. The third person narrator in 'Hanwell Senior' claims Hanwell Senior's desertion of his family in the late 1920s 'was never forgotten. It persists, a fleck of the late nineteen-twenties. It is recorded here by a descendent of Hanwell Snr of whom he could have had no notion, [...] No one can explain the process by which these things are retained while much else vanishes' (N. Pag.). The female narrator, Claire, reclaims, and reveals, in the last sentence of the story, her identity as 'a female Hanwell', as she attempts to represent this 'fleck' of history. For her, Hanwell Senior is a parody of negative English working-class stereotypes: as a younger man, he is a brash 'boyo, with charm in spades', occasionally capable of cruelty and who handles money and family responsibilities with a 'feckless and slapdash' attitude (N. Pag.). Such negative images persist in the story: when they finally meet following a long period of separation, Hanwell Senior barely restrains his 'satirical disgust' towards his adult son's marital problems with a wife who is mentally ill. The brief encounter reaffirms Hanwell Senior's callous boorishness which Hanwell clearly remembers from childhood memories in which his father would unequivocally view any of his son's difficulties and discomfort as emasculating signs of inherent weakness.

Smith asserts in the opening paragraph of 'Hanwell Senior' that being fathered like that would 'teach you a sad self-sufficiency, [...] and a brutal reticence of the heart. A reluctance to get going at all' (N. Pag.). In 'Hanwell in Hell', Hanwell's struggle to confront this personal legacy contributes to one of the story's most touching elements when read retrospectively after 'Hanwell Senior'. Hanwell movingly transforms the brutal rejection of his impassive, patriarchal father as he endeavours to rescue a sense of comforting domesticity following his wife's suicide (possibly from the mental illness to which Hanwell refers in 'Hanwell Senior'), which resulted in him being separated from his daughters. Unlike his father, Hanwell, 'cared for the domestic and lamented its loss; with it went all the things he cared for – women, the home, family' (26). In his small rented flat, which he sets up alone following his wife's death, he carefully displays feminine objects of English working-class domesticity: '[P]retty blue china plates hung above the doorway' and '[D]oilies [which] seemed to cover all the limited surfaces, and on top of them stray ornaments were lined up' (42). Small, embroidered pillows sit in chairs and a woman's fur was hung over the back of one of the chairs (44–5). Furthermore, Hanwell's stoic efforts to readdress his early sense of parental desertion by Hanwell Senior steeps the small personal tragedy revealed at the end of 'Hanwell in Hell' in pathos. At the end of the story, Hanwell has, with some measure of unanticipated desperation and connivance, sought the help of a stranger, the narrator of the story – whom he meets at the thuggish restaurant where Hanwell works as a dishwasher – to paint a room intended for his daughters in his dilapidated flat. However, because Hanwell is colour blind, he has mistakenly painted the room a hellish red rather than the sunny yellow he had imagined would cheer up his daughters, whom he and the narrator know will not turn up to live with him. The story is focalized through the narrator, Clive Black, who recounts the story of the red room to Claire who has solicited information about her father from Clive. The story closes with Clive's claim to Claire that '[N]ot many men can hope red yellow' (49). This last line conveys the transcendent and hopeful love Hanwell holds for his daughters despite his own material deprivation, a love which is particularly poignant in the face of Hanwell Senior's consistent physical absence and emotional neglect during Hanwell's childhood.

Thus, Hanwell strives, in his fractured relationship with his daughters, to rectify the worst excesses of his own working-class father. Lexi Stuckey argues that 'Hanwell in Hell' demonstrates a 'full blown hostility towards the multicultural genre that put her [Smith] on the literary map' (158). Yet I would argue that these stories concerning Hanwell have less to do with multicultural Britain, but more with redeeming the life of a working-class English father who perceives himself to have failed his children, and with endowing meaning and significance to an enduring Englishness in men, like Hanwell, who as Smith writes in 'Hanwell Senior' believe themselves to have merely 'existed in a small way' (N. Pag.). Similarly, Sharon Raynor holds a misplaced belief that in order for Hanwell to understand 'his own dispossession and fully comprehend his existence', Claire, his daughter, is 'pushed to the margins (of the narrative)'; her existence, on the other hand 'hinges on the renewal and acceptance of their culture by the patriarchal society' (154). Raynor's feminist reading of 'Hanwell in Hell' rests uncomfortably, however, with Smith's sensitivities to Hanwell's efforts to overcome English patriarchal values as embodied most clearly in Hanwell Senior. Thus, the Hanwell stories, alongside 'The Newspaper Man' enable a reassessment of the complex identities of white English working-class men within fictional narratives which can serve as sympathetic creative sites for alternative personal narratives. The two Hanwell stories are a tribute to another kind of inheritance which finds expression in art, in which families beget the sources for fictional works based on characters which are paradoxically both realistic and larger than the life they led. Indeed, these stories lend a public depth and dignity to a working-class father that he himself would probably have found difficult to privately conceive. In Smith's essay 'Accidental Hero', an account of her father's experience of World War II, she testifies to her father's quiet humility and recalcitrance in his modest insistence that 'he wasn't brave' (237). Hence, these stories are much less combative than redemptive and humanist, even as they are emotionally attune and critical of the limitations to forms of working-class English masculinity.

In particular, Smith conveys, in these stories, her understanding of one distinct element of post-war English masculinity through the comedic inheritance Harvey bequeaths to her. Harvey's love for grotesque comedy and a dark macabre existentialism also appears in Smith's continuation of the Hanwell family's story in *NW*. This interest in inherited epistemologies may well stem from Harvey's influence on Smith during her childhood. Remembering her father after his death, Smith describes Harvey's sense of humour in an article which she had sardonically titled 'Dead Man Laughing'. She fondly recollects Harvey having loved *Steptoe and Son*, a sitcom about two rag-and-bone men broadcast by the BBC in the early 1960s, in which '[E]ach episode ends with the son [...] submitting to a funk of existential despair. The sadder and more desolate the comedy, the better Harvey liked it' (239–40). Harvey also loved Tony Hancock, an English comedian popular during the 1950s and early 1960s, who finally took his own life and who in Smith's words was 'a comic wedded to despair, in his life as much as in his work' (240). We see much of this English form of ironic despondency throughout the short stories on Hanwell, in which life's irredeemable bleakness is both realistically portrayed and comically displaced through fiction. They are feelingly written than self-consciously clever, far more concerned with postmodern life's contingencies and a Britain which Harvey, 'found [...] hard' (253) than with representations of the youthful jubilance of twenty-first-century Britain for which Smith made a name for herself.

Conclusion

Smith's short stories explore Englishness in our global world. Whether through small-town America, cosmopolitan Paris or rustic Italy, Smith uses foreign settings to foreground particular facets of Englishness which only become more evocative and pronounced in circumstances that seem incongruous to the expectations of English codes of behaviour. In the stories set within Britain, Smith's celebration of multiculturalism is often more muted. Instead, these stories reveal a fixation with white English bourgeois life in a neo-liberal world, the personal and ethical compromises it exacts, and other forms of English working-class identity occluded by its tendentious grip on all facets of contemporary British life.

Bibliography

Bentley, Nick. 'Re-writing Englishness: Imagining the nation in Julian Barnes's *England, England* and Zadie Smith's *White Teeth*' *Textual Practice* 21(3) (2007): 483–504.

Boyd, William. 'A Short History of the Short Story'. *Prospect*. 10 July 2006. http://www.prospectmagazine.co.uk/magazine/william-boyd-short-history-of-the-short-story/ (accessed 29 January 2013).

Gunning, Dave. *Race and Antiracism in Black British and British Asian Literature*. Liverpool: Liverpool University Press, 2010.

Leyshon, Cressida. 'This Week in Fiction: Zadie Smith'. *The New Yorker: Page-Turner*. Online. 23 July 2012. http://www.newyorker.com/online/blogs/books/2012/07/this-week-in-fiction-zadie-smith.html (accessed 29 January 2013).

Lorentzen, Christian. 'Why am I so fucked up?'. Rev. of *NW* by Zadie Smith. *London Review of Books*. 8 November 2012: 21–2.

Phillips, Caryl. *A New World Order: Selected Essays*. London: Secker and Warburg, 2001.

Raynor, Sharon. 'From the Dispossessed to the Decolonized: From Samuel Selvon's *The Lonely Londoners* to Zadie Smith's "Hanwell in Hell"'. In *Zadie Smith: Critical Essays*. Tracey L. Walters (ed.). New York and Oxford: Peter Lang, 2008, 141–55.

Rushdie, Salman. *Imaginary Homelands: Essays and Criticism 1981–1991*. London, Granta, 1991.

San Jan Jr, E. *Beyond Postcolonial Theory*. London: Macmillan, 1998.

Smith, Zadie. 'Mirrored Box'. *The May Anthology of Oxford and Cambridge Short Stories 1995*. Ruth Scurr and Chris Taylor (eds). Oxford and Cambridge: Varsity and Cherwell, 1995, 125–41.

—'The Newspaper Man'. *The May Anthology of Oxford and Cambridge Short Stories 1996*. Nick Laird and Toby Smith (eds). Oxford and Cambridge: Varsity and Cherwell, 1996, 7–33.

—'Mrs Begum's Son and the Private Tutor'. *The May Anthology of Oxford and Cambridge Shorts Stories 1997*. Martha Kelly (ed.). Oxford and Cambridge: Varsity and Cherwell, 1997, 89–113.

—'Picnic, Lightning'. *The May Anthology of Oxford and Cambridge Short Stories 1997*. Martha Kelly (ed.). Oxford and Cambridge: Varsity and Cherwell, 1997, 115–22.

—'Stuart'. *The New Yorker*. 27 December 1999: 60–7.

—*White Teeth*. London: Penguin, 2001 [2000].

—(ed.). *Piece of Flesh*. London: Institute of Contemporary Arts, 2001.

—'The Trials of Finch'. *The New Yorker*. 23 and 30 December 2002: 116–23.

—'Zadie Smith with Gretchen Holbrook Gerzina (2000)'. *Writings Across Worlds: Contemporary Writers Talk*. Susheila Nasta (ed.). London: Routledge, 2004, 266–78.

—'Author's Note'. *Martha and Hanwell*. Penguin Books, 2005, vii–xi.

—'Hanwell in Hell'. In *Martha and Hanwell*. London: Penguin Books, 2005, 25–49.

—'Martha, Martha'. In *Martha and Hanwell*. London: Penguin Books, 2005, 1–24.

—'The Girl with Bangs'. *The Best of McSweeney's Vol. 1*. Dave Eggers (ed.). Penguin Books, 2005, 79–87.

—'Hanwell Senior'. *The New Yorker*. Online. 14 September 2007. http://www.newyorker.com/archive/2004/09/27/040927fi_fiction (accessed 29 January 2013).

—(ed.). *The Book of Other People*. London: Penguin Books, 2007.

—'Monsters'. *The New Yorker*. Online. 12 September 2011. http://www.newyorker.com/talk/2011/09/12/110912ta_talk_smith (accessed 29 January 2013).

—'Accidental Hero'. In *Changing my Mind: Occasional Essays*. London: Penguin Books, 2011, 232–8.

—'Dead Man Laughing'. In *Changing My Mind: Occasional Essays*. London: Penguin Books, 2011, 239–54.

—'Speaking in Tongues'. In *Changing My Mind: Occasional Essays*. London: Penguin Books, 2011, 133–50.

—*NW*. London: Hamish Hamilton, 2012.

Stuckey, Lexi. 'Red and Yellow, Black and White: Color-Blindness as Disillusionment in Zadie Smith's "Hanwell in Hell"'. *Zadie Smith: Critical Essays*. Tracey L. Walters (ed.). New York and Oxford: Peter Lang, 2008, 157–69.

Tew, Philip. *Zadie Smith*. London: Palgrave Macmillan, 2009.

Thompson, Molly. '"Happy Multicultural Land"? The Implications of an "Excess of Belonging" in Zadie Smith's *White Teeth*'. In Kadija Sesay (ed.). *Write Black, Write British: From Post Colonial to Black British Literature*. Hertford, England: Hansib, 2005, 122–40.

NOTES ON
CONTRIBUTORS

Brad Buchanan is Chair of the English Department at the California State University, Sacramento, an expert in Modernist and Contemporary British Literature. He has published two scholarly books: *Hanif Kureishi* (Palgrave Macmillan, 2007) and *Oedipus Against Freud: Myth and the End(s) of Humanism in Twentieth-Century British Literature* (University of Toronto Press, 2010), two books of poetry entitled *The Miracle Shirker* and *Swimming the Mirror*, and various writings in academic journals such as *Canadian Literature*, *Journal of Modern Literature* and *Twentieth Century Literature*.

Susan Alice Fischer is Professor of English at Medgar Evers College of The City University of New York. She is editor of the online journal *Literary London Journal* and co-editor of *Changing English: Studies in Culture and Education*, published by Routledge/Taylor & Francis. Her work has appeared in *Tulsa Studies in Women's Literature*, *The Women's Review of Books*, *Critical Engagements*, *Zadie Smith: Critical Essays* and *The Swarming Streets: Twentieth Century Representations of London*. Her research focuses largely on contemporary British literature.

Christopher Holmes is Assistant Professor of English at Ithaca College. Awarded the Roland G. D. Richardson Fellowship he completed his doctorate at Brown University. He has published on the novels of Ivan Vladislavic, Michael Ondaatje and Kazuo Ishiguro. He is currently at work on a book tentatively entitled 'At the Limit: The Impossible, Unfinishable Work of World Literature'. At Ithaca he teaches classes on the contemporary Anglophone novel, South African literature after Apartheid and literary theory.

Wendy Knepper is a Lecturer in English at Brunel University, London and was previously a Research Fellow at the Institute for the Study of the Americas at University of London (2007–9). For research on Patrick Chamoiseau, she was awarded a Social Science and Humanities Council of Canada postdoctoral fellowship (2003–5) in affiliation with Harvard and New York Universities. Her publications include two scholarly books:

Postcolonial Literature (Longman, 2011) and *Patrick Chamoiseau: A Critical Introduction* (University of Mississippi Press, 2012). She has also published various book chapters on crime fiction and postcolonial literature and articles in the *Journal of Postcolonial Writing*, *The Journal of Commonwealth Literature*, *PMLA* and *Small Axe* and. She is currently working on a critical introduction to Caribbean literary studies for Palgrave.

Lucienne Loh is Lecturer in English Literature at the University of Liverpool. Her first book is *Postcolonial Dislocations: Politics of the Country in Contemporary Literature* (Palgrave Macmillan, 2012). Other publications include essays on postcolonial writing in *Wasafiri* and *The Journal of Postcolonial Writing*, and she has forthcoming articles in *Interventions* and a special issue of *Textual Practice* on 'Postcolonial Literature and Challenges of the New Millennium', which Loh is co-editing. A founding participant of the Postcolonial Studies Association in 2008, she was on its Executive Committee till 2011. Current projects include one on black British heritage, part funded by the British Academy.

Lewis MacLeod is Associate Professor in the Department of English at Trent University, Canada. His research focuses on the transition between Modern and Postmodern cultures/literatures and on the function of ritual in secular cultures. His scholarly interests include postcolonialism, masculinities, narratology, as well as modern and postmodern British literature. His work has appeared in a variety of journals, including: *Modern Fiction Studies*, *Narrative*, *Critique*, *Yearbook of English Studies*, *ARIEL*, LIT, *Mosaic* and *The Journal of West Indian Literature*.

Magdalena Mączyńska is an Associate Professor in the Department of Literature and Language at Marymount Manhattan College, New York. Her field of study is contemporary fiction, with emphasis on British, Anglophone and urban writing. She has published articles on the work of Diran Adebayo, Martin Amis, David Lodge, China Mieville, Ian McEwan, Ben Okri, Will Self,and Zadie Smith. Currently she is working on a book examining appropriations of religious scriptures in twenty-first-century fiction.

Joanna O'Leary completed her doctorate examining contagion, genre and infectious disease in Victorian literature at Rice University in Houston, Texas. Her subsequent research focuses on representations of science and medicine in nineteenth-century British and American novels, particularly those by Charles Dickens, Henry James and Wilkie Collins. Other research interests include transatlanticism, twins, child mortality and food history. She has published in *Nineteenth-Century Gender Studies* and *Victorian Network*. Joanna received an A.B from Harvard University and completed an MA in English Literature at Boston University.

Tracey K. Parker earned her PhD at the University of Arkansas in 2008; her dissertation, *Pop Life: Images and Popular Culture in the Works of Hanif Kureishi and Zadie Smith* incorporates her research interests in British minority literature, postmodernism, cultural studies and postcolonial theory. She has taught at Auburn University, the University of Arkansas, Missouri State University, Columbus Technical College and Ozarks Technical College.

Ulrike Tancke has taught at Johannes Gutenberg-Universität Mainz, Germany, Lancaster University, UK, and also Universität Trier, Germany, where she was awarded a PhD in English Literature in 2006. She has published a monograph on sixteenth-century women's life writing, *'Bethinke Thy Selfe' in Early Modern England: Writing Women's Identities* (Rodopi, 2010), as well as various articles on early modern literature and contemporary British fiction. In 2010–11 she held a Research Fellowship at the Centre for Contemporary Writing at Brunel University, UK, funded by DAAD (*Deutscher Akademischer Austauschdienst/German Academic Exchange Service*) to pursue her current research project, which focuses on violence and trauma in British novels around the Millennium.

Philip Tew is both Professor in English (Post-1900 Literature) and Deputy Head for Research of the School of Arts at Brunel University, London, a fellow of the Royal Society of Arts, and a member of the Royal Society of Literature. His many publications include *B. S. Johnson: A Critical Reading* (Manchester University Press, 2001), *The Contemporary British Novel* (Continuum, 2004; rev. (ed.) 2007), *Jim Crace: A Critical Introduction* (Manchester University Press, 2006) and *Re-reading B. S. Johnson* (Palgrave Macmillan, 2007) co-edited with Glyn White. Recent books include: *Writers Talk: Conversations with Contemporary Novelists* (Continuum, 2008) co-edited with Fiona Tolan and Leigh Wilson; *Re-Envisioning the Pastoral* (Fairleigh Dickinson UP, 2009) co-edited with David James; *Zadie Smith* (Palgrave Macmillan, 2010); and *Well Done God! Selected Prose and Drama of B. S. Johnson* co-edited with Jonathan Coe and Julia Johnson (Picador, 2013).

Lynn Wells is Lynn Wells is Vice-President Academic of the First Nations University of Canada in Regina. Her wide research interests include Contemporary British fiction, contemporary culture, urban fiction, ethics and literature. Her two major book are *Allegories of Telling: Self-Referential Narrative in Contemporary British Fiction (*Rodopi, 2003) and *Ian McEwan* (Palgrave Macmillan, 2010). Her various essays include one in *Modern Fiction Studies* on A. S. Byatt's *Possession*, plus numerous chapters in various books including *British Fiction Today, Materialities of Twentieth-Century Narrative* and *Iconoclastic Departures: Mary Shelley After 'Frankenstein'*. She has contributed entries on contemporary fiction to a number of reference works, including *Cyclopedia of World Authors* and *Reader's Guide to Literature in English*.

INDEX